The Clinical
Documentation
Sourcebook

Practice Planners™ Series

Treatment *Planners*

The Complete Psychotherapy Treatment Planner

The Child & Adolescent Psychotherapy Treatment Planner

The Chemical Dependence Treatment Planner

The Continuum of Care Treatment Planner

The Couples Psychotherapy Treatment Planner

The Employee Assistance Treatment Planner

The Pastoral Counseling Treatment Planner

The Older Adult Psychotherapy Treatment Planner

The Behavioral Medicine Treatment Planner

Homework *Planners*

Brief Therapy Homework Planner

Brief Couples Therapy Homework Planner

Chemical Dependence Homework Planner

Child and Adolescent Homework Planner

Documentation *Sourcebooks*

Clinical Documentation Sourcebook

The Forensic Documentation Sourcebook

The Psychotherapy Documentation Primer

The Chemical Dependence Documentation Sourcebook

The Clinical Child Documentation Sourcebook

Couples & Family Clinical Documentation Sourcebook

The Clinical Documentation Sourcebook, Second Edition

The Clinical Documentation Sourcebook

A Comprehensive Collection of Mental Health Practice Forms, Handouts, and Records

Second Edition

Donald E. Wiger

John Wiley & Sons, Inc.

New York • Chichester • Weinheim • Brisbane • Singapore • Toronto

---

Note about Photocopy Rights

The publisher grants purchasers permission to reproduce handouts from this book for professional use with their clients.

Library of Congress Cataloging-in-Publication Data:

Wiger, Donald E., 1953–
    The clinical documentation sourcebook : a comprehensive collection
of mental health practice forms, handouts, and records / by Donald E.
Wiger. — 2nd ed.
        p.   cm. — (Practice planners series)
    Accompanied by one computer disk.
    ISBN 0-471-32692-5 (paper: alk. paper)
    1. Psychiatry—Medical records—Forms.   2. Mental health services—
Medical records—Forms.   I. Title.   II. Series: Practice planners.
    [DNLM: 1. Mental Health Services—forms.   2. Documentation—
methods—forms.   3. Medical Records—forms.   WM 30W654c 1999]
RC455.2.M38W54   1999
616.89′ 0068—dc21
DNLM/DLC
for Library of Congress   98-38798

Printed in the United States of America.

10   9   8   7   6   5   4   3   2   1

This second edition is dedicated to my loving wife, Debra.
There were so many times when I came home
from work exhausted from seeing clients, but still had to write
reports and then work on the book. You were always
there to say a kind word and rub my back. Thank you.
Let's go out to eat tonight. My mother will watch the children.

Practice Planner Series Preface

The practice of psychotherapy has a dimension that did not exist 30, 20, or even 15 years ago—accountability. Treatment programs, public agencies, clinics, and even group and solo practitioners must now justify the treatment of patients to outside review entities that control the payment of fees. This development has resulted in an explosion of paperwork.

Clinicians must now document what has been done in treatment, what is planned for the future, and what the anticipated outcomes of the interventions are. The books and software in this Practice Planner series are designed to help practitioners fulfill these documentation requirements efficiently and professionally.

The Practice Planner series is growing rapidly. It now includes not only the original *Complete Psychotherapy Treatment Planner* and the *Child and Adolescent Psychotherapy Treatment Planner,* but also *Treatment Planners* targeted to specialty areas of practice, including chemical dependency, the continuum of care, couples therapy, older adult treatment, employee assistance, pastoral counseling, and more.

In addition to the *Treatment Planners,* the series also includes *Therascribe®: The Computerized Assistant to Psychotherapy Treatment Planning* and *TheraBiller™: The Computerized Mental Health Officer Manager,* as well ad adjunctive books, such as the *Brief Therapy, Chemical Dependence, Couples,* and *Child Homework Planners, The Psychotherapy Documentation Primer,* and *Clinical, Forensic, Child, Couples and Family,* and *Chemical Dependence Documentation Sourcebooks*—containing forms and resources to aid in mental health practice management. The goal of the series is to provide practitioners with the resources they need in order to provide high-quality care in the era of accountability—or, to put it simply, we seek to help you spend more time on patients and less on paperwork.

ARTHUR E. JONGSMA, JR.
Grand Rapids, Michigan

Preface

The first edition of the *Clinical Documentation Sourcebook* aroused much interest in integrating psychological forms throughout the course of therapy. The ongoing examples of charting a client's progress were helpful to many clinicians. Several clinics have reported adopting the forms and have expressed a further interest in more explanation of clinical documentation. Thus, *The Clinical Documentation Primer*, a text that teaches specific documentation skills in diagnostic interviewing, treatment plans, and progress notes is published by John Wiley & Sons coinciding with publication of the second edition of this sourcebook.

This second edition has added 50 percent more mental health forms compared to the previous edition. Changes have included more emphasis on biopsychosocial information, treatment plan updates, progress reports, and outcome indices. An added emphasis in integrating and coordinating personal history information and mental status information helps reduce redundant information. Current forms are designed to meet JCAHO standards, thus both large and small mental health practices and organizations will benefit.

The following forms have been added:

Suicide Contract.

Termination Letter.

Initial Assessment—Adult.

Initial Assessment—Child.

Personal History Form—Adult.

Personal History Form—Child.

Emotional/Behavioral Update.

Biopsychosocial Report.

Diagnostic Assessment—Lower Functioning.

Treatment Review.

Treatment Update.

Clinical Outcomes Questionnaire.

Chart Review.

Contents

Contents

Chapter 3 Evaluation Forms and Procedures 3.1

Chapter 4 Treatment Plan Forms and Procedures 4.1

Contents

Chapter 5   Progress Notes and Prior Authorization Request Forms and Procedures 5.1

Chapter 6   Relationship Counseling Forms and Procedures 6.1

Introduction

Few mental health professionals have received graduate training in documentation procedures. Learning to write case notes, treatment plans, and other documentation is usually a trial-and-error process, often resulting in vague treatment plans, case notes, and therapy. Historically, case notes and treatment plans have been required in most mental health care settings, but few standardized procedures have been acknowledged. In many cases, the mere existence of various forms and documents in clients' files was sufficient.

Historically, documentation procedures in medical fields other than mental health have been quite stringent, requiring that specific interventions be accurately charted. Without such documentation, physicians and nurses are understandably vulnerable to litigation. But prior to the emergence of managed care, most mental health professions received little scrutiny by third-party payers in areas of accountability. Managed care changed the rules by raising the standards of documentation procedures in the mental health field.

For managed care companies to obtain contracts, they must attempt to provide the best services for the least money. Often, a few managed care companies cover a significant number of people in a given geographic area. To receive a sufficient number of referrals, mental health providers contract with these companies, but may become dissatisfied with demanding documentation rules and regulations.

Graduate training programs have concentrated on traditional therapeutic methods, teaching therapists to attend to clients, conceptualize cases, listen empathically, render interpretations, ease clients' emotional pain, provide direction, and slowly taper off the sessions to prevent relapse. Although such procedures and interventions are therapeutically necessary, third-party requirements rarely mention them because in themselves they do not necessarily document the efficacy and course of therapy. Instead, terms often not learned in graduate school such as "medical necessity," "functional impairment," and "discharge criteria" have become the criteria for continued services.

Procedural requirements and changes catalyzed by managed care for documentation of therapy have increased cognitive dissonance in mental health professionals. Dissonance has developed because therapists are being challenged by discrepancies between their established mental health procedures and seemingly conflicting new requirements that are often viewed as limiting the clinician's therapeutic freedom. The resulting cognitive dissonance leads to stress, discomfort, worry, and complaints. To say that managed care regulations and procedures have caused cognitive dissonance is an understatement like the observations that "Sigmund Freud had some sort of effect on psychology" or "Albert Einstein was smart."

It is possible to reduce cognitive dissonance by focusing on the benefits of documentation procedures. Effective documentation holds mental health professionals accountable for accurate diagnosis, concise treatment planning, case notes that follow the treatment plan, treatment reflecting the diagnosis, and documentation of the course of therapy.

Introduction

Effective case notes can be written in a manner that would enable a new therapist to review a file and clearly determine specific impairments, the effectiveness of previous treatment strategies, client compliance, progress and setbacks.

Treatment does not necessarily have to change, but documentation procedures validating the effectiveness of treatment must be learned in order for mental health services to survive in the world of managed care. The ethical implications of being accountable (or not being accountable) for work deserves attention.

Managed care has brought the mental health profession up to par with other health care professionals in accountability procedures. In other areas of health care, the "black box" treatment approach—in which specific interventions are not documented—would be considered unethical, not reimbursable, and open to litigation. Without clear documentation procedures there is little or no accountability, leaving professionals open to allegations of fraud due to lack of specific evidence that necessary services are being provided.

For example, one major managed care company (Blue Cross/Blue Shield) has established the following (selected) requirements and criteria for mental health services to be eligible for benefits:

1. "Services must be medically and/or therapeutically necessary." Medical necessity is determined by "the presence of significant impairment or dysfunction in the performance of activities and/or responsibilities of daily living as a result of a mental disorder." Note that the emphasis is on the impairment, not simply the diagnosis. Although most third-party payers require an Axis I diagnosis, it is the resulting impairment that is the focus of interventions.

2. "Therapeutic necessity is defined as services consistent with the diagnosis and impairment which are non-experimental in nature and can be reliably predicted to positively affect the patient's condition." Therapeutic interventions must have a positive track record for the particular diagnosis and impairments. Charting procedures that do not clearly and consistently reflect such interventions do not document therapeutic necessity.

3. "The intensity of treatment must be consistent with the acuity and severity of the patient's current level of impairment and/or dysfunction." Without regular documentation of current functioning (session by session) and a rationale for the intensity of treatment, no evidence exists.

4. "There must be documentation of reasonable progress consistent with the intensity of treatment and the severity of the disorder." Case notes must validate the effectiveness of the current therapeutic interventions and justify the frequency of sessions.

5. ". . . documented, specific evidence of a diagnosable mental disorder (based on current *DSM*). The diagnosis must be validated by *Diagnostic and Statistical Manual of Mental Disorders (DSM)* criteria. A diagnosis is more than an opinion: Specific symptoms must be documented according to current *DSM-IV* criteria.

6. "The treatment plan includes specific, objective, behavioral goals for discharge." Both the client and the therapist have agreed on discharge criteria, stated in behavioral measures.

7. Justification to continue treatment includes "persistence of significant symptoms and impairment or dysfunction resultant from mental illness which required continued treatment including impaired social, familial or occupational functioning or evidence of symptoms which reflects potential dangers to self, others and/or property." Case notes must regularly document the persistence of impairment. Without this documentation, there is no evidence and therefore the impairment and diagnosis no longer exist (as far as documentation is concerned). It is possible that

a significant impairment may exist, but if it is not appropriately documented, payment for services could be discontinued.

8. "Insufficient behavioral and/or dysfunctional evidence is present to support the current diagnosis." Not only must impairments be documented, but the DSM Axis I diagnosis must be documented with evidence throughout the course of therapy. If the diagnosis is not supported throughout the case notes, there is no evidence, and therefore third-party payment may be halted.

9. "Lack of therapeutic appropriateness and/or lack of therapeutic progress." Evidence of therapeutic gains and setbacks are required documentation procedures.

10. Noncovered services include services without a "definite treatment plan," services without corresponding documentation, medically unnecessary services, services without a diagnosable mental disorder, and several other uncovered services.

This summary of third-party documentation procedures indicates specific requirements that are designed to document the efficacy of therapy in such areas as validation of diagnosis, functional impairments, symptoms, treatment, client cooperation, and providing behavioral evidence of gains and setbacks in treatment. Benefits of learning these procedures range from increased prior authorization approval for additional sessions, to clearer focus in therapy, to audit survival.

Sample forms and related examples of several documentation procedures from the initial client contact to the discharge summary are included. Blank forms are provided along with several of the forms filled out. Unless a form is self-explanatory, explanations are provided on its use. Special emphasis is placed on treatment plans and case notes.

Organization

This book is organized into six chapters of forms and procedures in the areas of intake and termination, assessment for counseling, evaluations, treatment plans, case notes, and relationship counseling.

Brief explanations of each form are followed by blank forms, and where forms are complex, filled out forms are provided. Blank forms are provided on the disk in the back of the book. An ongoing case example of Judy Doe is used in many of the documentation procedures and forms.

Chapter 1

Intake and Termination Forms and Procedures

The mental health clinic's intake information forms elicit demographic and payment information about the client. They also communicate business, legal, and ethical issues and responsibilities. Although initial intake forms do not provide specific clinical information, they do provide an understanding of the responsibilities of both the client and the clinic. In each case, these forms are taken care of prior to the first counseling session. All insurance and financial agreements are contracted with the client before services begin. The clinic's financial policies must be clearly spelled out. In addition, the client should be made aware of, and agree to, the limits of confidentiality in a counseling session.

Common client questions are: "What if my insurance company does not pay?," "How confidential is the session?," "Do parents have the right to their children's records?," "What happens if payment is not received?," "What happens if suicide is mentioned?," and "What is the price of therapy?" These and other questions are not only answered, but also documented and signed. Any of these issues, if not covered, could lead to misunderstanding, subsequent premature termination of treatment, ethics changes, or a lawsuit. Intake forms provide clear communication between the client and clinic, with the aim of eliminating misunderstandings detrimental to the therapeutic process and clinic survival.

FORM 1
Initial Client Information Form

The initial intake information form (Form 1) is filled out at the time of the referral or initial client contact with the mental health care provider. Information solicited from the client includes basic demographic, plus insurance identification information. For insurance reasons, information requested from the client should minimally include:

- Policyholder information: name, date of birth, social security number, policy number.

- Similar information from family members receiving services.

- Name of employer.

- Name and telephone number of each third-party payer.

If the mental health care provider processes insurance information, it is crucial to verify benefits from the insurance company. Specific questions should be asked of the third party, minimally including the following:

- Persons covered by the policy.

- Deductible amount and amount currently satisfied.

- Co-payment amounts.

- Limits of policy.

- Covered/noncovered services (e.g., individual, family, relationship).

- Prior authorizations needed.

- Coverage and policies for testing.

- Supervision required for various providers.

- Type(s) of provider(s) covered for services (e.g., psychologist, social worker counselor).

- Policy anniversary date.

When this information is unclear or unknown, there is room for misunderstanding between the mental health care provider and the client. Clients usually believe that all services performed in therapy are covered by their insurance. But mental health benefits from several sources are decreasing, and only specific, limited services are now covered. For example, just a few years ago several third-party payers paid for testing; today testing is seldom considered a standard procedure and often needs prior approval. Another trend is that most managed-care companies approve only a few sessions at a time, while in the past few restrictions were made.

Initial insurance information provided by third-party payers is not a guarantee of benefits. Each mental health care provider should have a clear financial policy and payment contract (possibly on the same form) to explain conditions of payment in the event that the third-party payer denies payment.

FORM 2
Financial Policy Statement

Clinical skills are necessary, but not the sole component in the overall scope of mental health services. A concise, written financial policy is crucial to the successful operation of any practice. Clear financial policies and procedures eliminate much potential discord (and premature termination of services) between the client and the therapist and clinic. Clinics that thrive financially and are self-sufficient have few accounts receivable at any time. An adequate financial policy statement addresses the following:

- The client is ultimately responsible for payment to the clinic. The clinic can not guarantee insurance benefits. (*Note:* Some managed-care contracts forbid client payment to the clinic for noncovered services without permission.)

- Clinics that bill insurance companies should convey to clients the fact that billing third-party payers is simply a service—not a responsibility—of the clinic.

- There are time limits in waiting for insurance payments, after which the client must pay the clinic. Some clinics collect the entire amount initially from the client and reimburse the client when insurance money is received.

- The clinic's policy regarding payment for treatment of minors should be noted.

- The policy regarding payment for charges not covered by third-party payers should be addressed.

- The financial policy form should be signed by the person(s) responsible for payment.

- Assignment of benefit policies should be addressed.

- The financial policy statement should specify when payments are due and policies for nonpayment.

- Methods of payment should be listed.

Request clients to read and sign the financial policy statement (Form 2) prior to the first session. Some mental health providers ask clients to come to the first session 15 to 20 minutes early to review the initial policies and procedures. Take care of all financial understandings with the client before the first session begins; otherwise, valuable session time might be taken up reviewing financial issues.

FORM 3
Payment Contract for Services

Along with the financial policy statement, the payment contract is vital for the clinic's financial survival. Without a payment contract, clients are not clearly obligated to pay for mental health services.

The following payment contract meets federal criteria for a truth in lending disclosure statement for professional services and provides a release of information to bill third parties (Form 3).

The contract lists professional fees that will be charged. (A clinical hour should be defined by the number of minutes it covers rather than stating "per hour"). Interest rates on late payments must be disclosed. Other services provided by the mental health care provider must also be listed, and costs should be disclosed. Fees for services such as testing should be listed, either by the test or at an hourly rate for testing and interpretation time. The contract should cover specific clinic policies regarding missed appointments, outside consultations, and other potential fees related to the mental health care provider.

The mental health care provider may choose to include or omit estimated insurance benefits in the payment contract. Since the mental health clinic is not directly affiliated with the third-party payer and their changing policies, it is important to clearly state that payment is due regardless of decisions made by the third-party payer and that the client is financially responsible to the clinic for any amounts not paid by the third-party payer within a certain time frame.

FORM 4
Limits of Confidentiality Form

Accountability in the intake session goes far beyond providing an accurate diagnosis. Legal and ethical considerations must be addressed prior to eliciting personal intake information. As "informed consumers" of mental health services, clients are entitled to know how confidential their records are. Few people are aware of the potential risks of having a recorded Axis I diagnosis and how such a record might adversely affect the client.

While several books have been written regarding the ethics of informed consent, there are additional areas of informed consent usually not addressed in the intake process that could lead to litigation. Therapists should have a written document addressing the limits of confidentiality that is to be signed by the client (Form 4). Thirteen areas of confidentiality are noted below. The first seven are commonly known, while the remaining items are seldom considered.

1. *Duty to warn and protect.* When a client discloses intentions or a plan to harm another person, health care professionals are required to warn the intended victim and report this information to legal authorities. In cases in which the client discloses or implies a plan for suicide, health care professionals are required to notify legal authorities and make reasonable attempts to warn the family of the client.

2. *Abuse of children and vulnerable adults.* If a client states or suggests that he or she is abusing or has recently abused a child or vulnerable adult, or a child or vulnerable adult is in danger of abuse, health care professionals are required to report this information to the appropriate social service and/or legal authorities.

3. *Prenatal exposure to controlled substances.* Health care professionals are required to report admitted prenatal exposure to controlled substances that are potentially harmful. State laws may vary.

4. *In the event of a client's death.* In the event of a client's death, the spouse or parents of a deceased client have a right to gain access to their child's or spouse's records.

5. *Professional misconduct.* Professional misconduct by a health care professional must be reported by other health care professionals. If a professional or legal disciplinary meeting is held regarding the health care professional's actions, related records may be released in order to substantiate disciplinary concerns.

6. *Court orders.* Health care professionals are required to release records of clients when a court order has been issued.

7. *Minors/guardianship.* Parent or legal guardians of nonemancipated minor clients have the right to gain access to the client's records.

8. *Collection agencies.* Although the use of collection agencies is not considered unethical, there may be ethical concerns if a client is not informed that the clinic uses collection agencies when fees are not paid in a timely manner. If use of a collection agency causes a client's credit report to list the name of the counseling agency, it is not uncommon for the client to threaten a lawsuit against a therapist claiming the confidentiality has been violated.

   A clear financial policy signed by the client prior to receiving services in crucial in the operation of a clinic. Clear financial policies and procedures eliminate much potential discord (and premature termination of services) between the client and the therapist and clinic. Clinics which thrive financially and are self sufficient have few accounts receivable.

9. *Third-party payers.* Many clients using insurance to pay for services are not aware of potential drawbacks. They may not realize which of their mental health records may be available to third-party payers. Insurance companies may require and be entitled to information such as dates of service, diagnosis, treatment plans, descriptions of impairment, progress of therapy, case notes and summaries. The documented existence of an Axis I diagnosis could have adverse future effects on such areas as insurance benefits.

10. Professional consultations. Clients should be informed if their cases are discussed in staff meetings or professional consultations. Assure them that no identifying information will be disclosed.

11. *Typing/dictation services.* Confidentiality might be violated when anyone other than the therapist types psychological reports. In many cases office staff have access to records. There have been several cases in which office personnel have reviewed files of relatives, neighbors, and other acquaintances. This is difficult to prevent, so inform clients that clerical personnel might have access to records and are held accountable for confidentiality. Records should be available within a clinic only on a "need to know" basis.

12. *Couples, family, and relationship counseling.* Separate files should be kept for each person involved in any conjoint or family counseling. If more than one person's records are kept in one file, it is possible that a serious breach of confidentiality could take place. For example, when couples enter counseling for marital issues, there is a potential for divorce and a child custody battle. If one of the partners requests "their file" and receives confidential material about the spouse, confidentiality has been violated. A clear policy indicating the agency's procedures in such situations is needed.

13. *Telephone calls, answering machines, and voice mail.* In the event that the agency or mental health professional must telephone the client for purposes such as appointment cancellations,

reminders, or to give/receive information, efforts must be made to preserve confidentiality. The therapist should ask the client to list where the agency may phone the client and what identifying information can be used.

FORM 5
Preauthorization for
Health Care Form

Charge cards are an effective means of collecting fees for professional services. The following form provides several benefits (Form 5). It allows the clinic to automatically bill the charge-card company for third-party payments not received after a set number of (often 60) days. It eliminates expensive—and often ineffective—billing to the client and successive billing to the insurance company. It further allows the clinic to bill the charge-care company for recurring amounts such as co-payments. This policy is often welcomed by clients because it eliminates the need to write a check each time services are received.

Most banks offer both VISA and MasterCard dealer status, but established credit is needed. Some therapists have become vendors for credit-card companies by offering to back the funds with a secured interest-bearing account (e.g., $500) for a set period while their credit becomes established with the bank.

Fees for being a charge-card dealer vary and may be negotiated, so competitive shopping for a bank is suggested. Some banks charge a set percentage of each transaction, while others include several hidden fees. The process is simpler though when the same bank is used in which the mental health professional has a checking account, because charge account receipts are generally deposited into a checking account.

FORM 6
Release of Information
Consent Form

The Release of Information Consent Form incorporates both legal and ethical obligations between the mental health professional and the client (Form 6). No information about clients should be discussed with anyone without that person's written permission, except information listed in the Limits of Confidentiality form (e.g., suicide, abuse, and so forth). A violation of confidentiality could lead to ethical, professional, and legal problems.

Clients have the right to know how the information will be used and which files will be released. A release of information is valid for one year, but may be cancelled at any time.

The legal guardians of children must sign the release. No release is necessary for children who are emancipated. It is necessary to find out if a vulnerable adult has a designated guardian (e.g., state or private guardianship, family).

This release form allows for a two-way release of information (to and from various providers). Some agencies and some clients prefer to fill out a separate release for each transaction.

FORM 7
Suicide Contract

A suicide contract serves several purposes. Although it is not a legal contract, it represents the client's commitment to take responsible actions when feeling suicidal. It is a signed agreement between the client and the therapist that suicide will not take place. It further provides evidence that the therapist has provided help for the client.

Most therapists ask clients to keep the contract with them at all times. It contains important contact telephone numbers that may not otherwise be immediately available or thought of during a crisis period. It also represents the therapist's commitment to the client, by providing means to contact the therapist in times of emergency or crisis.

FORM 8
Discharge Summary Form

The Discharge Summary Form (Form 8) is intended to summarize the effects of therapy. It lists the initial and final diagnoses, dates of service, progress, and reasons for termination. It provides a brief overview of changes in symptomology and the client's level of functioning as the result of therapy. Both the client's and therapist's evaluation are included.

Material from the Discharge Summary is helpful in assessing outcome measures. For example, changes in diagnosis, GAF, and current stressors can provide quantifiable information deemed necessary by several managed care organizations and third-party reviewers. An evaluation of the reasons for termination may help the clinic assess the quality, type, and number of services provided by both individual therapists and the clinic. Such information is helpful in clinic planning.

FORM 9
Termination Letter

The Termination Letter (Form 9) is sent to the client when services from the therapist or clinic are no longer being utilized. It serves at least two purposes. First, it is designed to free the clinic from any responsibility for any of the client's actions (which had nothing to do with the therapy received) after therapy has taken place. A clinic may bear some responsibility for a nonterminated client. Second, it provides a transition point to the client.

Certain ethical principles must be considered at a termination. Terminating a client is not abandoning a client. A proper termination implies that sufficient progress was made or attempted at the clinic, and the client is ready for a change to treatment elsewhere, or has made sufficient progress so that treatment is no longer necessary.

The clinic should provide the client with resources at termination to handle emergencies or crises. There may include crisis hot-line numbers, hospitals, walk-in clinics, or availability of the therapist or clinic in the future. Clearly document in progress notes that this information was provided to the client.

At the time of termination, the therapist should document the reason for termination and the estimated risk of relapse. Relapse is beyond the clinic's control. Therefore, the therapist should assure the client that help is available if needed in the future.

Some therapists suggest that the client receives periodic "booster sessions" such as at 6 months, then 12 months. It is important to clearly explain to a client the purpose of termination and that a termination letter will be sent, even though there may be booster sessions in the future.

Form 1   Initial Client Information

Name: _____   Intake date: _____   Time: _____

Address: _____   Therapist requested: ___ Y   ___ N

_____   Therapist: _____   Office: _____

Source of referral: _____   Type(s) of service: _____

Phone number: _____   Work phone: _____   Date of birth: ____/____/____

(___)   Primary insurance company: _____

Address: _____   City: _____   State: _____   Zip: _____

Phone number: _____   Persons covered: _____

Contact person: _____   M&F covered: _____

Policy holder: _____   Policy number: _____

Employer/Group: _____   SS number: _____

PROVISIONS: Client pays $ _____ Deductible amount   Amount satisfied: $ _____

Insurance pays _____ % for visits ___ - ___ and _____ % for visits ___ - ___

Type(s) of providers covered: _____   Supervision: _____

Prior authorization needed: _____

Effective date: _____   Policy anniversary: _____

Coverage for testing: _____   Annual limit: _____

Other third-party coverage: _____

Address: _____   City: _____   State: _____   Zip: _____

Phone number: _____   Persons covered: _____

Contact person: _____   M&F covered: _____

Policy holder: _____   Policy number: _____

Other provisions: _____

_____

(___)   Personal payment amount: $ _____   Terms: _____

Payment method (Insurance and cash clients; deductibles, co-payments, etc.)

___ Check   ___ Cash   ___ Charge card (type) _____   Number: _____

Cardholder's name: _____   Expires: _____

Completed procedures: ___ Entered system   Date: _____

___ Confirmed insurance   Date: _____

___ Confirmed with client   Date: _____

Form 1A   Initial Client Information

(Completed)

Name: _Judy Doe_   Intake date: _3/8/2001_   Time: _9:00 A.M._

Address: _123 Main St._   Therapist requested: ___ Y _X_ N

___Pleasantville, NJ 99999___   Therapist: _DLB_   Office: _SP_

Source of referral: _YP_   Type(s) of service: _Individual_

Phone number: _555-5555_   Work phone: _555-5544_   Date of birth: _7_ / _6_ / _1948_

(_X_) Primary insurance company: _United Cross Healthcare_

        Address: _5678 9th St._   City: _Pleasantville_   State: _NJ_   Zip: _99998_

Phone number: _555-5555_   Persons covered: _All family members_

Contact person: _Sheryl Sperry_   M&F covered: _No_

Policy holder: _Judy Doe_   Policy number: _1234567_

Employer/Group: _Pleasantville School Dis. 22_   SS number: _999-99-9999_

PROVISIONS: Client pays $ _100_ Deductible amount   Amount satisfied: $ _50_

            Insurance pays _80_ % for visits _1_ - _10_ and _75_ % for visits _11_ - _30_

Type(s) of providers covered: _Indiv, Family, Group, Assessment_   Supervision: _None if licensed_

Prior authorization needed: _After session 5 need PA. All testing_

Effective date: _Jan. 1, 1999_   Policy anniversary: _Dec. 31, 1999_

Coverage for testing: _Annual limit: $400_   Annual limit: _(total) $2,000.00_

Other third-party coverage: _None_

Address: _____ City: _____ State: _____ Zip: _____

Phone number: _____   Persons covered: _____

Contact person: _____   M&F covered: _____

Policy holder: _____   Policy number: _____

Other provisions: _____

_____

(_X_) Personal payment amount: $ _____   Terms: _as incurred_

Payment method (Insurance and cash clients; deductibles, co-payments, etc.)

___ Check   ___ Cash   _X_ Charge card (type) _Discover_   Number: _1234-5678-9012-3456_

Cardholder's name: _Judy Doe_   Expires: _8/02/2002_

Completed procedures: _X_ Entered system   Date: _3/5/1999_

                        _X_ Confirmed insurance   Date: _3/5/1999_

                        _X_ Confirmed with client Date: _3/5/1999_

Form 2 Financial Policy

The staff at (_____) (hereafter referred to as the clinic) are committed to providing caring and professional mental health care to all of our clients. As part of the delivery of mental health services we have established a financial policy which provides payment policies and options to all consumers. The financial policy of the clinic is designed to clarify the payment policies as determined by the management of the clinic.

The Person Responsible for Payment of Account is required to sign the form, *Payment Contract for Services,* which explains the fees and collection policies of the clinic. Your insurance policy, if any, is a contract between you and the insurance company; we are not part of the contract with you and your insurance company.

As a service to you, the clinic will bill insurance companies and other third-party payers, but can not guarantee such benefits or the amounts covered, and is not responsible for the collection of such payments. In some cases insurance companies or other third-party payers may consider certain services as not reasonable or necessary or may determine that services are not covered. In such cases the Person Responsible for Payment of Account is responsible for payment of these services. We charge our clients the usual and customary rates for the area. Clients are responsible for payments regardless of any insurance company's arbitrary determination of usual and customary rates.

The Person Responsible for Payment (as noted in the Payment Contract for Services) will be financially responsible for payment of such services. The Person Responsible for Payment of Account is financially responsible for paying funds not paid by insurance companies or third-party payers after 60 days. Payments not received after 120 days are subject to collections. A 1% per month interest rate is charged for accounts over 60 days.

Insurance deductibles and co-payments are due at the time of service. Although it is possible that mental health coverage deductible amounts may have been met elsewhere (e.g., if there were previous visits to another mental health provider since January of the current year that were prior to the first session at the clinic), this amount will be collected by the clinic until the deductible payment is verified to the clinic by the insurance company or third-party provider.

All insurance benefits will be assigned to this clinic (by insurance company or third-party provider) unless the Person Responsible for Payment of Account pays the entire balance each session.

Clients are responsible for payments at the time of services. The adult accompanying a minor (or guardian of the minor) is responsible for payments for the child at the time of service. Unaccompanied minors will be denied nonemergency service unless charges have been preauthorized to an approved credit plan, charge card, or payment at the time of service.

Missed appointments or cancellations less than 24 hours prior to the appointment are charged at a rate noted in the Payment Contract for Services.

Payment methods include check, cash, or the following charge cards: _____ .
Clients using charge cards may either use their card at each session or sign a document allowing the clinic to automatically submit charges to the charge card after each session.

Questions regarding the financial policies can be answered by the Office Manager.

I (we) have read, understand, and agree with the provisions of the Financial Policy.

Person responsible for account: _____ Date: ____/____/_____

Co-responsible party: _____ Date: ____/____/_____

Form 3   Payment Contract for Services

Name(s): _____

Address: _____ City: _____ State: _____ Zip: _____

Bill to: Person responsible for payment of account: _____

Address: _____ City: _____ State: _____ Zip: _____

Federal Truth in Lending Disclosure Statement for Professional Services

Part One   **Fees for Professional Services**

I (we) agree to pay _____ , hereafter referred to as the clinic, a rate of $ _____ per clinical unit (defined as 45–50 minutes for assessment, testing, and individual, family and relationship counseling).

A fee of $ _____ is charged for group counseling. The fee for testing includes scoring and report-writing time.

A fee of $ _____ is charged for missed appointments or cancellations with less that 24 hours' notice.

Part Two   **Clients with Insurance (Deductible and Co-payment Agreement)**

This clinic has been informed by either you or your insurance company that your policy contains (but is not limited to) the following provisions for mental health services:

Estimated Insurance Benefits

1) $ _____ Deductible amount (paid by insured party)
2) Co-payment _____ % ($ _____ /clinical unit) for first _____ visits.
3) Co-payment _____ % ($ _____ /clinical unit) up to _____ visits.
4) The policy limit is _____ per year: ___ annual ___ calendar

We suggest you confirm these provisions with the insurance company. The Person Responsible for Payment of Account shall make payment for services which are not paid by your insurance policy, all co-payments, and deductibles. We will also attempt to verify these amounts with the insurance company.

Your insurance company may not pay for services that they consider to be nonefficacious, not medically or therapeutically necessary, or ineligible (not covered by your policy, or the policy has expired or is not in effect for you or other people receiving services). If the insurance company does not pay the estimated amount, you are responsible for the balance. The amounts charged for professional services are explained in Part One above.

Part Three   **All Clients**

Payments, co-payments, and deductible amounts are due at the time of service. There is a 1% per month (12% Annual Percentage Rate) interest charge on all accounts that are not paid within 60 days of the billing date.

I HEREBY CERTIFY that I have read and agree to the conditions and have received a copy of the Federal Truth in Lending Disclosure Statement for Professional Services.

Person responsible for account: _____ Date: _____/_____/_____

Release of Information Authorization to Third Party

I (we) authorize _____ to disclose case records (diagnosis, case notes, psychological reports, testing results, or other requested material) to the above listed third-party payer or insurance company for the purpose of receiving payment directly to _____ .

I (we) understand that access to this information will be limited to determining insurance benefits, and will be accessible only to persons whose employment is to determine payments and/or insurance benefits. I (we) understand that I (we) may revoke this consent at any time by providing written notice, and after one year this consent expires. I (we) have been informed what information will be given, its purpose, and who will receive it. I (we) certify that I (we) have read and agree to the conditions and have received a copy of this form.

Person(s) responsible for account: _____ Date: _____/_____/_____

Person(s) receiving services: _____ Date: _____/_____/_____

Person(s) or guardian(s): _____ Date: _____/_____/_____

Form 4   Limits of Confidentiality

The contents of a counseling, intake, or assessment session are considered to be confidential. Both verbal information and written records about a client cannot be shared with another party without the written consent of the client or the client's legal guardian. It is the policy of this clinic not to release any information about a client without a signed release of information. Noted exceptions are as follows:

Duty to Warn and Protect

When a client discloses intentions or a plan to harm another person, the health care professional is required to warn the intended victim and report this information to legal authorities. In cases in which the client discloses or implies a plan for suicide, the health care professional is required to notify legal authorities and make reasonable attempts to notify the family of the client.

Abuse of Children and Vulnerable Adults

If a client states or suggests that he or she is abusing a child (or vulnerable adult) or has recently abused a child (or vulnerable adult), or a child (or vulnerable adult) is in danger of abuse, the health care professional is required to report this information to the appropriate social service and/or legal authorities.

Prenatal Exposure to Controlled Substances

Health care professionals are required to report admitted prenatal exposure to controlled substances that are potentially harmful.

In the Event of a Client's Death

In the event of a client's death, the spouse or parents of a deceased client have a right to access their child's or spouse's records.

Professional Misconduct

Professional misconduct by a health care professional must be reported by other health care professionals. In cases in which a professional or legal disciplinary meeting is being held regarding the health care professional's actions, related records may be released in order to substantiate disciplinary concerns.

Court Orders

Health care professionals are required to release records of clients when a court order has been placed.

Minors/Guardianship

Parents or legal guardians of nonemancipated minor clients have the right to access the client's records.

Other Provisions

When fees for services are not paid in a timely manner, collection agencies may be utilized in collecting unpaid debts. The specific content of the services (e.g., diagnosis, treatment plan, case notes, testing) is not disclosed. If a debt remains unpaid it may be reported to credit agencies, and the client's credit report may state the amount owed, time frame, and the name of the clinic.

Insurance companies and other third-party payers are given information that they request regarding services to clients. Information which may be requested includes type of services, dates/times of services, diagnosis, treatment plan, description of impairment, progress of therapy, case notes, and summaries.

Information about clients may be disclosed in consultations with other professionals in order to provide the best possible treatment. In such cases the name of the client, or any identifying information, is not disclosed. Clinical information about the client is discussed.

In some cases notes and reports are dictated/typed within the clinic or by outside sources specializing (and held accountable) for such procedures.

When couples, groups, or families are receiving services, separate files are kept for individuals for information disclosed that is of a confidential nature. The information includes (a) testing results, (b) information given to the mental health professional not in the presence of other person(s) utilizing services, (c) information received from other sources about the client, (d) diagnosis, (e) treatment plan, (f) individual reports/summaries, and (h) information that has been requested to be separate. The material disclosed in conjoint family or couples sessions, in which each party discloses such information in each other's presence, is kept in each file in the form of case notes.

In the event in which the clinic or mental health professional must telephone the client for purposes such as appointment cancellations or reminders, or to give/receive other information, efforts are made to preserve confidentiality. Please list where we may reach you by phone and how you would like us to identify ourselves. For example, you might request that when we phone you at home or work, we do not say the name of the clinic or the nature of the call, but rather the mental health professional's first name only.

If this information is not provided to us (below), we will adhere to the following procedure when making phone calls: First we will ask to speak to the client (or guardian) without identifying the name of the clinic. If the person answering the phone asks for more identifying information we will say that it is a personal call. We will not identify the clinic (to protect confidentiality). If we reach an answering machine or voice mail we will follow the same guidelines.

Please check where you may be reached by phone. Include phone numbers and how you would like us to identify ourselves when phoning you.

___ HOME   Phone number: _____
How should we identify ourselves? _____
May we say the clinic name? ___ Yes   ___ No

___ WORK   Phone number: _____
How should we identify ourselves? _____
May we say the clinic name? ___ Yes   ___ No

___ OTHER   Phone number: _____
How should we identify ourselves? _____
May we say the clinic name? ___ Yes   ___ No

I agree to the above limits of confidentiality and understand their meanings and ramifications.

Client's name (please print): _____

Client's (or guardian's) signature: _____ Date: ____/____/_____

Form 5   Preauthorization for Health Care

I authorize (_____) to keep my signature on file and to charge my
_____ (type of charge card) account for:

___ All balances not paid by insurance or other third-party payers after 60 days. This total amount
cannot exceed $ _____ .

___ Recurring charges (ongoing treatment) as per amounts stated in the signed Payment Contract for
Services with this clinic.

I assign my insurance benefits to the provider listed above. I understand that this form is valid for one
year unless I cancel the authorization through written notice to this clinic.

Client's name: _____

Cardholder's name: _____

Cardholder's billing address: _____

               City: _____ State: _____ Zip: _____

Charge card number _____ Expiration date: _____

Cardholder's signature: _____ Date: ____/____/_____

Form 6 Release of Information Consent

I, _____ , authorize _____ to:

___ (send) ___ (receive) the following ___ (to) ___ (from) the following agencies or people:

Name: _____

Address: _____ City: _____ State: _____ Zip: _____

Name: _____

Address: _____ City: _____ State: _____ Zip: _____

Name: _____

Address: _____ City: _____ State: _____ Zip: _____

___ Academic testing results	___ Psychological testing results
___ Behavior programs	___ Service plans
___ Case notes	___ Summary reports
___ Intelligence testing results	___ Vocational testing results
___ Medical reports	___ Entire record
___ Personality profiles	___ Other (specify) _____
___ Progress reports	_____
___ Psychological reports	_____

The above information will be used for the following purposes:

___ Planning appropriate treatment or program

___ Continuing appropriate treatment or program

___ Determining eligibility for benefits or program

___ Case review

___ Updating files

___ Other (specify) _____

I understand that I may revoke this consent at any time by providing written notice, and after one year this consent automatically expires. I have been informed what information will be given, its purpose, and who will receive the information.

Client's signature: _____ Date: ____/____/_____

Parent/guardian signature: _____ Date: ____/____/_____

Witness (if client is unable to sign): _____ Date: ____/____/_____

Person informing client of rights: _____ Date: ____/____/_____

Mail to: _____

Address: _____ City: _____ State: _____ Zip: _____

Form 7   Suicide Contract

Date: _____

I, _____ , (client), hereby contract with _____
(therapist), that I will take the following actions if I feel suicidal.

1. I will not attempt suicide.

2. I will phone _____ at _____ .

3. If I do not reach _____ , I will phone any of the following services:

<table>
<tr><td>Name/Agency</td><td>Phone</td></tr>
<tr><td>_____</td><td>_____</td></tr>
<tr><td>_____</td><td>_____</td></tr>
<tr><td>_____</td><td>_____</td></tr>
<tr><td>_____</td><td>_____</td></tr>
<tr><td>_____</td><td>_____</td></tr>
</table>

4. I will further seek social supports from any of the following people:

<table>
<tr><td>Name</td><td>Phone</td></tr>
<tr><td>_____</td><td>_____</td></tr>
<tr><td>_____</td><td>_____</td></tr>
<tr><td>_____</td><td>_____</td></tr>
<tr><td>_____</td><td>_____</td></tr>
<tr><td>_____</td><td>_____</td></tr>
</table>

5. If none of these actions are helpful or not available, I will check-in the ER at one of the following:

<table>
<tr><td>Hospital</td><td>Address</td><td>Phone</td></tr>
<tr><td>_____</td><td>_____</td><td>_____</td></tr>
<tr><td>_____</td><td>_____</td><td>_____</td></tr>
<tr><td>_____</td><td>_____</td><td>_____</td></tr>
<tr><td>_____</td><td>_____</td><td>_____</td></tr>
<tr><td>_____</td><td>_____</td><td>_____</td></tr>
</table>

6. If I am not able I will phone 911, or 0 for help.

Client's signature: _____ Date: ____/____/_____

Therapist's signature: _____ Date: ____/____/_____

Form 8   Discharge Summary

Client's name: _____ DOB: _____ Case # _____

Initial Diagnosis   Axis I _____ Code # _____

Axis II _____ Code # _____

Axis III _____ Code # _____

Axis IV _____

Axis V   GAF _____

Discharge Diagnosis   Axis I _____ Code # _____

Axis II _____ Code # _____

Axis III _____ Code # _____

Axis IV _____

Axis V   GAF _____

Services and Termination Status

Opening date: _____   Termination date: _____   Total number of sessions: _____

Which of the following services were used during client's stay?

___ Individual   ___ Group   ___ Family   ___ Marital   ___ Psychiatric

___ Psych. Testing   ___ Other (specify) _____

Overall Status at Termination

___ Marked improvement ___ Moderate improvement ___ No change ___ Regressed ___ Unknown

Reason(s) for Termination

___ Discharged as planned   ___ Terminated against therapist's advice

___ Referred for other services   ___ Therapist is leaving the clinic or area

___ No longer making appointments   ___ Insufficient progress in therapy

___ Have missed excessive appointments   ___ Client is leaving the area

___ Other _____

Presenting Problem and Assessment

(Subjective Evaluation: Summarize specific symptomatology, onset, duration, and frequency of Sx's. Include client's assessment of presenting problem and reason(s) for seeking services. Also include factors such as family or environmental factors affecting functioning.)

_____

_____

_____

_____

_____

Clinical Course

(Impact of services upon each problem identified in Treatment Plan. What the client and therapist did to become healthy and was there any improvement in client's condition in regards to specific problem areas.)

_____
_____
_____
_____
_____
_____

Medical/Psychiatric Status

(Was the client seen by the psychiatrist for either a psychiatric evaluation or for medications. Discharge meds, dosages, instructions.)

_____
_____
_____
_____

Post-Termination Plan

(Include referrals, appointments, disposition, client's reaction.)

_____
_____
_____
_____
_____

Client's Statement Regarding Satisfaction of Treatment Rendered

_____
_____
_____
_____
_____

Endorsements

Therapist signature/certification: _____   Date: ____/____/_____

I concur with the Final Diagnosis and Termination Plan, as delineated.

Comments: _____
_____

Supervisor signature/certification: _____   Date: ____/____/_____

Form 8A   Discharge Summary

(Completed)

Client's name: _Judy Doe_   DOB: _7/6/1948_   Case # _DJ 030899_

Initial Diagnosis   Axis I   _Major Dep. Mod. Recurrent_   Code # _296.32_

Axis II   _Deferred_   Code # _799.9_

Axis III   _Defer to physician_   Code # _____

Axis IV   _Marital, social, occupational problems_

Axis V   GAF _55_

Discharge Diagnosis   Axis I   _Major Dep. Recurrent (full remission)_   Code # _296.32_

Axis II   _No diagnosis_   Code # _V71.09_

Axis III   _Defer to physician_   Code # _____

Axis IV   _Mild occupational problems_

Axis V   GAF _74_

Services and Termination Status

Opening date: _3/8/1999_   Termination date: _1/8/2000_   Total number of sessions: _30_

Which of the following services were used during client's stay?

_X_ Individual   ___ Group   ___ Family   _X_ Marital   ___ Psychiatric

___ Psych. Testing   ___ Other (specify) _____

Overall Status at Termination

___ Marked improvement   _X_ Moderate improvement   ___ No change   ___ Regressed   ___ Unknown

Reason(s) for Termination

_X_ Discharged as planned   ___ Terminated against therapist's advice

___ Referred for other services   ___ Therapist is leaving the clinic or area

___ No longer making appointments   ___ Insufficient progress in therapy

___ Have missed excessive appointments   ___ Client is leaving the area

___ Other _____

Presenting Problem and Assessment

(Subjective Evaluation: Summarize specific symptomatology, onset, duration, and frequency of Sx's. Include client's assessment of presenting problem and reason(s) for seeking services. Also include factors such as family or environmental factors affecting functioning.)

Depressed mood most of time with extreme social withdrawal resulting in missing work and loss

of friends in past year. Exacerbated by marital discord. Wants to return to previous functioning.

_____

_____

_____

1.20

Clinical Course

(Impact of services upon each problem identified in Treatment Plan. What the client and therapist did to become healthy and was there any improvement in client's condition in regards to specific problem areas.)

(1) Regular exercise and nutrition led to increased energy level. (2) Self-esteem gradually increased as step-by-step behavioral assignments and assertiveness training yielded positive results. (3) Analyzing dysfunctional thoughts led to viewing situations more positively.

Medical/Psychiatric Status

(Was the client seen by the psychiatrist for either a psychiatric evaluation or for medications. Discharge meds, dosages, instructions.)

4/1/1999—Placed on Prozac 30 mg by Dr. Holtz. No side effects. Gradual improvement in mood stabilization over next 3–4 weeks. Remains on Prozac. Med check-ups as per physician.

Post-Termination Plan

(Include referrals, appointments, disposition, client's reaction.)

Therapist is available for future needs. Names of 3 crisis centers given to client. She feels satisfied with the course of therapy status.

Client's Statement Regarding Satisfaction of Treatment Rendered

She states that she is satisfied with the treatment and outcomes and agrees with discharge status.

Endorsements

Therapist signature/certification: *Darlene Benton, PhD*   Date: *1 / 7 / 2000*

I concur with the Final Diagnosis and Termination Plan, as delineated.

Comments: *Discharge seems appropriate.*

Supervisor signature/certification: *Sharon Bell, PhD*   Date: *1 / 9 / 2000*

Form 9   Termination Letter

Name: _____   Date: _____

Address: _____

City, State, Zip: _____

Dear (name of client) _____:

We thank you for using our services. Our records indicate that you are no longer receiving counseling at our clinic due to:

___ Discharged as planned   ___ Terminated against therapist's advice

___ Referred for other services   ___ Therapist is leaving the clinic or area

___ No longer making appointments   ___ Insufficient progress in therapy

___ Have missed excessive appointments   ___ Client is leaving the area

___ Other _____

If you are in need of further services at this time, or in the future, please feel free to phone us to discuss continuing services or a referral.

Sincerely,

Therapist: _____   Date: _____/_____/_____

Chapter 2

Assessment for
Counseling Forms
and Procedures

FORMS 10 and 11
Initial Assessment Forms

Two initial assessment forms are provided, adults (Form 10) and children (Form 11). The initial assessment material is gathered during the first session with the client. The goal of the first session is to establish and document a diagnosis, identify functional impairments, and determine respective onsets, frequencies, durations, intensities, and examples of *DSM-IV (Diagnostic and Statistical Manual of Mental Disorders, 4th ed.),* symptoms and impairments. Statements comparing current to previous functioning are also helpful.

The information attained is tentative and generally based on one session, but many third-party reimbursers require this information prior to the second session. The form allows for the presenting problem, background information, history, biopsychosocial information, mental status, and a rule-in/rule-out procedure for various diagnoses. Client strengths and weaknesses are also assessed to be incorporated into the treatment plan.

The initial assessment is a screening device to help determine the need for services. It is revised as more information is collected in subsequent sessions. The usual time needed to collect the information is one hour. *The Clinical Documentation Primer* (Wiger, Wiley, 1999), provides specific training in conducting a diagnostic interview and mental status exam.

Intake information provides necessary information for the treatment plan and validates the diagnosis. Unless the intake material sufficiently supports a diagnosis according to the *DSM-IV,* it is vulnerable to rejection by a third party. The specific functional impairments documented in the intake material may include social, family, occupational, affective, physical, cognitive, sexual, educational, biopsychological, and other areas of impairment that support the diagnosis.

Treatment, according to several third-party criteria, becomes the process of alleviated functional impairments. Documentation is generally requested to be in behavioral terms (usually quantifiable, observable, and measurable). Thus, intake notes should specifically list baseline rates of behavior for later comparisons of progress and setbacks. Baseline rates are also needed to help determine objective discharge criteria.

Judy Doe's (our case example) initial assessment lists both background and current information about the client. Both types of information are necessary for therapy, but observations regarding the current functional impairments are more needed for third-party documentation and accountability procedures. The Initial Assessment Form for Judy Doe (Form 10a) contains the therapist's documentation statements.

Judy Doe's initial assessment statements help to document a diagnosis, describe the client's mental health condition, provide a baseline for certain depressive behaviors, and reflect issues to be dealt with in therapy.

Five Sources of Information Available from the Intake Session(s)

The mental health intake procedure serves several purposes, including rapport building, information gathering, diagnosis, and setting up the treatment plan, each of which is necessary for accurate documentation. Information is available from at least five sources, including:

1. Diagnostic interview and mental status examination (observations by the clinician).

2. Testing (standardized, objective measures).

3. Self-report information (questionnaires filled out by the client).

4. Historical documents (past behaviors).

5. Collateral information (other people involved in the client's life).

1. *The Diagnostic Interview and Mental Status Examination.* The diagnostic interview is subject to limitations of validity and reliability. It is as valid as the diagnostic category. Some diagnoses have clear *DSM-IV* criteria and are more easily identified than others. For example, a major depressive episode is clearly defined in the *DSM-IV;* but several other disorders seem to be less clearly defined, causing the differential diagnosis to be more tentative and less valid.

The interview is as reliable as the clinician's knowledge of psychopathology. A vague knowledge of *DSM-IV* symptomology and differential diagnoses limits specificity, leading to erratic treatment. Mental health professionals can increase the reliability of their diagnoses by increasing their knowledge of psychopathology.

The interview should clearly document the onset, frequency, duration, and intensity of each symptom. Without this information, there would be problems in differential diagnosis. For example, a diagnosis of dysthymic disorder cannot be given unless the person has been depressed for at least two years. Without documentation of a history of depression for this time period, dysthymia is not adequately documented. A misdiagnosis could lead to improper treatment. Treatment for dysthymia is not the same as treatment for other types of depression such as single-episode major depression, bipolar disorder, or an adjustment disorder with depressed mood.

2. *Testing.* It is the clinician's responsibility to choose tests that are valid measures of the behaviors in question. That is, the test must measure what it purports to measure. Some clinics have administered the same battery of tests to all clients, whatever the reason for therapy or evaluation. Current contracts with third-party payers stipulate that if a test is administered there must be documented verification that the information derived for the particular test is medically necessary for accurate treatment. Clients should be informed that services such as testing or other procedures may not be covered by third-party payers. Payment contracts and financial policies should cover such provisions.

Standardized testing may be used as a documentation procedure in at least three ways: norm-referenced, criterion-referenced, and self-referenced. The same test can be used for all three purposes.

In norm-referenced testing, a person's test performance is compared with a normal population or a reference group. Most test distributions follow a normal curve in which the greatest number of people score at the 50th percentile and increasingly fewer people's scores approach the extremes. Scores are generally reported as standard scores. For example, most intelligence tests (e.g., Wechsler Adult Intelligence Scale–Revised [WAIS-III]) have a mean of 100 (i.e., average intelligence quotient [IQ] = 100) and a standard deviation of 15. Approximately 68 percent of test takers score within one standard deviation from the mean (i.e., 68 percent of the population have an IQ between 85 and 115). Increasingly fewer people score higher or lower if the test follows a normal curve.

Criterion-referenced testing involves setting cutoff scores based on diagnostic categories. Referring to the previous example, WAIS-R criterion scores have been set as follows:

Standard Score (IQ)	Category
69 and below	Mentally retarded or mentally deficient
70–79	Borderline
80–89	Low average
90–109	Average
110–119	High average
120–129	Superior
130 and above	Very superior

In self-referenced testing, an individual's test scores are compared over time. For example, some therapists ask clients to fill out a brief test periodically (e.g., Beck Depression Inventory). Scores are charted throughout therapy and progress is measured by affective changes depicted by test scores. Self-referenced testing could be charted as in Figure 2.1.

3. *Self-Report Information.* Additional information may be obtained by asking the client to fill out a biographical information form either prior to the initial interview or after the intake session (and returned prior to the second session). This information is especially helpful because the client is able to spend sufficient time in private delineating various historical, familial, medical, and mental health concerns. Also, using simple graphs such as those depicted in Figure 2.2, the client can furnish examples of impairment involving a wide range of mental health and behavioral symptoms. The information provided converts to treatment plan objectives.

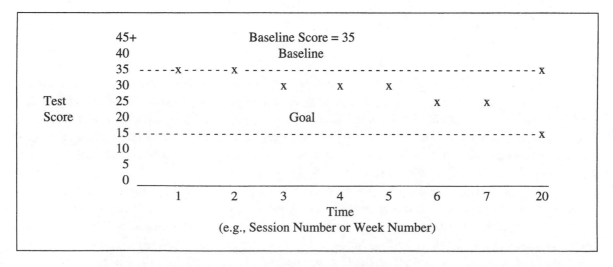

Figure 2.1 Graph of Therapeutic Progress Using Self-Referenced Testing.

2.4

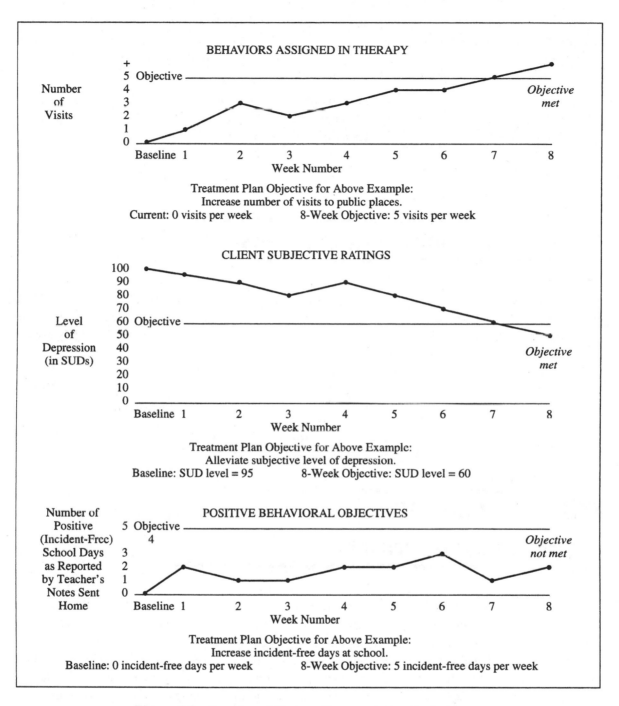

Figure 2.2 Samples of Various Documentation Techniques.

4. *Historical Documents.* Reports and evaluations by other professionals are quite helpful in documenting the client's mental health history. These are generally obtained from other professionals, schools, and agencies or, at times, brought in by the client. They must be requested in writing and the request form signed by the client. (See Release of Information Consent Form on page 1.16).

5. *Collateral Information.* Collateral information is data disclosed by others in the assessment session. For example, a parent might supply background information about a child, or a stroke victim's spouse might provide information about functioning before and after the stroke.

Background Information Forms

The first edition of this text included Biographical Information Forms for adults (Form 12) and children (Form 13). The form is filled out by the client, or client's caregiver, outside of the session. The information is integrated into the global assessment. The Biographical Information Form has been widely used in clinics that are not under JCAHO guidelines.

Two additional forms, Adult Personal History (Form 14) and Child/Adolescent Personal History Forms (Form 15) have been added to address JCAHO guidelines. Clinicians would use either the Biographical Information Form or the Personal History Form, but not both, because of overlap.

FORMS 12 and 13
Biographical Information

The Biographical Information Form is an effective means of documenting material not fully covered in the intake session. It is suggested that the client return this information to the therapist within a few days and before the second session. The first session (intake session) is intended to elicit specific diagnostic information. The second session (treatment planning session) is designed to collaboratively agree on the treatment plan with the client. Clients are given this form during the first session and asked to have it completed at least two days prior to the second session so that the therapist has sufficient time to review the information provided.

Both child and adult biographical information forms are provided. The child version is filled out by the parents. Each is written in terms consistent with *DSM-IV.*

The Biographical Information Form (Form 12) asks clients to provide a wide range of information such as personal, counseling, medical, and family history. The relative importance of this information often depends on the therapist's frame of reference. The form lists specific *DSM-IV*-related thoughts and behaviors for which the client rates the degree of concern. The client is further asked to comment on impairing concerns taking place frequently. The section titled "Symptoms" is modeled after the *DSM-IV.*

The last page gives the client an opportunity to list strengths and weaknesses and specific difficulties needing interventions.

The Biographical Information Form filled out by Judy Doe (Form 12a) documents her diagnosis and provides additional information for treatment planning. Examples of important diagnostic information provided by Judy Doe in her Biographical Information Form are as follows:

BIF Line #	Answer Provided by Client
20	Previously in counseling for depression
22	Depressed for the past year, but historical depression
30	Good health
35	No medications
69	Notes frequent occurrence of the following thoughts:

	Life is hopeless.	I want to die.
	I am lonely.	I can't concentrate.
	No one cares about me.	I am so depressed.
	I am a failure.	I have no emotions.

70	Endorses the following symptoms/impairments:	
	Avoiding people	Sexual difficulties
	Depression	Sick often
	Distractibility	Sleeping problems
	Fatigue	Suicidal thoughts
	Hopelessness	Withdrawing
	Loneliness	Worrying

The Biographical Information Form is written in *DSM-IV* terminology and designed to validate diagnostic criteria and subsequent impairments. As in the intake session, the information is incorporated into the treatment plan and subsequent interventions.

Similar to the adult biographical information form, the children's version (Form 13) initially elicits background data. Additional information such as developmental history is included. The form lists several *DSM-IV* impairments categorized by the following topics:

Items 1–9	Oppositional defiant disorder
Items 10–21	Conduct disorder
Items 22–36	Attention deficit hyperactivity disorder (ADHD)
Items 37–50	Various learning and mental health issues

FORMS 14 and 15
Personal History Forms

These forms are usually filled out prior to the initial assessment session. The Personal History Form—Adult (Form 14) is filled out by adult clients, while the Personal History Form—Child/Adolescent (Form 15) is filled out by the child's caregiver. Each form is written in the same order as the Initial Assessment and the Biopsychosocial Information Form. Thus, the clinician can quickly reference both the Personal History Form and Initial Assessment Form when completing summary reports or psychological evaluations.

Like the Biographical Information Form, the Personal History Form is designed in conjunction with the *DSM-IV*. The Personal History Forms are specifically designed to fit JCAHO standards for background information.

FORM 16
Emotional/Behavioral Assessment

The Emotional/Behavioral Assessment Form (Form 16) is primarily used for children and people diagnosed with developmental disabilities. It is designed to solicit information about the client's current level of emotional expression, positive behaviors, behaviors targeted for change, and recent stressors. It further helps set treatment plan goals.

FORM 17
Emotional/Behavioral Update

The Emotional/Behavioral Update (Form 17) is filled out by a caregiver of the client. It is used to inform the therapist of specific current emotional/behavioral problems areas that are current. Without knowledge of specific ongoing issues, the therapy could easily be off-track or not relevant to issues that are fresh in the client's memory.

Caution and sound judgment are needed as to whether and how to incorporate the information from this form into therapy. It can work positively when the client (usually a child or low-functioning adult such as mentally retarded) has difficulty relating current issues and welcomes the interventions of trusted others. It may be problematic if the client views the shared information as an alliance between the caregiver and therapist resulting in an unbalanced relationship.

FORM 18
Biopsychosocial Report

The Biopsychosocial Report (Form 18) provides background information in several areas of the client's life. Much of the information is obtained in the initial interview, and additions and revisions are made throughout therapy. Information covered includes biological (or physical), psychological, and social. Biological information includes any background material such as information about the client's family, development, education, employment, legal, and other medical history. Psychological information focuses on previous and current psychological status and treatment. Social information includes the client's social relationships and supports. Each area of biopsychosocial information collected should include both strengths and weaknesses.

The order of information in the Biopsychosocial Report is written in the same order as the information in the Personal History Forms. This procedure saves much time and effort when coordinating clinical information and in report writing.

Some therapists choose to collect this information by the first two sessions, while others fill it in as the information unfolds, usually within the first six sessions. Biopsychosocial information is very important for clinics subject to JCAHO guidelines. The report concludes with an integrated summary of information gathered. It is designed to be written after the sixth client visit, rather than after the first or second session. It is strong in following JCAHO guidelines, but weak in providing up-front information as per managed care guidelines.

FORM 19
Diagnostic Assessment Report

The Diagnostic Assessment Report (Form 19) is similar to the Biopsychosocial Report, but is based on clinical information and mental status, more than on biopsychosocial information. It is designed to be written after the first or second visit. It tends to satisfy managed care requirements of providing assessment information up-front.

The Diagnostic Assessment Report is designed to summarize the intake and assessment material, providing clear documentation of the client's current mental health condition—presenting problem, history, current functional impairments, and mental status. The report includes specific examples of frequency, duration, and intensity of symptoms.

In the Diagnosis Validation section of the form, the therapist may use diagnostic material such as testing, biographical data, collateral information, and intake material to document the diagnosis. This section may be especially helpful for an adult, for forensics, and in justifying the need for further services.

This form is useful in at least two ways: (1) it helps the therapist to keep on target in documenting the diagnosis and treatment, and (2) is helpful to send this form in to third-party payers along with their request form for additional service authorization.

The Diagnosis Assessment Report for Judy Doe (Form 19a) provides clear validation of supporting material for a diagnosis of major depression. Information provided in the form is a summary of the previous assessment material.

FORM 20
Diagnostic Assessment—
Lower Functioning

This Diagnostic Assessment Form (Form 20) is designed for people with concerns such as mental retardation or severe delays in adaptive functioning. Many states require periodic evaluations for individuals with delayed adaptive functioning. In many cases, most of the evaluation will involve little or no communication with the client (due to poor insight or lack of comprehension).

The diagnostic information in such cases comes from caregivers, previous records, observations, and testing, when possible. Generally, the higher the level of functioning, the less need there is for this form. The Diagnostic Assessment—Lower Functioning Form is routinely used for clients with mental retardation. Information is divided into eight categories that often serve as an outline for a write up or psychological evaluation which concludes with a summary and recommendations:

Background Information	Observations
Medical Concerns	Previous Testing
Present Behaviors	Present Testing
Emotional Issues	Clinical Diagnosis

Form 10   Initial Assessment—Adult

Client's name: _____   Date: _____

Starting time: _____   Ending time: _____   Duration: _____

PART A.   BIOPSYCHOSOCIAL ASSESSMENT

1. Presenting Problem

_____

_____

_____

_____

2. Signs and Symptoms (DSM based) . . . Resulting in Impairment(s)

(Include current examples; for treatment planning, e.g., social, occupational, affective, cognitive, physical)

_____

_____

_____

_____

3. History of Presenting Problem

Events, precipitating factors or incidents leading to need for services: _____

_____

_____

_____

Frequency/duration/severity/cycling of symptoms: _____

_____

_____

_____

Was there a clear time when Sx worsened? _____

Family mental health history: _____

_____

_____

_____

4. Current Family and Significant Relationships   (See Personal History Form)

Strengths/support: _____

Stressors/problems: _____

Recent changes: _____

Changes desired: _____

Comment on family circumstances: _____

5. Childhood/Adolescent History (See Personal History Form)

(Developmental milestones, past behavioral concerns, environment abuse, school, social, mental health.)

_____

_____

_____

_____

6. Social Relationships (See Personal History Form)

Strengths/support: _____

Stressors/problems: _____

Recent changes: _____

Changes desired: _____

7. Cultural/Ethnic (See Personal History Form)

Strengths/support: _____

Stressors/problems: _____

Beliefs/practices to incorporate into therapy: _____

8. Spiritual/Religious (See Personal History Form)

Strengths/support: _____

Stressors/problems: _____

Beliefs/practices to incorporate into therapy: _____

Recent changes: _____

Changes desired: _____

9. Legal (See Personal History Form)

_____

_____

Status/impact/stressors: _____

10. Education (See Personal History Form)

Strengths: _____

Weaknesses: _____

11. Employment/Vocational (See Personal History Form)

Strengths/support: _____

Stressors/problems: _____

12. Military (See Personal History Form)

_____

Current impact: _____

13. Leisure/Recreational (See Personal History Form)

Strengths/support: _____

Recent changes: _____

Changes desired: _____

14. Physical Health   (See Personal History Form)

_____

_____

Physical factors affecting mental condition: _____

_____

15. Chemical Use History   (See Personal History Form)

_____

_____

Patient's perception of problem: _____

_____

16. Counseling/Prior Treatment History   (See Personal History Form)

_____

_____

Benefits of previous treatment: _____
Setbacks of previous treatment: _____

PART B.   DIAGNOSITC INTERVIEW

Mood

(Rule-in and rule-out signs and symptoms: validate with _DSM_)

Predominant mood during interview: _____

Current Concerns (give examples of impairments (i), severity (s), frequency (f), duration (d)

Adjustment Disorder

(w/in 3 months of identified stressor, Sx persist < 6 months after stressor, marked distressed)

___ Depressed   ___ Anxiety   ___ Mixed anxiety & depression   ___Conduct

___ Emotions & conduct   ___ Unspecified

Specify disturbance: ___ Acute (<6 months)   ___ Chronic (>6 months) _____

_____

Impairment(s): ___ social ___ occupational/educational ___ affective ___ cognitive ___ other
Examples of impairment(s): _____

_____

Major Depression (2 or more wks): ___ Usually depressed or ___ anhedonia. (4+ of following):

___ wght + / (-) 5%/month   ___ appetite + / (-)   ___ sleep + / (-)   ___ psychomotor + / (-)

___ fatigue   ___ worthlessness/guilt   ___ concentration   ___ death/suicidal ideation

Other: ___ crying spells   ___ withdrawal   ___ add'l. sx _____

_____

Impairment(s): ___ social ___ occupational/educational ___ affective ___ cognitive ___ other
Examples of impairment(s): _____

_____

Dysthymia (2 or more years): ___ depressed most of time. (2+ of following)

___ low/high appeitie or eating   ___in/hypersomnia   ___low energy/fatigue   ___ low self-esteem

___ low concentration/decisions   ___ hopelessness   ___ other

_____

Impairment(s): ___ social ___ occupational/educational ___ affective ___ cognitive ___ other

Examples of impairment(s): _____

_____

Mania (3+):

___ grandiosity   ___ low sleep   ___ talkative   ___ flight of ideas   ___distractibility

___ goals/agitation   ___excessive pleasure

_____

Impairment(s): ___ social ___ occupational/educational ___ affective ___ cognitive ___ other

Examples of impairment(s): _____

_____

Panic Attacks (4+, abrupt development of):

___ palpitations ___ sweating ___ trembling ___ shortness of breath ___ feeling of choking

___ chest pain ___ nausea ___dizziness ___ light-headed ___ derealization

___ fear of losing control ___ fear of dying ___numbness ___ chills/hot flashes

_____

Impairment(s): ___ social ___ occupational/educational ___ affective ___ cognitive ___ other

Examples of impairment(s): _____

_____

Anxiety (GAD: 3+, most of time, 6 months):

___ restlessness   ___ easily fatigued   ___ concentration   ___ irritability

___ muscle tension   ___ sleep disturbance

_____

Impairment(s): ___ social ___ occupational/educational ___ affective ___ cognitive ___ other

Examples of impairment(s): _____

_____

Other Diagnostic Concerns or Behavioral Issues

(E.g., ___ dissociation ___ eating ___ sleep ___ impulse control ___ thought disorders ___ anger

___ relationships ___ cognitive ___ phobias ___ substance abuse ___ medical conditions

___ somatization ___ phobias ___ sexual ___ PTSD, etc.)

_____

Impairment(s): ___ social ___ occupational/educational ___ affective ___ cognitive ___ other

Examples of impairment(s): _____

_____

USE ADDITIONAL PAPER AS NECESSARY

2.14

Mental Status

(Check appropriate level of impairment: N/A or OK signifies no known impairment. Comment on significant areas of impairment.)

Appearance	N/A or OK	Slight	Moderate	Severe
Unkempt, disheveled	(__)	(__)	(__)	(__)
Clothing, dirty, atypical	(__)	(__)	(__)	(__)
Odd phys. characteristics	(__)	(__)	(__)	(__)
Body odor	(__)	(__)	(__)	(__)
Appears unhealthy	(__)	(__)	(__)	(__)
Posture	N/A or OK	Slight	Moderate	Severe
Slumped	(__)	(__)	(__)	(__)
Rigid, tense	(__)	(__)	(__)	(__)
Body Movements	N/A or OK	Slight	Moderate	Severe
Accelerated, quick	(__)	(__)	(__)	(__)
Decreased, slowed	(__)	(__)	(__)	(__)
Restlessness, fidgety	(__)	(__)	(__)	(__)
Atypical, unusual	(__)	(__)	(__)	(__)
Speech	N/A or OK	Slight	Moderate	Severe
Rapid	(__)	(__)	(__)	(__)
Slow	(__)	(__)	(__)	(__)
Loud	(__)	(__)	(__)	(__)
Soft	(__)	(__)	(__)	(__)
Mute	(__)	(__)	(__)	(__)
Atypical (e.g., slurring)	(__)	(__)	(__)	(__)
Attitude	N/A or OK	Slight	Moderate	Severe
Domineering, controlling	(__)	(__)	(__)	(__)
Submissive, dependent	(__)	(__)	(__)	(__)
Hostile, challenging	(__)	(__)	(__)	(__)
Guarded, suspicious	(__)	(__)	(__)	(__)
Uncooperative	(__)	(__)	(__)	(__)
Affect	N/A or OK	Slight	Moderate	Severe
Inappropriate to thought	(__)	(__)	(__)	(__)
Increased liability	(__)	(__)	(__)	(__)
Blunted, dull, flat	(__)	(__)	(__)	(__)
Euphoria, elation	(__)	(__)	(__)	(__)
Anger, hostility	(__)	(__)	(__)	(__)
Depression, sadness	(__)	(__)	(__)	(__)
Anxiety	(__)	(__)	(__)	(__)
Irritability	(__)	(__)	(__)	(__)

Perception	N/A or OK	Slight	Moderate	Severe
Illusions	(__)	(__)	(__)	(__)
Auditory hallucinations	(__)	(__)	(__)	(__)
Visual hallucinations	(__)	(__)	(__)	(__)
Other hallucinations	(__)	(__)	(__)	(__)
Cognitive	N/A or OK	Slight	Moderate	Severe
Alertness	(__)	(__)	(__)	(__)
Attn. span, distractibility	(__)	(__)	(__)	(__)
Short-term memory	(__)	(__)	(__)	(__)
Long-term memory	(__)	(__)	(__)	(__)
Judgment	N/A or OK	Slight	Moderate	Severe
Decision making	(__)	(__)	(__)	(__)
Impulsivity	(__)	(__)	(__)	(__)
Thought Content	N/A or OK	Slight	Moderate	Severe
Obsessions/compulsions	(__)	(__)	(__)	(__)
Phobic	(__)	(__)	(__)	(__)
Depersonalization	(__)	(__)	(__)	(__)
Suicidal ideation	(__)	(__)	(__)	(__)
Homicidal ideation	(__)	(__)	(__)	(__)
Delusions	(__)	(__)	(__)	(__)

Estimated level of intelligence: _____

Orientation: ___ Time   ___ Place   ___ Person

Able to hold normal conversation? ___ Yes   ___ No

Eye contact: _____

Level of insight:

___ Complete denial   ___ Slight awareness

___ Blames others   ___ Blames self

___ Intellectual insight, but few changes likely

___ Emotional insight, understanding, change can occur

Client's view of actions needed to change: _____

Comments

_____

_____

_____

_____

_____

_____

_____

PART C.   DIAGNOSIS VALIDATION

Diagnosis 1: _____   Code: _____

DSM Criteria

_____

_____

_____

Examples of impairment/dysfunction: _____

_____

_____

Additional validation (e.g., testing, previous records, self-report): _____

_____

_____

_____

Diagnosis 2: _____   Code: _____

DSM Criteria

_____

_____

_____

Examples of impairment/dysfunction: _____

_____

_____

Additional validation (e.g. testing, previous records, self-report): _____

_____

_____

_____

Diagnosis 3: _____   Code: _____

DSM Criteria

_____

_____

_____

Examples of impairment/dysfunction: _____

_____

_____

Additional validation (e.g. testing, previous records, self-report): _____

_____

_____

_____

	Diagnosis	Code

Axis I   1: _____   _____

              2: _____   _____

              3: _____   _____

Axis II   1: _____   _____

              2: _____   _____

Axis III   _____   _____

Axis IV   _____

Axis V   Current GAF = _____   Highest past year GAF = _____

Prognosis: ___ Poor   ___ Marginal   ___ Guarded   ___ Moderate   ___ Good   ___ Excellent

Qualifiers to prognosis: ___ Med compliance   ___ Tx compliance   ___ Home environment

   ___ Activity changes   ___ Behavioral changes   ___ Attitudinal changes   ___ Education/training

___ Other: _____

Treatment Considerations

Is the patient appropriate for treatment? ___ Yes   ___ No

If no, explain and indicate referral made: _____

Tx modality: ___ Indiv.   ___ Conjoint   ___ Family   ___ Collateral   ___ Group

Frequency: _____   _____   _____   _____   _____

If Conjoint, Family or Collateral, specify with whom: _____

Adjunctive Services Needed: ___ Physical exam   ___ School records

                               ___ Laboratory tests (specify): _____

                               ___ Patient records (specify): _____

Therapist's Questions/Concerns/Comments: ___ Psychiatric evaluation   ___ Psychological testing

_____

_____

_____

Therapist's signature/credentials: _____   Date: ____/____/_____

Supervisor's Remarks

_____

_____

_____

Supervisor's signature/credentials: _____   Date: ____/____/_____

Therapist's Response to Supervisor's Remarks

_____

_____

_____

Therapist's signature/credentials: _____   Date: ____/____/_____

2.18

Form 10A   Initial Assessment—Adult

(Completed)

Client's name: _Judy Doe_   Date: _3/8/1999_

Starting time: _10:00 A.M._   Ending time: _11:30 A.M._   Duration: _90 min._

PART A.   BIOPSYCHOSOCIAL ASSESSMENT

1. Presenting Problem

Missing increasingly more time at work, avoiding friends, marital conflict. "I just can't snap out of this depression."

2. Signs and Symptoms (DSM based) . . . Resulting in Impairment(s)

(Include current examples; for treatment planning, e.g., social, occupational, affective, cognitive, physical)

Usually fatigued, depressed and has low motivation to go to work, resulting in occupational impairment. Avoiding most of her close friends, rarely answers the door or telephone. Increasing anger outbursts toward spouse, with decreased sexual activity, resulting in marital relationship problems and possible divorce. Has unintentionally lost 20# in past 6 months.

3. History of Presenting Problem

Events, precipitating factors or incidents leading to need for services: _Previous history of diagnosis of Major Depression in 1968 due to coping with a relationship break-up. Current relationship issues are exacerbating similar problems._

Frequency/duration/severity/cycling of symptoms: _Feels depressed 3 out of 4 days, most of the day, especially in the morning. Symptoms increase when feeling stressed or after a conflict with spouse or family members._

Was there a clear time when Sx worsened? _One year ago with increased marital conflict_

Family mental health history: _Functional family of origin. No family history of depression._

4. Current Family and Significant Relationships   (See Personal History Form)

Strengths/support: _Very supportive family of origin_

Stressors/problems: _Marital conflict, intrusive mother and older sister_

Recent changes: _Spouse threatening divorce_

Changes desired: _To be less dependent on others, increase assertiveness_

Comment on family circumstances: _Family of origin may interfere with marriage_

5. **Childhood/Adolescent History** (See Personal History Form)

(Developmental milestones, past behavioral concerns, environment abuse, school, social, mental health.)

Normal childhood development, often dependent on others. No history of abuse or neglect.

Above average grades in school.

6. **Social Relationships** (See Personal History Form)

Strengths/support: *History of social activities*

Stressors/problems: *Avoid all previous friends*

Recent changes: *Has dropped all social activities*

Changes desired: *Return to premorbid functioning*

7. **Cultural/Ethnic** (See Personal History Form)

Strengths/support: *Mainstream culture*

Stressors/problems: *No*

Beliefs/practices to incorporate into therapy: *No*

8. **Spiritual/Religious** (See Personal History Form)

Strengths/support: *States that belief in God prevents suicide*

Stressors/problems: *None*

Beliefs/practices to incorporate into therapy: *None*

Recent changes: *None*

Changes desired: *None*

9. **Legal** (See Personal History Form)

No history of legal issues

Status/impact/stressors: *None*

10. **Education** (See Personal History Form)

Strengths: *Superior academic achievement when in high school*

Weaknesses: *None*

11. **Employment/Vocational** (See Personal History Form)

Strengths/support: *Steady employment as teacher, history of good job.*

Stressors/problems: *Currently feels "burnt out"*

12. **Military** (See Personal History Form)

N/A

Current impact:

13. **Leisure/Recreational** (See Personal History Form)

Strengths/support: *History of exercising, bowling and being active*

Recent changes: *Has stopped all such activities*

Changes desired: *Return to previous functioning*

14. Physical Health (See Personal History Form)

History of good health. Currently experiences weight loss, increased headaches, fatigue,
decrease libido, and poor sleep

Physical factors affecting mental condition: _Vegetative symptoms of depression_

15. Chemical Use History (See Personal History Form)

Light social drinking. No history of drug or alcohol abuse. No treatment history, no DWI.
No job loss.

Patient's perception of problem: _Not a problem_

16. Counseling/Prior Treatment History (See Personal History Form)

1968 counseling after relationship break-up. Successful treatment with individual counseling.

Benefits of previous treatment: _Returned to previous functioning_
Setbacks of previous treatment: _None known_

PART B.   DIAGNOSITC INTERVIEW

Mood

(Rule-in and rule-out signs and symptoms: validate with *DSM*)

Predominant mood during interview: _Depressed_

Current Concerns (give examples of impairments (i), severity (s), frequency (f), duration (d)

Adjustment Disorder

(w/in 3 months of identified stressor, Sx persist < 6 months after stressor, marked distressed)

___ Depressed   ___ Anxiety   ___ Mixed anxiety & depression   ___Conduct

___ Emotions & conduct   ___ Unspecified

Specify disturbance: ___ Acute (<6 months)   ___ Chronic (>6 months)   _Denies_

Impairment(s): ___ social ___ occupational/educational ___ affective ___ cognitive ___ other
Examples of impairment(s): _____

Major Depression (2 or more wks): _X_ Usually depressed or _X_ anhedonia. (4+ of following):

_X_ wght + / (-) 5%/month   _X_ appetite + / (-)   _X_ sleep + / (-)   _X_ psychomotor + / (-)

_X_ fatigue   _X_ worthlessness/guilt   _X_ concentration   _X_ death/suicidal ideation

Other: ___ crying spells   _X_ withdrawal   ___ add'l. sx _____

Impairment(s): _X_ social _X_ occupational/educational _X_ affective ___ cognitive ___ other
Examples of impairment(s): _Avoiding and losing friends, impending divorce. Sad most of the time._
Can't focus on lesson plans (teacher).

Dysthymia (2 or more years): ___ depressed most of time. (2+ of following)

___ low/high appeitie or eating   ___ in/hypersomnia   ___ low energy/fatigue   ___ low self-esteem

___ low concentration/decisions   ___ hopelessness   ___ other

_____ *Denies* _____

Impairment(s): ___ social ___ occupational/educational ___ affective ___ cognitive ___ other

Examples of impairment(s): _____

_____

Mania (3+):

___ grandiosity   ___ low sleep   ___ talkative   ___ flight of ideas   ___ distractibility

___ goals/agitation   ___ excessive pleasure

_____ *Denies* _____

Impairment(s): ___ social ___ occupational/educational ___ affective ___ cognitive ___ other

Examples of impairment(s): _____

_____

Panic Attacks (4+, abrupt development of):

___ palpitations ___ sweating ___ trembling ___ shortness of breath ___ feeling of choking

___ chest pain ___ nausea ___ dizziness ___ light-headed ___ derealization

___ fear of losing control ___ fear of dying ___ numbness ___ chills/hot flashes

_____ *Denies* _____

Impairment(s): ___ social ___ occupational/educational ___ affective ___ cognitive ___ other

Examples of impairment(s): _____

_____

Anxiety (GAD: 3+, most of time, 6 months):

___ restlessness   ___ easily fatigued   ___ concentration   ___ irritability

___ muscle tension   ___ sleep disturbance

_____ *Denies* _____

Impairment(s): ___ social ___ occupational/educational ___ affective ___ cognitive ___ other

Examples of impairment(s): _____

_____

Other Diagnostic Concerns or Behavioral Issues

(E.g., ___ dissociation ___ eating ___ sleep ___ impulse control ___ thought disorders ___ anger

___ relationships ___ cognitive ___ phobias ___ substance abuse ___ medical conditions

___ somatization ___ phobias ___ sexual ___ PTSD, etc.)

_____ *Each ruled out* _____

Impairment(s): ___ social ___ occupational/educational ___ affective ___ cognitive ___ other

Examples of impairment(s): _____

_____

USE ADDITIONAL PAPER AS NECESSARY

2.22

Mental Status

(Check appropriate level of impairment: N/A or OK signifies no known impairment. Comment on significant areas of impairment.)

Appearance	N/A or OK	Slight	Moderate	Severe
Unkempt, disheveled	(__)	(_X_)	(__)	(__)
Clothing, dirty, atypical	(_X_)	(__)	(__)	(__)
Odd phys. characteristics	(_X_)	(__)	(__)	(__)
Body odor	(_X_)	(__)	(__)	(__)
Appears unhealthy	(__)	(_X_)	(__)	(__)

Posture	N/A or OK	Slight	Moderate	Severe
Slumped	(__)	(__)	(_X_)	(__)
Rigid, tense	(__)	(__)	(_X_)	(__)

Body Movements	N/A or OK	Slight	Moderate	Severe
Accelerated, quick	(_X_)	(__)	(__)	(__)
Decreased, slowed	(__)	(__)	(_X_)	(__)
Restlessness, fidgety	(__)	(_X_)	(__)	(__)
Atypical, unusual	(_X_)	(__)	(__)	(__)

Speech	N/A or OK	Slight	Moderate	Severe
Rapid	(_X_)	(__)	(__)	(__)
Slow	(__)	(__)	(_X_)	(__)
Loud	(_X_)	(__)	(__)	(__)
Soft	(__)	(__)	(_X_)	(__)
Mute	(_X_)	(__)	(__)	(__)
Atypical (e.g., slurring)	(_X_)	(__)	(__)	(__)

Attitude	N/A or OK	Slight	Moderate	Severe
Domineering, controlling	(_X_)	(__)	(__)	(__)
Submissive, dependent	(__)	(__)	(_X_)	(__)
Hostile, challenging	(_X_)	(__)	(__)	(__)
Guarded, suspicious	(__)	(_X_)	(__)	(__)
Uncooperative	(_X_)	(__)	(__)	(__)

Affect	N/A or OK	Slight	Moderate	Severe
Inappropriate to thought	(_X_)	(__)	(__)	(__)
Increased liability	(_X_)	(__)	(__)	(__)
Blunted, dull, flat	(__)	(__)	(__)	(_X_)
Euphoria, elation	(_X_)	(__)	(__)	(__)
Anger, hostility	(_X_)	(__)	(__)	(__)
Depression, sadness	(__)	(__)	(__)	(_X_)
Anxiety	(__)	(_X_)	(__)	(__)
Irritability	(__)	(__)	(_X_)	(__)

Perception	N/A or OK	Slight	Moderate	Severe
Illusions	(X)	(_)	(_)	(_)
Auditory hallucinations	(X)	(_)	(_)	(_)
Visual hallucinations	(X)	(_)	(_)	(_)
Other hallucinations	(X)	(_)	(_)	(_)
Cognitive	N/A or OK	Slight	Moderate	Severe
Alertness	(_)	(X)	(_)	(_)
Attn. span, distractibility	(_)	(_)	(X)	(_)
Short-term memory	(_)	(X)	(_)	(_)
Long-term memory	(_)	(X)	(_)	(_)
Judgment	N/A or OK	Slight	Moderate	Severe
Decision making	(_)	(_)	(X)	(_)
Impulsivity	(X)	(_)	(_)	(_)
Thought Content	N/A or OK	Slight	Moderate	Severe
Obsessions/compulsions	(X)	(_)	(_)	(_)
Phobic	(X)	(_)	(_)	(_)
Depersonalization	(X)	(_)	(_)	(_)
Suicidal ideation	(_)	(_)	(X)	(_)
Homicidal ideation	(X)	(_)	(_)	(_)
Delusions	(X)	(_)	(_)	(_)

Estimated level of intelligence: _IQ = (110-120)_

Orientation: _X_ Time   _X_ Place   _X_ Person

Able to hold normal conversation? _X_ Yes   ___ No

Eye contact: _Moderate_

Level of insight:

    ___ Complete denial   ___ Slight awareness

    ___ Blames others   _X_ Blames self

    ___ Intellectual insight, but few changes likely

    ___ Emotional insight, understanding, change can occur

Client's view of actions needed to change: _Meds & counseling_

Comments

Very low energy; often cried; psycho-motor retardation; very low self-concept; cried often during interview; slumped posture entire interview.

PART C.   DIAGNOSIS VALIDATION

Diagnosis 1: _Major depression recurrent, moderate, w/o psychotic features_   Code: _296.32_

DSM Criteria

Depressed most of the time past year, no pleasure, weight loss, low appetite, sleep disturbance,

fatigue, feels worthless, decreased concentration, suicidal ideation.

Examples of impairment/dysfunction: _Loss of friends, withdrawn. Decreased performance and_

attendance at work.

Additional validation (e.g., testing, previous records, self-report): _MMPI-2 = (2-4-7 profile)—_

Depressed anxious; BDI score = 32—severe depression

Diagnosis 2: _____   Code: _____

DSM Criteria

Examples of impairment/dysfunction: _____

Additional validation (e.g. testing, previous records, self-report): _____

Diagnosis 3: _____   Code: _____

DSM Criteria

Examples of impairment/dysfunction: _____

Additional validation (e.g. testing, previous records, self-report): _____

	Diagnosis	Code

Axis I 1: _Major depression, recurrent, moderate w/o psychotic features_   _296.32_

2: _____   _____

3: _____   _____

Axis II 1: _Deferred_   _V71.09_

2: _____   _____

Axis III   _Defer to physician_   _____

Axis IV   _Marital discord, occupational social problems_

Axis V   Current GAF = _55_   Highest past year GAF = _75_

Prognosis: ___ Poor   ___ Marginal   ___ Guarded   _X_ Moderate   ___ Good   ___ Excellent

Qualifiers to prognosis: _X_ Med compliance   _X_ Tx compliance   _X_ Home environment

_X_ Activity changes   ___ Behavioral changes   ___ Attitudinal changes   ___ Education/training

___ Other: _____

Treatment Considerations

Is the patient appropriate for treatment? _X_ Yes   ___ No

If no, explain and indicate referral made: _____

Tx modality: _X_ Indiv.   ___ Conjoint   ___ Family   ___ Collateral   ___ Group

Frequency: _weekly_   _____   _____   _____   _____

If Conjoint, Family or Collateral, specify with whom: _____

Adjunctive Services Needed: _X_ Physical exam   ___ School records

___ Laboratory tests (specify): _____

___ Patient records (specify): _____

Therapist's Questions/Concerns/Comments: _X_ Psychiatric evaluation   _X_ Psychological testing

Is marital counseling appropriate? _____

_____

_____

Therapist's signature/credentials: _Darlene Benton, PhD_   Date: _3 / 8 / 1999_

Supervisor's Remarks

First work on stabilizing mood and alleviating depression. Share information with psychiatrist.

Concur with diagnosis.

_____

Supervisor's signature/credentials: _Sharon Bell, PhD_   Date: _3 / 12 / 1999_

Therapist's Response to Supervisor's Remarks

None

_____

_____

Therapist's signature/credentials: _Darlene Benton, PhD_   Date: _3 / 12 / 1999_

Form 11   Initial Assessment—Child (< age 18)

Client's name: _____   Date: _____

Starting time: _____   Ending time: _____   Duration: _____

PART A.   BIOPSYCHOSOCIAL ASSESSMENT

1. **Presenting Problem**

   (Client's brief statement as to reason for seeking services, in behavioral terms)

   _____

   _____

   Onset: _____   Frequency: _____

   Duration: _____   Severity: ___ Mild   ___ Moderate   ___ Severe   ___Remission

2. **Signs and Symptoms (*DSM-IV* based) and Resulting in Impairment(s)**

   (e.g., social, occupational, affective, cognitive, physical)

   _____

   _____

   _____

   _____

   _____

   _____

   _____

3. **History of Presenting Problem**

   Events, precipitating factors, stressors, and/or incidents leading to need for services: _____

   _____

   _____

   _____

   Was there a clear time when Sx worsened? _____

   Family mental health history: _____

   _____

   _____

   _____

4. **Current Family and Significant Relationships**   (See Personal History Form)

   Strengths/support: _____

   Stressors/problems: _____

   Recent changes: _____

   Changes desired: _____

   Comment on family circumstances: _____

5. Childhood/Adolescent History   (See Personal History Form)

(Developmental milestones, past behavioral concerns, environment, abuse, school, social, mental health)

_____
_____
_____

6. Social Relationships   (See Personal History Form)

Strengths/support: _____
Stressors/problems: _____
Recent changes: _____
Changes desired: _____

7. Cultural/Ethnic   (See Personal History Form)

_____
Strengths/support: _____
Stressors/problems: _____
Beliefs/practices to incorporate into therapy: _____

8. Spiritual/Religious   (See Personal History Form)

_____
Strengths/support: _____
Stressors/problems: _____
Beliefs/practices to incorporate into therapy: _____
Recent changes: _____
Changes desired: _____

9. Legal   (See Personal History Form)

_____
Status/impact/stressors: _____
_____

10. Education   (See Personal History Form)

_____
In special education? ___ No ___ Yes (describe) :_____
Strengths: _____
Weaknesses: _____

11. Employment/Vocational   (See Personal History Form)

_____
Strengths/support: _____
Stressors/problems: _____

12. Leisure/Recreational   (See Personal History Form)

Strengths/support: _____
Recent changes: _____
Changes desired: _____

13. Physical Health (See Personal History Form)

_____

_____

Physical factors affecting mental condition: _____

_____

14. Chemical Use History (See Personal History Form)

_____

_____

Patient's perception of problem: _____

_____

15. Counseling/Prior Treatment History (See Personal History Form)

_____

_____

Benefits of previous treatment: _____

Setbacks of previous treatment: _____

PART B. DIAGNOSITC INTERVIEW

Mood

(Rule-in and rule-out signs and symptoms: validate with _DSM_)

Predominant mood during interview: _____

Current Concerns (give examples of impairments (i), severity (s), frequency (f), duration (d))

Adjustment Disorder

(w/in 3 months of identified stressor, Sx persist < 6 months after stressor, marked distress)

___ Depressed   ___ Anxiety   ___ Mixed anxiety & depression   ___Conduct

___ Emotions & conduct   ___ Unspecified

Specify disturbance: ___ Acute (<6 months)   ___ Chronic (>6 months) _____

_____

Impairment(s): ___ social ___ occupational/educational ___ affective ___ cognitive ___ other

Examples of impairment(s): _____

_____

Major Depression (2 or more wks): ___ Usually depressed or ___ anhedonia. (4+ of following):

___ wght + / (-) 5%/month   ___ appetite + / (-)   ___ sleep + / (-)   ___ psychomotor + / (-)

___ fatigue   ___ worthlessness/guilt   ___ concentration   ___ death/suicidal ideation

Other: ___ crying spells   ___ withdrawal   ___ add'l. sx _____

_____

Impairment(s): ___ social ___ occupational/educational ___ affective ___ cognitive ___ other

Examples of impairment(s): _____

_____

Dysthymia (2 or more years): ___ depressed most of time. (2+ of following):
___ low/high appeitie or eating ___in/hypersomnia ___low energy/fatigue ___ low self-esteem
___ low concentration/decisions ___ hopelessness ___ other

_____

Impairment(s): ___ social ___ occupational/educational ___ affective ___ cognitive ___ other
Examples of impairment(s): _____

_____

Anxiety (GAD: 3+, most of time, 6 months):
___ restlessness ___ easily fatigued ___ concentration ___ irritability
___ muscle tension ___ sleep disturbance

_____

Impairment(s): ___ social ___ occupational/educational ___ affective ___ cognitive ___ other
Examples of impairment(s): _____

_____

ODD (Pattern of negativistic, hostile, and defiant behaviors > 6 months: 4+ of following):
___ loses temper ___ argues with adults ___actively defies adult's requests ___ deliberately
annoys people ___ blames others for own mistakes or misbehavior ___ touchy/easily annoyed
___ angry/resentful ___spiteful/vindictive. 1+ impairment: ___ social ___ academic ___ occupational

_____

Conduct Repetitive/persistent behavior violating rights of others. 3+ (past 12 mo. 1 in past 6 mos.):
___ Aggression to people/animals: ___ bullies, threatens, intimidates ___ initiates physical fights
___ has used harmful weapon. Physically cruel to: ___ people ___ animals ___ stolen while
confronting victim ___ forces sexual activity. Destruction of property: ___ deliberate fire setting
(intended damage) ___ deliberate property destruction. Deceitfulness or theft: ___ broken into
someone's property ___ often lies/cons ___ has stolen without confrontation. Serious violation of
rules: ___ stays out at night against parents' rules before age 13 ___ has run away 2+ or one extended
___ often truant before age 13. 1+ impairment: ___ social ___ academic ___ occupational

_____

ADHD Inattention: 6+ Sx, 6+ months:
___ poor attn/careless mistakes ___ difficult sustaining attn. ___ not listen when spoken to
___ not follow through ___ difficult organizing, avoids tasks requiring sustained mental effort
___ loses things ___ easily distracted ___ forgetful and/or Hyperactivity/impulsivity. 6+ hyperactivity
___ fidgety ___ leaves seat often ___ runs/climbs ___difficult being quiet ___ "on the go"
___ talks excessively. Impulsivity: ___ blurts out answers ___ difficulty awaiting turn ___ interrupts.
___ some SX < 7. 1+ impairment: ___ social ___ academic ___ occupational

_____

Other Diagnostic Concerns or Behavioral Issues
(e.g., ___ dissociation ___ eating ___ sleep ___ impulse control ___ thought disorders ___ anger
___ relationships ___ cognitive ___ phobias ___ substance abuse ___ medical conditions
___ somatization ___ sexual ___ PTSD, etc.)

_____

Impairment(s): ___ social ___ occupational/educational ___ affective ___ cognitive ___ other
Examples of impairment(s): _____

_____

USE ADDITIONAL PAPER AS NECESSARY

Mental Status

(Check appropriate level of impairment: N/A or OK signifies no known impairment. Comment on significant areas of impairment.)

Appearance	N/A or OK	Slight	Moderate	Severe
Unkempt, disheveled	(__)	(__)	(__)	(__)
Clothing, dirty, atypical	(__)	(__)	(__)	(__)
Odd phys. characteristics	(__)	(__)	(__)	(__)
Body odor	(__)	(__)	(__)	(__)
Appears unhealthy	(__)	(__)	(__)	(__)

Posture	N/A or OK	Slight	Moderate	Severe
Slumped	(__)	(__)	(__)	(__)
Rigid, tense	(__)	(__)	(__)	(__)

Body Movements	N/A or OK	Slight	Moderate	Severe
Accelerated, quick	(__)	(__)	(__)	(__)
Decreased, slowed	(__)	(__)	(__)	(__)
Restlessness, fidgety	(__)	(__)	(__)	(__)
Atypical, unusual	(__)	(__)	(__)	(__)

Speech	N/A or OK	Slight	Moderate	Severe
Rapid	(__)	(__)	(__)	(__)
Slow	(__)	(__)	(__)	(__)
Loud	(__)	(__)	(__)	(__)
Soft	(__)	(__)	(__)	(__)
Mute	(__)	(__)	(__)	(__)
Atypical (e.g., slurring)	(__)	(__)	(__)	(__)

Attitude	N/A or OK	Slight	Moderate	Severe
Domineering, controlling	(__)	(__)	(__)	(__)
Submissive, dependent	(__)	(__)	(__)	(__)
Hostile, challenging	(__)	(__)	(__)	(__)
Guarded, suspicious	(__)	(__)	(__)	(__)
Uncooperative	(__)	(__)	(__)	(__)

Affect	N/A or OK	Slight	Moderate	Severe
Inappropriate to thought	(__)	(__)	(__)	(__)
Increased liability	(__)	(__)	(__)	(__)
Blunted, dull, flat	(__)	(__)	(__)	(__)
Euphoria, elation	(__)	(__)	(__)	(__)
Anger, hostility	(__)	(__)	(__)	(__)
Depression, sadness	(__)	(__)	(__)	(__)
Anxiety	(__)	(__)	(__)	(__)
Irritability	(__)	(__)	(__)	(__)

Perception	N/A or OK	Slight	Moderate	Severe
Illusions	(__)	(__)	(__)	(__)
Auditory hallucinations	(__)	(__)	(__)	(__)
Visual hallucinations	(__)	(__)	(__)	(__)
Other hallucinations	(__)	(__)	(__)	(__)

Cognitive	N/A or OK	Slight	Moderate	Severe
Alertness	(__)	(__)	(__)	(__)
Attn. span, distractibility	(__)	(__)	(__)	(__)
Short-term memory	(__)	(__)	(__)	(__)
Long-term memory	(__)	(__)	(__)	(__)

Judgment Issues	N/A or OK	Slight	Moderate	Severe
Decision making	(__)	(__)	(__)	(__)
Impulsivity	(__)	(__)	(_-_)	(__)

Thought Content	N/A or OK	Slight	Moderate	Severe
Obsessions/compulsions	(__)	(__)	(__)	(__)
Phobic	(__)	(__)	(__)	(__)
Depersonalization	(__)	(__)	(__)	(__)
Suicidal ideation	(__)	(__)	(__)	(__)
Homicidal ideation	(__)	(__)	(__)	(__)
Delusions	(__)	(__)	(__)	(__)

Estimated level of intelligence: _____

Orientation: ___ Time   ___ Place   ___ Person

Able to hold normal conversation? ___ Yes   ___ No

Eye contact: _____

Level of insight:

    ___ Complete denial   ___ Slight awareness

    ___ Blames others   ___ Blames self

    ___ Intellectual insight, but few changes likely

    ___ Emotional insight, understanding, change can occur

Client's view of actions needed to change: _____

Comments

_____

_____

_____

_____

_____

_____

_____

PART C. DIAGNOSIS VALIDATION

Diagnosis 1: _____ Code: _____

DSM criteria:

_____

_____

_____

Examples of impairment/dysfunction: _____

_____

_____

_____

Additional validation (e.g., testing, previous records, self-report): _____

_____

_____

_____

Diagnosis 2: _____ Code: _____

DSM Criteria

_____

_____

_____

Examples of impairment/dysfunction: _____

_____

_____

_____

Additional validation (e.g. testing, previous records, self-report): _____

_____

_____

_____

Diagnosis 3: _____ Code: _____

DSM Criteria

_____

_____

_____

Examples of impairment/dysfunction: _____

_____

_____

_____

Additional validation (e.g. testing, previous records, self-report): _____

_____

_____

_____

	Diagnosis	Code

Axis I   1: _____   _____

           2: _____   _____

           3: _____   _____

Axis II   1: _____   _____

           2: _____   _____

Axis III   _____   _____

Axis IV   _____

Axis V   Current GAF = _____   Highest past year GAF = _____

Prognosis: ___ Poor   ___ Marginal   ___ Guarded   ___ Moderate   ___ Good   ___ Excellent

Qualifiers to prognosis: ___ Med compliance   ___ Tx compliance   ___ Home environment

   ___ Activity changes   ___ Behavioral changes   ___ Attitudinal changes   ___ Education/training

___ Other: _____

Treatment Considerations

Is the patient appropriate for treatment? ___ Yes   ___ No

If no, explain and indicate referral made: _____

Tx modality: ___ Indiv.   ___ Conjoint   ___ Family   ___ Collateral   ___ Group

Frequency: _____   _____   _____   _____   _____

If Conjoint, Family or Collateral, specify with whom: _____

Adjunctive Services Needed: ___ Physical exam   ___ School records

                            ___ Laboratory tests (specify): _____

                            ___ Patient records (specify): _____

Therapist's Questions/Concerns/Comments: ___ Psychiatric evaluation   ___ Psychological testing

_____

_____

_____

Therapist's signature/credentials: _____   Date: ___/___/_____

Supervisor's Remarks

_____

_____

_____

Supervisor's signature/credentials: _____   Date: ___/___/_____

(Certifies diagnosis, treatment plan, level of care, mental status evaluation, and therapist assignment)

Therapist's Remarks to Supervisor's Remarks

_____

_____

_____

Therapist's signature/credentials: _____   Date: ___/___/_____

Client's name: _William Olden_   Date: _____4/4/1999_____

Starting time: _____3:00 P.M._____   Ending time: _____3:58 P.M._____   Duration: _____58 min._____

PART A.   BIOPSYCHOSOCIAL ASSESSMENT

1. **Presenting Problem**

   (Client's brief statement as to reason for seeking services, in behavioral terms)

   Often suspended from school for "sassing teachers." Disrespectful to parents. Hits and

   bullies other children.

   Onset: _age 12–13 (2 years ago)_   Frequency: _almost daily_

   Duration: _varies_   Severity: ___ Mild   _X_ Moderate   ___ Severe   ___Remission

2. **Signs and Symptoms (*DSM-IV* based) and Resulting in Impairment(s)**

   (e.g., social, occupational, affective, cognitive, physical)

   Argues with teacher and aid 2–3x/day resulting in frequent in-school suspensions at least

   4x/week. Refuses to do homework or participate in any class assignments, resulting in 3

   failing grades last term. Initiates fights in school or in neighborhood at least 3x/week,

   resulting in having no friends, thus, increased frustration and anger. "Trashes" room of

   sister after disagreements average of 1x/week. Temper tantrums (yelling, swearing, stomping)

   at home when told to do chores or anything he doesn't want to do.

3. **History of Presenting Problem**

   Events, precipitating factors, stressors, and/or incidents leading to need for services:

   Parents divorce led to some behavior problems, but dramatic increase in defiance when

   mother remarried. Very defiant toward step-father.

   Was there a clear time when Sx worsened? _1st time corrected by step-father._

   Family mental health history: _No mental health treatment. Biological father has history of_

   alcoholism and domestic violence charges toward mother.

4. **Current Family and Significant Relationships**   (See Personal History Form)

   Strengths/support: _Mother, step-father and sister get along. Willing to help._

   Stressors/problems: _Occasional visits to father lead to increased violence._

   Recent changes: _Mainly mother's remarriage 2 years ago._

   Changes desired: _Cooperative in school and at home. Learn to cope._

   Comment on family circumstances: _His behaviors causing marital conflict._

5. **Childhood/Adolescent History**   (See Personal History Form)

(Developmental milestones, past behavioral concerns, environment, abuse, school, social, mental health)

   No unusual developmental concerns. Prior to parents divorce, no behavioral/emotional

   incidents. No history of abuse, but observe much verbal and physical abuse from father to

   mother. Used to have stable friendships prior to age 13.

6. **Social Relationships**   (See Personal History Form)

Strengths/support: *Used to have friends; positive memories*

Stressors/problems: *No friends at this time*

Recent changes: *Gradual loss of 3 previous friends*

Changes desired: *Stabilize friendships. Stop bullying peers*

7. **Cultural/Ethnic**   (See Personal History Form)

   Native-American

Strengths/support: *Family practices traditional tribal beliefs/traditions*

Stressors/problems: *Some teasing by peers due to "pow-wows"*

Beliefs/practices to incorporate into therapy: *Tribe as support system*

8. **Spiritual/Religious**   (See Personal History Form)

   Non-organized. Incorporation of nature

Strengths/support: *Family teaching and practices*

Stressors/problems: *Some teasing by peers*

Beliefs/practices to incorporate into therapy: *Respect for all*

Recent changes: *None*

Changes desired: *Ok*

9. **Legal**   (See Personal History Form)

   No formal arrests but brought home by police 4 times in past year for fighting/bullying.

Status/impact/stressors: *Recent warning by school police officer that next incident will*

   result in arrest.

10. **Education**   (See Personal History Form)

   In 10th grade, Dalton School mainstreamed, but is being considered for EBD program.

In special education? *X* No ___ Yes (describe) : *But grades have decreased significantly*

Strengths: *Recent intelligence testing: WISC-III IQ of 115.*

Weaknesses: *Not completing assignments or tests.*

11. **Employment/Vocational**   (See Personal History Form)

   N/A

Strengths/support: _____

Stressors/problems: _____

12. **Leisure/Recreational**   (See Personal History Form)

Strengths/support: *History of being athletic, good runner, well-conditioned*

Recent changes: *No longer involved in sports or exercising*

Changes desired: *Become involved in cooperative sports*

13. Physical Health   (See Personal History Form)

   Good health. No significant illnesses. Normal height and weight _____

   _____

   Physical factors affecting mental condition: _ None known_ _____

   _____

14. Chemical Use History   (See Personal History Form)

   Mother states that she has been missing small amounts of alcohol at times. _____

   _____

   Patient's perception of problem: _ Denies_ _____

   _____

15. Counseling/Prior Treatment History   (See Personal History Form)

   No formal counseling. A few visits to school counselor as part of suspensions, but would _____

   not talk about issues. _____

   Benefits of previous treatment: _ N/A_ _____

   Setbacks of previous treatment: _ N/A_ _____

PART B.   DIAGNOSITC INTERVIEW

Mood

(Rule-in and rule-out signs and symptoms: validate with *DSM*)

Predominant mood during interview: _____

Current Concerns (give examples of impairments (i), severity (s), frequency (f), duration (d))

Adjustment Disorder

   (w/in 3 months of identified stressor, Sx persist < 6 months after stressor, marked distress)

   ___ Depressed   ___ Anxiety   ___ Mixed anxiety & depression   _X_ Conduct

   ___ Emotions & conduct   ___ Unspecified

Specify disturbance: ___ Acute (<6 months)   _X_ Chronic (>6 months) _ Parental divorce and_

soon remarriage of mother has led to dramatic increases in conduct problems _____

Impairment(s): _X_ social _X_ occupational/educational ___ affective ___ cognitive ___ other

Examples of impairment(s): _ Behavioral outbursts, defiance, temper tantrums_ _____

_____

Major Depression (2 or more wks): ___ Usually depressed or ___ anhedonia. (4+ of following):

   ___ wght + / (-) 5%/month   ___ appetite + / (-)   ___ sleep + / (-)   ___ psychomotor + / (-)

   ___ fatigue   ___ worthlessness/guilt   ___ concentration   ___ death/suicidal ideation

Other: ___ crying spells   ___ withdrawal   ___ add'l. sx _____

_____ *Denies* _____

Impairment(s): ___ social ___ occupational/educational ___ affective ___ cognitive ___ other

Examples of impairment(s): _____

_____

Dysthymia (2 or more years): ___ depressed most of time. (2+ of following):
___ low/high appeitie or eating ___in/hypersomnia ___low energy/fatigue ___ low self-esteem
___ low concentration/decisions ___ hopelessness ___ other

_____ *Denies* _____

Impairment(s): ___ social ___ occupational/educational ___ affective ___ cognitive ___ other
Examples of impairment(s): _____
_____

Anxiety (GAD: 3+, most of time, 6 months):
___ restlessness ___ easily fatigued ___ concentration ___ irritability
___ muscle tension ___ sleep disturbance

_____ *Denies* _____

Impairment(s): ___ social ___ occupational/educational ___ affective ___ cognitive ___ other
Examples of impairment(s): _____
_____

ODD (Pattern of negativistic, hostile, and defiant behaviors > 6 months: 4+ of following):
_X_ loses temper _X_ argues with adults _X_ actively defies adult's requests ___ deliberately
annoys people _X_ blames others for own mistakes or misbehavior ___ touchy/easily annoyed
_X_ angry/resentful _X_ spiteful/vindictive. 1+ impairment: _X_ social _X_ academic ___ occupational
_*Onset: 2 years ago. Daily arguing with teachers and family. Refuses to do anything.*_____

Conduct Repetitive/persistent behavior violating rights of others. 3+ (past 12 mo. 1 in past 6 mos.):
___ Aggression to people/animals: _X_ bullies, threatens, intimidates _X_ initiates physical fights
___ has used harmful weapon. Physically cruel to: ___ people ___ animals ___ stolen while
confronting victim ___ forces sexual activity. Destruction of property: ___ deliberate fire setting
(intended damage) ___ deliberate property destruction. Deceitfulness or theft: ___ broken into
someone's property ___ often lies/cons ___ has stolen without confrontation. Serious violation of
rules: ___ stays out at night against parents' rules before age 13 ___ has run away 2+ or one extended
___ often truant before age 13. 1+ impairment: ___ social ___ academic ___ occupational
_*Features—not full diagnosis.*_____

ADHD Inattention: 6+ Sx, 6+ months:
___ poor attn/careless mistakes ___ difficult sustaining attn. ___ not listen when spoken to
___ not follow through ___ difficult organizing, avoids tasks requiring sustained mental effort
___ loses things ___ easily distracted ___ forgetful and/or Hyperactivity/impulsivity. 6+ hyperactivity
___ fidgety ___ leaves seat often ___ runs/climbs ___difficult being quiet ___ "on the go"
___ talks excessively. Impulsivity: ___ blurts out answers ___ difficulty awaiting turn ___ interrupts.
___ some SX < 7. 1+ impairment: ___ social ___ academic ___ occupational

_____ *Denies* _____

Other Diagnostic Concerns or Behavioral Issues
(e.g., ___ dissociation ___ eating ___ sleep ___ impulse control ___ thought disorders ___ anger
___ relationships ___ cognitive ___ phobias ___ substance abuse ___ medical conditions
___ somatization ___ sexual ___ PTSD, etc.)
_____

Impairment(s): ___ social ___ occupational/educational ___ affective ___ cognitive ___ other
Examples of impairment(s): _____
_____

USE ADDITIONAL PAPER AS NECESSARY

Mental Status

(Check appropriate level of impairment: N/A or OK signifies no known impairment. Comment on significant areas of impairment.)

Appearance	N/A or OK	Slight	Moderate	Severe
Unkempt, disheveled	(__)	(X)	(__)	(__)
Clothing, dirty, atypical	(__)	(X)	(__)	(__)
Odd phys. characteristics	(X)	(__)	(__)	(__)
Body odor	(X)	(__)	(__)	(__)
Appears unhealthy	(X)	(__)	(__)	(__)

Posture	N/A or OK	Slight	Moderate	Severe
Slumped	(X)	(__)	(__)	(__)
Rigid, tense	(__)	(X)	(__)	(__)

Body Movements	N/A or OK	Slight	Moderate	Severe
Accelerated, quick	(__)	(X)	(__)	(__)
Decreased, slowed	(__)	(X)	(__)	(__)
Restlessness, fidgety	(__)	(__)	(X)	(__)
Atypical, unusual	(X)	(__)	(__)	(__)

Speech	N/A or OK	Slight	Moderate	Severe
Rapid	(X)	(__)	(__)	(__)
Slow	(X)	(__)	(__)	(__)
Loud	(__)	(__)	(X)	(__)
Soft	(__)	(__)	(__)	(__)
Mute	(X)	(__)	(__)	(__)
Atypical (e.g., slurring)	(X)	(__)	(__)	(__)

Attitude	N/A or OK	Slight	Moderate	Severe
Domineering, controlling	(__)	(__)	(X)	(__)
Submissive, dependent	(X)	(__)	(__)	(__)
Hostile, challenging	(__)	(__)	(X)	(__)
Guarded, suspicious	(__)	(__)	(X)	(__)
Uncooperative	(__)	(__)	(__)	(X)

Affect	N/A or OK	Slight	Moderate	Severe
Inappropriate to thought	(X)	(__)	(__)	(__)
Increased liability	(__)	(__)	(X)	(__)
Blunted, dull, flat	(X)	(__)	(__)	(__)
Euphoria, elation	(X)	(__)	(__)	(__)
Anger, hostility	(__)	(__)	(X)	(__)
Depression, sadness	(X)	(__)	(__)	(__)
Anxiety	(X)	(__)	(__)	(__)
Irritability	(__)	(__)	(__)	(X)

Perception	N/A or OK	Slight	Moderate	Severe
Illusions	(X)	(__)	(__)	(__)
Auditory hallucinations	(X)	(__)	(__)	(__)
Visual hallucinations	(X)	(__)	(__)	(__)
Other hallucinations	(X)	(__)	(__)	(__)
Cognitive	N/A or OK	Slight	Moderate	Severe
Alertness	(X)	(__)	(__)	(__)
Attn. span, distractibility	(__)	(X)	(__)	(__)
Short-term memory	(X)	(__)	(__)	(__)
Long-term memory	(X)	(__)	(__)	(__)
Judgment Issues	N/A or OK	Slight	Moderate	Severe
Decision making	(__)	(X)	(__)	(__)
Impulsivity	(__)	(__)	(X)	(__)
Thought Content	N/A or OK	Slight	Moderate	Severe
Obsessions/compulsions	(X)	(__)	(__)	(__)
Phobic	(X)	(__)	(__)	(__)
Depersonalization	(X)	(__)	(__)	(__)
Suicidal ideation	(X)	(__)	(__)	(__)
Homicidal ideation	(X)	(__)	(__)	(__)
Delusions	(X)	(__)	(__)	(__)

Estimated level of intelligence: _average_

Orientation: _X_ Time   _X_ Place   _X_ Person

Able to hold normal conversation? _X_ Yes   ___ No

Eye contact: _Poor_

Level of insight:

    ___ Complete denial   ___ Slight awareness

    _X_ Blames others   ___ Blames self

    ___ Intellectual insight, but few changes likely

    ___ Emotional insight, understanding, change can occur

Client's view of actions needed to change: _"Nothing, except have dad back"_

Comments

_ Very loud in waiting room with threats to walk home. Several statements about desire to get out_

_ of his "stupid family." Seemed to smile when mother discussed current behavioral issues._

_ Threatened to leave session three times. Appeared angry, frustrated and agitated. Very persistant._

PART C. DIAGNOSIS VALIDATION

Diagnosis 1: _Oppositional Defiant Disorder_   Code: _313.81_

DSM criteria:

Loses temper easily and often, daily arguing with adults, very defiant toward adults when simple

requests made. Usually blames others for own mistakes, usually angry and spiteful toward family.

Examples of impairment/dysfunction: _No friends, failing in school._

Additional validation (e.g., testing, previous records, self-report): _School reports indicate 17_

in–school suspensions in past month.

Diagnosis 2: _Adjustment Disorder: conduct, chronic_   Code: _309.3_

DSM Criteria

Stressor: parental divorce and remarriage of mother. During past 2 years increased stressors

which compound each other. Since that time dramatic conduct problems.

Examples of impairment/dysfunction: _Behavioral outbursts, bullying, fighting._

Additional validation (e.g. testing, previous records, self-report): _School reports indicate being_

sent home 2 times in past month for bullying.

Diagnosis 3: _____   Code: _____

DSM Criteria

Examples of impairment/dysfunction: _____

Additional validation (e.g. testing, previous records, self-report): _____

	Diagnosis	Code

Axis I   1: _Oppositional Defiant Disorder_   _313.81_

           2: _Adj. Disorder: conduct, chronic_   _309.3_

           3: _____

Axis II   1: _No diagnosis_   _V71.09_

           2: _____

Axis III   _Defer to physician_

Axis IV   _Social, family, and academic problems_

Axis V   Current GAF = _58_   Highest past year GAF = _65_

Prognosis: ___ Poor   ___ Marginal   ___ Guarded   _X_ Moderate   ___ Good   ___ Excellent

Qualifiers to prognosis: ___ Med compliance   _X_ Tx compliance   _X_ Home environment

   ___ Activity changes   _X_ Behavioral changes   _X_ Attitudinal changes   ___ Education/training

   ___ Other: _____

Treatment Considerations

Is the patient appropriate for treatment? _X_ Yes   ___ No

If no, explain and indicate referral made: _____

Tx modality: _X_ Indiv.   ___ Conjoint   _X_ Family   ___ Collateral   ___ Group

Frequency: _weekly_   _____   _2x/mo_   _____   _____

If Conjoint, Family or Collateral, specify with whom: _mother, step-father, sister_

Adjunctive Services Needed: _X_ Physical exam   _X_ School records

                   ___ Laboratory tests (specify): _____

                   ___ Patient records (specify): _____

Therapist's Questions/Concerns/Comments: ___ Psychiatric evaluation   _X_ Psychological testing

   (1) Would in-home family counseling be helpful?

   (2) What about our anger management group?

Therapist's signature/credentials: _Charles W. Wollat, MSW_   Date: _4_ / _4_ / _1999_

Supervisor's Remarks

   (1) Yes, perhaps after a few family sessions here

   (2) Probably helpful

Supervisor's signature/credentials: _Samuel Jones, LICSW_   Date: _4_ / _4_ / _1999_

(Certifies diagnosis, treatment plan, level of care, mental status evaluation, and therapist assignment)

Therapist's Remarks to Supervisor's Remarks

   None

Therapist's signature/credentials: _Charles W. Wollat, MSW_   Date: _4_ / _12_ / _1999_

Form 12　Biographical Information Form—Adult

Instructions: To assist us in helping you, please fill out this form as fully and openly as possible. All private information is held in strictest confidence within legal limits. If certain questions do not apply to you, leave them blank.

Personal History

1) Name: _____ 2) Age: _____ 3) Gender: ___ M ___ F

4) Address: _____ City: _____ State: _____ Zip: _____

5) Weight: _____ 6) Height: _____ 7) Eye color: _____ 8) Hair color: _____ 9) Race: _____

10) Today's date: _____ 11) Date of birth: _____ 12) Years of education: _____

13) Occupation: _____ 14) Home phone: _____ 15) Business phone: _____

16) Present marital status:

  ___ 1) never married   ___ 5) separated

  ___ 2) engaged to be married   ___ 6) divorced and not remarried

  ___ 3) married now for first time   ___ 7) widowed and not remarried

  ___ 4) married now after first time   ___ 8) other (specify) _____

17) If married, are you living with your spouse at present? ___ Yes ___ No

18) If married, years married to present spouse: _____

Counseling History

19) Are you receiving counseling services at present? ___ Yes ___ No

  If Yes, please briefly describe: _____

_____

20) Have you received counseling in the past? ___ Yes ___ No

  If Yes, please briefly describe: _____

_____

21) What is (are) your main reason(s) for this visit? _____

_____

_____

22) How long has this problem persisted (from #21)? _____

_____

_____

23) Under what conditions do your problems usually get worse? _____

_____

_____

24) Under what conditions are your problems usually improved? _____

_____

_____

25) How did you hear about this clinic, or who referred you? _____

_____

_____

26) Name and address of your primary physician:

Physician's name: _____

Address: _____

27) List any major illnesses and/or operations you have had: _____

_____

_____

28) List any physical concerns you are having at present (e.g., high blood pressure, headaches, dizziness, etc.): _____

_____

_____

29) List any other physical concerns you are having at present: _____

_____

_____

30) When was your most recent complete physical exam? _____

Results of physical exam: _____

_____

31) On average how many hours of sleep do you get daily? _____

32) Do you have trouble falling asleep at night? ___ Yes   ___ No

If Yes, describe: _____

_____

33) Have you gained/lost over ten pounds in the past year? ___ Yes ___ No, ___ gained ___ lost

If Yes, was the gain/loss on purpose? ___ Yes   ___ No

34) Describe your appetite (during the past week):

___ poor appetite   ___ average appetite   ___ large appetite

35) What medications (and dosages) are you taking at present, and for what purpose?

Medication	Purpose
_____	_____
_____	_____
_____	_____
_____	_____

36) What is your present religious affiliation?

___ 1) Catholic

___ 2) Jewish

___ 3) Protestant (specify denomination if any) _____

___ 4) None, but I believe in God

___ 5) Atheist or agnostic

___ 6) Other (please specify) _____

37) How important is religious commitment to you?

Unimportant   Average importance   Extremely important

   1   2   3   4   5   6   7

38) Do you desire to have your religious beliefs and values incorporated into the counseling process?

___ Yes ___ No ___ Not sure   (If Yes, please explain): _____

_____

39) Mother's age: _____   If deceased, how old were you when she died? _____

40) Father's age: _____   If deceased, how old were you when he died? _____

41) If your parents separated or divorced, how old were you then? _____

42) Number of brother(s) _____   Their ages: _____ _____ _____ _____ _____ _____

43) Number of sister(s) _____   Their ages: _____ _____ _____ _____ _____ _____

44) I was child number _____ in a family of _____ children.

45) Were you adopted or raised with parents other than your natural parents? ___ Yes ___ No

46) Briefly describe your relationship with your brothers and/or sisters: _____

_____

_____

47) Which of the following best describes the family in which you grew up?

Warm and accepting   Average   Hostile and fighting

   1   2   3   4   5   6   7   8   9

48) Which of the following best describes the way in which your family raised you?

Allowed me to be   Attempted to

very independent   Average   control me

   1   2   3   4   5   6   7   8   9

Your Mother (or mother substitute)

49) Briefly describe your mother: _____

_____

_____

50) How did she discipline you? _____

_____

_____

51) How did she reward you? _____

_____

_____

52) How much time did she spend with you when you were a child?

___ much   ___ average   ___ little

53) Your mother's occupation when you were a child: _____

___ stayed home   ___ worked outside part-time   ___ worked outside full-time

54) How did you get along with your mother when you were a child?

___ poorly   ___ average   ___ well

55) How do you get along with your mother now?

___ poorly   ___ average   ___ well

56) Did you mother have any problems (e.g., alcoholism, violence, etc.) that may have affected your childhood development? ___ Yes   ___ No

If Yes, please describe: _____

_____

57) Is there anything unusual about your relationship with your mother? ___ Yes   ___ No

If Yes, please describe: _____

_____

58) Describe overall how your mother treated the following people as you were growing up:

(Circle one answer for each)

Your mother's treatment of:	Poor			Average			Excellent
1) You	1	2	3	4	5	6	7
2) Your family	1	2	3	4	5	6	7
3) Your father	1	2	3	4	5	6	7

Your Father (or father substitute)

59) Briefly describe your father: _____

_____

_____

60) How did he discipline you? _____

_____

_____

61) How did he reward you? _____

_____

_____

62) How much time did he spend with you when you were a child?

___ much   ___ average   ___ little

63) Your father's occupation when you were a child: _____

___ stayed home   ___ worked outside part-time   ___ worked outside full-time

64) How did you get along with your father when you were a child?

___ poorly   ___ average   ___ well

65) How do you get along with your father now?

___ poorly   ___ average   ___ well

66) Did you father have any problems (e.g., alcoholism, violence) that may have affected your childhood development? ___ Yes   ___ No

If Yes, please describe: _____

_____

67) Is there anything unusual about your relationship with your father? ___ Yes   ___ No

If Yes, please describe: _____

_____

68) Describe overall how your father treated the following people as you were growing up:

(Circle one answer for each)

Your father's treatment of:	Poor			Average			Excellent
1) You	1	2	3	4	5	6	7
2) Your family	1	2	3	4	5	6	7
3) Your mother	1	2	3	4	5	6	7

Thoughts and Behaviors

69) Please check how often the following thoughts occur to you:

1) Life is hopeless. ___ Never ___ Rarely ___ Sometimes ___ Frequently
2) I am lonely. ___ Never ___ Rarely ___ Sometimes ___ Frequently
3) No one cares about me. ___ Never ___ Rarely ___ Sometimes ___ Frequently
4) I am a failure. ___ Never ___ Rarely ___ Sometimes ___ Frequently
5) Most people don't like me. ___ Never ___ Rarely ___ Sometimes ___ Frequently
6) I want to die. ___ Never ___ Rarely ___ Sometimes ___ Frequently
7) I want to hurt someone. ___ Never ___ Rarely ___ Sometimes ___ Frequently
8) I am so stupid. ___ Never ___ Rarely ___ Sometimes ___ Frequently
9) I am going crazy. ___ Never ___ Rarely ___ Sometimes ___ Frequently
10) I can't concentrate. ___ Never ___ Rarely ___ Sometimes ___ Frequently
11) I am so depressed. ___ Never ___ Rarely ___ Sometimes ___ Frequently
12) God is disappointed in me. ___ Never ___ Rarely ___ Sometimes ___ Frequently
13) I can't be forgiven. ___ Never ___ Rarely ___ Sometimes ___ Frequently
14) Why am I so different? ___ Never ___ Rarely ___ Sometimes ___ Frequently
15) I can't do anything right. ___ Never ___ Rarely ___ Sometimes ___ Frequently
16) People hear my thoughts. ___ Never ___ Rarely ___ Sometimes ___ Frequently
17) I have no emotions. ___ Never ___ Rarely ___ Sometimes ___ Frequently
18) Someone is watching me. ___ Never ___ Rarely ___ Sometimes ___ Frequently
19) I hear voices in my head. ___ Never ___ Rarely ___ Sometimes ___ Frequently
20) I am out of control. ___ Never ___ Rarely ___ Sometimes ___ Frequently

Please comment (e.g., examples, frequency, duration, effects on you) about each of the above thought that occur frequently or are a concern to you. Use the back of this sheet is necessary.

_____
_____
_____
_____
_____
_____
_____
_____
_____

2.47

Symptoms

70) Check the behaviors and symptoms that occur to you more often than you would like them to take place:

___ aggression	___ fatigue	___ sexual difficulties
___ alcohol dependence	___ hallucinations	___ sick often
___ anger	___ heart palpitations	___ sleeping problems
___ antisocial behavior	___ high blood pressure	___ speech problems
___ anxiety	___ hopelessness	___ suicidal thoughts
___ avoiding people	___ impulsivity	___ thoughts disorganized
___ chest pain	___ irritability	___ trembling
___ depression	___ judgment errors	___ withdrawing
___ disorientation	___ loneliness	___ worrying
___ distractibility	___ memory impairment	___ other (specify)
___ dizziness	___ mood shifts	_____
___ drug dependence	___ panic attacks	_____
___ eating disorder	___ phobias/fears	_____
___ elevated mood	___ recurring thoughts	_____

Please give examples of how each of the symptoms you checked impairs your ability to function (e.g., socially, emotionally, occupationally, physically). Use the back of this sheet if necessary.

_____

_____

_____

_____

_____

_____

_____

_____

_____

_____

71) List your five greatest strengths:

1) _____

2) _____

3) _____

4) _____

5) _____

72) List your five greatest weaknesses:

1) _____

2) _____

3) _____

4) _____

5) _____

73) List your main social difficulties: _____

_____

_____

_____

_____

74) List your main love and sex difficulties: _____

_____

_____

_____

_____

75) List your main difficulties at school or work: _____

_____

_____

_____

_____

76) List your main difficulties at home: _____

_____

_____

_____

_____

77) List your behaviors you would like to change: _____

_____

_____

_____

_____

78) Additional information you believe would be helpful: _____

_____

_____

_____

_____

PLEASE RETURN THIS AND OTHER ASSESSMENT MATERIALS TO THIS
OFFICE AT LEAST TWO DAYS BEFORE YOUR NEXT APPOINTMENT.

Form 12A Biographical Information Form—Adult
(Completed)

Instructions: To assist us in helping you, please fill out this form as fully and openly as possible. All private information is held in strictest confidence within legal limits. If certain questions do not apply to you, leave them blank.

Personal History

1) Name: _Judy Doe_   2) Age: _50_   3) Gender: ___ M _X_ F

4) Address: _1234 Main St._   City: _Pleasantville_   State: _NJ_   Zip: _99999_

5) Weight: _148_ 6) Height: _5–3_ 7) Eye color: _Bl_ 8) Hair color: _Br_ 9) Race: _Cau_

10) Today's date: _3/12/1999_   11) Date of birth: _7/6/1948_   12) Years of education: _16_

13) Occupation: _Teacher_   14) Home phone: _555-5555_   15) Business phone: _555-5544_

16) Present marital status:

    ___ 1) never married   ___ 5) separated

    ___ 2) engaged to be married   ___ 6) divorced and not remarried

    _X_ 3) married now for first time   ___ 7) widowed and not remarried

    ___ 4) married now after first time   ___ 8) other (specify) _____

17) If married, are you living with your spouse at present? _X_ Yes ___ No

18) If married, years married to present spouse: _22_

Counseling History

19) Are you receiving counseling services at present? ___ Yes _X_ No

    If Yes, please briefly describe: _____

_____

20) Have you received counseling in the past? _X_ Yes ___ No

    If Yes, please briefly describe: _In 1968 when in college I had a stressful relationship breakup. I went through therapy for about one year for depression._

21) What is (are) your main reason(s) for this visit? _I am depressed. I just don't care about things at home or at work._

22) How long has this problem persisted (from #21)? _Mainly in the past year, but I've been this way before in my life._

23) Under what conditions do your problems usually get worse? _When there are too many demands placed on me._

24) Under what conditions are your problems usually improved? _When I'm alone._

25) How did you hear about this clinic, or who referred you? ___*Yellow pages*___
_____
_____

26) Name and address of your primary physician:

Physician's name: ___*Dr. Hope Wellby*___

Address: ___*The Clinic*___

27) List any major illnesses and/or operations you have had: *None*___
_____
_____

28) List any physical concerns you are having at present (e.g., high blood pressure, headaches, dizziness, etc.): ___*Occasional headaches*___
_____
_____

29) List any other physical concerns you are having at present: ___*None*___
_____
_____

30) When was your most recent complete physical exam? ___*5 years ago*___

Results of physical exam: ___*Good health*___
_____

31) On average how many hours of sleep do you get daily? ___*5*___

32) Do you have trouble falling asleep at night? _*X*_ Yes ___ No

If Yes, describe: ___*It often takes a few hours just to fall asleep. I don't know why.*___
_____

33) Have you gained/lost over ten pounds in the past year? _*X*_ Yes ___ No, ___ gained _*X*_ lost

If Yes, was the gain/loss on purpose? ___ Yes _*X*_ No

34) Describe your appetite (during the past week):

_*X*_ poor appetite ___ average appetite ___ large appetite

35) What medications (and dosages) are you taking at present, and for what purpose?

Medication	Purpose
None	

36) What is your present religious affiliation?

___ 1) Catholic

___ 2) Jewish

___ 3) Protestant (specify denomination if any) _____

_*X*_ 4) None, but I believe in God

___ 5) Atheist or agnostic

___ 6) Other (please specify) _____

37) How important is religious commitment to you?

Unimportant   Average importance   Extremely important

    1   2   3   4   5   (6)   7

38) Do you desire to have your religious beliefs and values incorporated into the counseling process?

___ Yes   _X_ No   ___ Not sure   (If Yes, please explain): _____

_____

39) Mother's age: _____71_____   If deceased, how old were you when she died? _____

40) Father's age: __*Deceased*__   If deceased, how old were you when he died? _____39_____

41) If your parents separated or divorced, how old were you then? _____

42) Number of brother(s) __2__   Their ages: _51_   _42_   ____   ____   ____   ____

43) Number of sister(s) __2__   Their ages: _46_   _44_   ____   ____   ____   ____

44) I was child number __5__ in a family of __5__ children.

45) Were you adopted or raised with parents other than your natural parents? ___ Yes   _X_ No

46) Briefly describe your relationship with your brothers and/or sisters: __*We got along well.*__

    __*Typical family ups and downs.*__ _____

_____

47) Which of the following best describes the family in which you grew up?

Warm and accepting   Average   Hostile and fighting

   1   (2)   3   4   5   6   7   8   9

48) Which of the following best describes the way in which your family raised you?

Allowed me to be   Attempted to

very independent   Average   control me

   1   2   3   4   5   6   (7)   8   9

Your Mother (or mother substitute)

49) Briefly describe your mother: __*Kind, giving, did too much for others.*__

_____

_____

50) How did she discipline you? __*Sent me to my room and lectured me.*__

_____

_____

51) How did she reward you? __*Go shopping, extra allowance money.*__

_____

_____

52) How much time did she spend with you when you were a child?

___ much   _X_ average   ___ little

53) Your mother's occupation when you were a child: __*Worked in a bakery*__

___ stayed home   ___ worked outside part-time   _X_ worked outside full-time

54) How did you get along with your mother when you were a child?

___ poorly   ___ average   _X_ well

55) How do you get along with your mother now?

___ poorly   ___ average   _X_ well

56) Did you mother have any problems (e.g., alcoholism, violence, etc.) that may have affected your childhood development? ___ Yes _X_ No

If Yes, please describe: _____

_____

57) Is there anything unusual about your relationship with your mother? ___ Yes _X_ No

If Yes, please describe: _____

_____

58) Describe overall how your mother treated the following people as you were growing up:

(Circle one answer for each)

Your mother's treatment of:	Poor			Average			Excellent
1) You	1	2	3	4	5	(6)	7
2) Your family	1	2	3	4	5	(6)	7
3) Your father	1	2	3	4	5	(6)	7

Your Father (or father substitute)

59) Briefly describe your father: ___*Fun, but stern*_____

_____

_____

60) How did he discipline you? ___*Light spanking or grounded*_____

_____

_____

61) How did he reward you? ___*Money, toys, dolls, etc.*_____

_____

_____

62) How much time did he spend with you when you were a child?

___ much   _X_ average   ___ little

63) Your father's occupation when you were a child: _*TV repairman*_____

___ stayed home   ___ worked outside part-time   _X_ worked outside full-time

64) How did you get along with your father when you were a child?

___ poorly   ___ average   _X_ well

65) How do you get along with your father now?

___ poorly   ___ average   _X_ well

66) Did you father have any problems (e.g., alcoholism, violence) that may have affected your childhood development? _?_ Yes _?_ No

If Yes, please describe: ___*Drank socially on weekends. May have been intoxicated at times*___

_____

67) Is there anything unusual about your relationship with your father? ___ Yes _X_ No

If Yes, please describe: _____

_____

2.53

68) Describe overall how your father treated the following people as you were growing up:

(Circle one answer for each)

Your father's treatment of:	Poor			Average			Excellent
1) You	1	2	3	4	5	6	(7)
2) Your family	1	2	3	4	5	6	(7)
3) Your mother	1	2	3	4	5	6	(7)

Thoughts and Behaviors

69) Please check how often the following thoughts occur to you:

	Never	Rarely	Sometimes	Frequently
1) Life is hopeless.	___ Never	___ Rarely	___ Sometimes	_X_ Frequently
2) I am lonely.	___ Never	___ Rarely	___ Sometimes	_X_ Frequently
3) No one cares about me.	___ Never	___ Rarely	___ Sometimes	_X_ Frequently
4) I am a failure.	___ Never	___ Rarely	___ Sometimes	_X_ Frequently
5) Most people don't like me.	___ Never	___ Rarely	_X_ Sometimes	___ Frequently
6) I want to die.	___ Never	___ Rarely	___ Sometimes	_X_ Frequently
7) I want to hurt someone.	___ Never	_X_ Rarely	___ Sometimes	___ Frequently
8) I am so stupid.	___ Never	___ Rarely	_X_ Sometimes	___ Frequently
9) I am going crazy.	___ Never	_X_ Rarely	___ Sometimes	___ Frequently
10) I can't concentrate.	___ Never	___ Rarely	___ Sometimes	_X_ Frequently
11) I am so depressed.	___ Never	___ Rarely	___ Sometimes	_X_ Frequently
12) God is disappointed in me.	___ Never	___ Rarely	_X_ Sometimes	___ Frequently
13) I can't be forgiven.	___ Never	___ Rarely	_X_ Sometimes	___ Frequently
14) Why am I so different?	___ Never	___ Rarely	_X_ Sometimes	___ Frequently
15) I can't do anything right.	___ Never	___ Rarely	_X_ Sometimes	___ Frequently
16) People hear my thoughts.	_X_ Never	___ Rarely	___ Sometimes	___ Frequently
17) I have no emotions.	___ Never	___ Rarely	___ Sometimes	_X_ Frequently
18) Someone is watching me.	_X_ Never	___ Rarely	___ Sometimes	___ Frequently
19) I hear voices in my head.	_X_ Never	___ Rarely	___ Sometimes	___ Frequently
20) I am out of control.	_X_ Never	___ Rarely	___ Sometimes	___ Frequently

Please comment (e.g., examples, frequency, duration, effects on you) about each of the above thought that occur frequently or are a concern to you. Use the back of this sheet is necessary.

I just don't care about anything. I don't want to be around others, go to work, or even get up in the morning. When people ask me how I'm doing, I just want to say, "fine" and find a place to hide. I'm a loser, so why should I try to get ahead? No one cares—they just care about themselves. Maybe I should just quit teaching. What can people learn from me? Usually I just feel nothing inside and don't care. Often I want to die, but that's not right. It's like I'm around lots of people, but still alone. What's the use?

Symptoms

70) Check the behaviors and symptoms that occur to you more often than you would like them to take place:

___ aggression	_X_ fatigue	_X_ sexual difficulties
___ alcohol dependence	___ hallucinations	_X_ sick often
___ anger	___ heart palpitations	_X_ sleeping problems
___ antisocial behavior	___ high blood pressure	___ speech problems
___ anxiety	_X_ hopelessness	_X_ suicidal thoughts
_X_ avoiding people	___ impulsivity	___ thoughts disorganized
___ chest pain	___ irritability	___ trembling
_X_ depression	___ judgment errors	_X_ withdrawing
___ disorientation	_X_ loneliness	_X_ worrying
_X_ distractibility	___ memory impairment	___ other (specify)
___ dizziness	___ mood shifts	_____
___ drug dependence	___ panic attacks	_____
___ eating disorder	___ phobias/fears	_____
___ elevated mood	___ recurring thoughts	_____

Please give examples of how each of the symptoms you checked impairs your ability to function (e.g., socially, emotionally, occupationally, physically). Use the back of this sheet if necessary.

My friends are not visiting me. When my husband is upset I get down. I don't want to be around others because they know what a loser I am. Why am I always so sick and tired? I can't keep my mind on anything anymore. I no longer have any interest in sex. I worry all the time about money, people, and what is in the future. When I get too upset, I look for an argument. I'm sure I'll lost my job. I won't commit suicide, but no one would notice if I did. Lately, when I teach, I will be talking about a subject and forget what I have told the students and feel really stupid. Lately, I've gotten up in the morning and felt too sick to go work.

71) List your five greatest strengths:
   1) _Good provider_
   2) _Religious beliefs_
   3) _Honest_
   4) _____
   5) _____

72) List your five greatest weaknesses:
   1) _Impatient_
   2) _Hard to take much pressure_
   3) _Give up too easily_
   4) _Intolerant of other people's differences_
   5) _____

2.55

73) List your main social difficulties: *I don't feel like being around other people. I don't want to meet new people. What do I have to offer?*

74) List your main love and sex difficulties: *I have no interest in sex anymore. No one can make me happy. Why would anyone love me? What do I have to offer? I feel no love toward my spouse.*

75) List your main difficulties at school or work: *I used to enjoy teaching, but now I dread seeing students and colleagues. Nothing happens. No one cares. I don't care either.*

76) List your main difficulties at home: *Frustrated with husband because he treats me like a child. Children won't help out and it's hard to keep up around the house.*

77) List your behaviors you would like to change: *Be more motivated, happy, and friendly (the way I used to be).*

78) Additional information you believe would be helpful: *If this counseling doesn't help, I'll probably lose my job and marriage. I'm going nowhere.*

PLEASE RETURN THIS AND OTHER ASSESSMENT MATERIALS TO THIS OFFICE AT LEAST TWO DAYS BEFORE YOUR NEXT APPOINTMENT.

Form 13   Biographical Information Form—Child

Instructions: To assist us in helping your child, please fill out this form as fully and openly as possible. All private information is held in strictest confidence within legal limits. If certain questions do not apply to the child, leave them blank.

Information supplied by: _____   Relationship: _____

Personal History

1) Child's name: _____   2) Age: _____   3) Gender: ___ M   ___ F

4) Weight: _____   5) Height: _____   6) Eye color: _____   7) Hair color: _____   8) Race: _____

9) Address: _____   City: _____   State: _____   Zip: _____

10) Today's date: _____   11) Date of birth: _____

12) Home phone: _____   13) Year in school: _____

14) Has the child been involved in previous counseling? ___ Yes   ___ No

    If Yes, please describe: _____

_____

15) Why is the child coming to counseling? _____

_____

16) How long has this problem persisted (from #15)? _____

17) Under what conditions do the problems usually get worse? _____

_____

18) Under what conditions are the problems usually improved? _____

_____

Medical History

19) Name and address of your primary physician:

    Physician's name: _____

    Address: _____   City: _____   State: _____   Zip: _____

    Most recent physical exam: _____   Results: _____

20) List any major illnesses and/or operations: _____

_____

21) List any physical concerns occurring at present: (e.g., high blood pressure, headaches, dizziness):

_____

_____

22) List any physical concerns (e.g., head trauma, seizures) experienced in the past: _____

_____

23) On average how many hours does the child sleep daily? _____

24) Does the child have trouble falling asleep at night? ___ Yes ___ No

If Yes, how long has this been a problem? _____

25) Describe the child's appetite (during the past week):

___ poor appetite ___ average appetite ___ large appetite

26) What medications (and dosages) are you taking at present, and for what purpose? _____

_____

Family History

27) Mother's age: _____ If deceased, how old was the child when she passed away? _____

28) Father's age: _____ If deceased, how old was the child when he passed away? _____

29) If parents separated or divorced, how old was the child then? _____

30) Number of brother(s) _____ Their ages: _____ _____ _____ _____ _____ _____

31) Number of sister(s) _____ Their ages: _____ _____ _____ _____ _____ _____

32) I was child number _____ in a family of _____ children.

33) Is the child adopted or raised with parents other than biological parents? ___ Yes ___ No

34) Briefly describe the child's relationship with brothers and/or sisters:

Biological siblings: _____

_____

Step and/or half siblings: _____

_____

Other: _____

_____

35) What is the family relationship between the child and his/her custodial parents?

___ Single parent mother ___ Single parent father ___ Parents unmarried

___ Parents married, together ___ Parents divorced ___ Parents separated

___ With mother and stepfather ___ With father and stepmother

___ Child adopted ___ Other, describe: _____

36) Is there a history or recent occurrence(s) of child abuse to this child? ___ Yes ___ No

If Yes, which type(s) of abuse? ___ Verbal ___ Physical ___ Sexual

Comments: _____

_____

_____

_____

_____

37) Parents' occupations: Mother: _____ Father: _____

38) Briefly describe the style of parenting used in the household: _____

_____

_____

_____

_____

Developmental History

39) Briefly describe any problems in the child's mother's pregnancy and/or childbirth: _____
_____

40) Please fill in when the following developmental milestones took place?

Behavior	Age began	Comments
Walking	_____	_____
Talking	_____	_____
Toilet trained	_____	_____

41) List any drugs used by mother of father at time of conception, or by mother during pregnancy:
_____

42) Please rate your opinion of the child's development (compared to others the same age) in the following areas:

	Below average	About average	Above average
Social	_____	_____	_____
Physical	_____	_____	_____
Language	_____	_____	_____
Intellectual	_____	_____	_____
Emotional	_____	_____	_____

For each type of development that you rated above as *below* average, please describe current areas of concern. Be specific.

_____
_____

43) List the child's three greatest strengths:
1) _____
2) _____
3) _____

44) List the child's three greatest weaknesses or needed areas of improvement:
1) _____
2) _____
3) _____

45) List the child's main difficulties in school:
1) _____
2) _____
3) _____

46) List the child's main difficulties at home:
1) _____
2) _____
3) _____

47) Briefly describe the child's friendships: _____
_____
_____

48) What report card grades does the child usually receive? _____
Have theses changed lately? ___ Yes ___ No   If Yes, how? _____

49) Briefly describe the child's hobbies and interests: _____
_____

50) Describe how the child is disciplined: _____
_____

51) For what reasons is the child disciplined: _____
_____

Behaviors of Concern

52) Please check how often the following behaviors occur. Those occurring FREQUENTLY or of special concern may be described on the next page.

1) Loses temper easily	___ Never	___ Rarely	___ Sometimes	___ Frequently
2) Argues with adults	___ Never	___ Rarely	___ Sometimes	___ Frequently
3) Refuses adults' requests	___ Never	___ Rarely	___ Sometimes	___ Frequently
4) Deliberately annoys people	___ Never	___ Rarely	___ Sometimes	___ Frequently
5) Blames others for own mistakes	___ Never	___ Rarely	___ Sometimes	___ Frequently
6) Easily annoyed by others	___ Never	___ Rarely	___ Sometimes	___ Frequently
7) Angry/resentful	___ Never	___ Rarely	___ Sometimes	___ Frequently
8) Spiteful/vindictive	___ Never	___ Rarely	___ Sometimes	___ Frequently
9) Defiant	___ Never	___ Rarely	___ Sometimes	___ Frequently
10) Bullies/teases others	___ Never	___ Rarely	___ Sometimes	___ Frequently
11) Initiates fights	___ Never	___ Rarely	___ Sometimes	___ Frequently
12) Uses a weapon	___ Never	___ Rarely	___ Sometimes	___ Frequently
13) Physically cruel to people	___ Never	___ Rarely	___ Sometimes	___ Frequently
14) Physically cruel to animals	___ Never	___ Rarely	___ Sometimes	___ Frequently
15) Stealing	___ Never	___ Rarely	___ Sometimes	___ Frequently
16) Forced sexual activity	___ Never	___ Rarely	___ Sometimes	___ Frequently
17) Intentional arson	___ Never	___ Rarely	___ Sometimes	___ Frequently
18) Burglary	___ Never	___ Rarely	___ Sometimes	___ Frequently
19) "Cons" other people	___ Never	___ Rarely	___ Sometimes	___ Frequently
20) Runs away from home	___ Never	___ Rarely	___ Sometimes	___ Frequently
21) Truant at school	___ Never	___ Rarely	___ Sometimes	___ Frequently
22) Doesn't pay attention to details	___ Never	___ Rarely	___ Sometimes	___ Frequently
23) Several careless mistakes	___ Never	___ Rarely	___ Sometimes	___ Frequently
24) Does not listen when spoken to	___ Never	___ Rarely	___ Sometimes	___ Frequently
25) Doesn't finish chores/homework	___ Never	___ Rarely	___ Sometimes	___ Frequently
26) Difficulty organizing tasks	___ Never	___ Rarely	___ Sometimes	___ Frequently
27) Loses things	___ Never	___ Rarely	___ Sometimes	___ Frequently
28) Easily distracted	___ Never	___ Rarely	___ Sometimes	___ Frequently
29) Forgetful in daily activities	___ Never	___ Rarely	___ Sometimes	___ Frequently
30) Fidgety/squirmy	___ Never	___ Rarely	___ Sometimes	___ Frequently
31) Difficulty remaining seated	___ Never	___ Rarely	___ Sometimes	___ Frequently
32) Runs/climbs around excessively	___ Never	___ Rarely	___ Sometimes	___ Frequently
33) Difficulty playing quietly	___ Never	___ Rarely	___ Sometimes	___ Frequently
34) Hyperactive	___ Never	___ Rarely	___ Sometimes	___ Frequently
35) Difficulty awaiting turn	___ Never	___ Rarely	___ Sometimes	___ Frequently
36) Interrupts others	___ Never	___ Rarely	___ Sometimes	___ Frequently
37) Problems pronouncing words	___ Never	___ Rarely	___ Sometimes	___ Frequently

38) Poor grades in school	___ Never	___ Rarely	___ Sometimes	___ Frequently
39) Expelled from school	___ Never	___ Rarely	___ Sometimes	___ Frequently
40) Drug abuse	___ Never	___ Rarely	___ Sometimes	___ Frequently
41) Alcohol consumption	___ Never	___ Rarely	___ Sometimes	___ Frequently
42) Depression	___ Never	___ Rarely	___ Sometimes	___ Frequently
43) Shy/avoidant/withdrawn	___ Never	___ Rarely	___ Sometimes	___ Frequently
44) Suicide threats/attempts	___ Never	___ Rarely	___ Sometimes	___ Frequently
45) Fatigued	___ Never	___ Rarely	___ Sometimes	___ Frequently
46) Anxious/nervous	___ Never	___ Rarely	___ Sometimes	___ Frequently
47) Excessive worrying	___ Never	___ Rarely	___ Sometimes	___ Frequently
48) Sleep disturbance	___ Never	___ Rarely	___ Sometimes	___ Frequently
49) Panic attacks	___ Never	___ Rarely	___ Sometimes	___ Frequently
50) Mood shifts	___ Never	___ Rarely	___ Sometimes	___ Frequently

53) For each of the behaviors noted earlier as occurring FREQUENTLY, or if it causes significant impairment, write a brief description of how it impacts the child's or other people's lives. Give examples. Use the back of this page as needed.

Behaviors of concern   Impact on child or others

_____   _____
_____   _____
_____   _____
_____   _____
_____   _____
_____   _____
_____   _____
_____   _____
_____   _____
_____   _____
                                  _____
                                  _____
                                  _____

54) Briefly describe the child's way of expressing the following emotions or behaviors:

Anger: _____

Happiness: _____

Sadness: _____

Anxiety: _____

55) List the child's behaviors that you would like to see change: _____

_____

56) Additional information you believe would be helpful: _____

_____

PLEASE RETURN THIS AND OTHER ASSESSMENT MATERIALS TO THIS
OFFICE AT LEAST TWO DAYS BEFORE YOUR NEXT APPOINTMENT.

Form 13A   Biographical Information Form—Child

(Completed)

Instructions: To assist us in helping your child, please fill out this form as fully and openly as possible. All private information is held in strictest confidence within legal limits. If certain questions do not apply to the child, leave them blank.

Information supplied by: _Lisa Watters_   Relationship: _Mother_

Personal History

1) Child's name: _Christine Watters_   2) Age: _6_   3) Gender: ___ M _X_ F

4) Weight: _64_   5) Height: _44_   6) Eye color: _Brn_   7) Hair color: _Blk_ 8) Race: _Afr–Am_

9) Address: _4567 Hayward St._   City: _Tacoma_   State: _WA_ Zip: _99889_

10) Today's date: _4/2/1999_   11) Date of birth: _3/6/1993_

12) Home phone: _555-8899_   13) Year in school: _1st_

14) Has the child been involved in previous counseling? ___ Yes _X_ No

If Yes, please describe: _____

_____

15) Why is the child coming to counseling? _Disruptive behaviors. ADHD. Won't sit still. Needs to learn how to settle down._

16) How long has this problem persisted (from #15)? _About 3 years_

17) Under what conditions do the problems usually get worse? _When she does not get her way._

18) Under what conditions are the problems usually improved? _When she is not under any stress and things are calm._

Medical History

19) Name and address of your primary physician:

Physician's name: _Dr. Shawn Rellings_

Address: _45678 Hayward St._   City: _Tacoma_   State: _WA_ Zip: _99889_

Most recent physical exam: _Last year_   Results: _Good health_

20) List any major illnesses and/or operations: _None_

_____

21) List any physical concerns occurring at present: (e.g., high blood pressure, headaches, dizziness): _None_

_____

22) List any physical concerns (e.g., head trauma, seizures) experienced in the past: _None_

_____

23) On average how many hours does the child sleep daily? _9_

24) Does the child have trouble falling asleep at night? _X_ Yes _____ No

If Yes, how long has this been a problem? ___*3–4 years*___

25) Describe the child's appetite (during the past week):

___ poor appetite   _X_ average appetite   ___ large appetite

26) What medications (and dosages) are you taking at present, and for what purpose? ___*None*___

Family History

27) Mother's age: ___*32*___   If deceased, how old was the child when she passed away? _____

28) Father's age: ___*39*___   If deceased, how old was the child when he passed away? _____

29) If parents separated or divorced, how old was the child then? _____

30) Number of brother(s) ___*1*___   Their ages: ___*4*___ _____ _____ _____ _____ _____

31) Number of sister(s) ___*1*___   Their ages: ___*10*___ _____ _____ _____ _____ _____

32) I was child number ___*2*___ in a family of ___*3*___ children.

33) Is the child adopted or raised with parents other than biological parents? ___ Yes _X_ No

34) Briefly describe the child's relationship with brothers and/or sisters:

Biological siblings: ___*Increasingly annoying them. Picks on little brother. Tattles on older*___
___*sister all the time. Usually get along when supervised.*___

Step and/or half siblings: _____

Other: _____

35) What is the family relationship between the child and his/her custodial parents?

___ Single parent mother   ___ Single parent father   ___ Parents unmarried

_X_ Parents married, together   ___ Parents divorced   ___ Parents separated

___ With mother and stepfather   ___ With father and stepmother

___ Child adopted   ___ Other, describe: _____

36) Is there a history or recent occurrence(s) of child abuse to this child? ___ Yes _X_ No

If Yes, which type(s) of abuse? ___ Verbal ___ Physical ___ Sexual

Comments: _____
_____
_____
_____
_____

37) Parents' occupations: Mother: ___*Home catalog business*___   Father: ___*Insurance sales*___

38) Briefly describe the style of parenting used in the household: ___*Children are expected to behave*___
___*and obey their parents. When they don't listen or they disobey, they are sent to their room*___
___*for about one hour. When they behave they are praised. We have set rules and do not*___
___*"reason" with the children. But as they get older they will be given more liberties to learn*___
___*responsibility.*___

Developmental History

39) Briefly describe any problems in the child's mother's pregnancy and/or childbirth: ___None___

___

40) Please fill in when the following developmental milestones took place?

Behavior	Age began	Comments
Walking	13 months	It seemed like she ran before she walked.
Talking	20 months	Hasn't stopped since then.
Toilet trained	4 years	

41) List any drugs used by mother of father at time of conception, or by mother during pregnancy:

___None___

42) Please rate your opinion of the child's development (compared to others the same age) in the following areas:

	Below average	About average	Above average
Social	X		
Physical		X	
Language		X	
Intellectual		X	
Emotional	X		

For each type of development that you rated above as *below* average, please describe current areas of concern. Be specific.

___Social—Immature, often teased by classmates___

___Emotional—Temper tantrums when feeling too stressed___

43) List the child's three greatest strengths:

1) ___Enjoys sports___

2) ___Good health___

3) ___Want to be good___

44) List the child's three greatest weaknesses or needed areas of improvement:

1) ___Often refuses to do what she is asked___

2) ___Won't pay attention___

3) ___Schoolwork___

45) List the child's main difficulties in school:

1) ___Making friends___

2) ___Completing work___

3) ___Sitting still___

46) List the child's main difficulties at home:

1) ___Completing tasks___

2) ___Going to bed___

3) ___Hyperactive___

47) Briefly describe the child's friendships: ___One best friend for past year. Has brought people___ ___from school home, but friendships do not last very long. Teased by several children at___ ___school.___

48) What report card grades does the child usually receive? ___"Needs improvement."___

Have theses changed lately? ___ Yes ___X___ No   If Yes, how? _____

49) Briefly describe the child's hobbies and interests: _Video games, coloring. Sometimes will do_
    puzzles with little brother. Loves playing outside.

50) Describe how the child is disciplined: _Sent to room. Loses privileges. Never spanked._

51) For what reasons is the child disciplined: _Disobeying, not doing homework, picking on_
    sister.

Behaviors of Concern

52) Please check how often the following behaviors occur. Those occurring FREQUENTLY or of
    special concern may be described on the next page.

1)	Loses temper easily	___ Never	___ Rarely	_X_ Sometimes	___ Frequently
2)	Argues with adults	___ Never	___ Rarely	_X_ Sometimes	___ Frequently
3)	Refuses adults' requests	___ Never	___ Rarely	_X_ Sometimes	___ Frequently
4)	Deliberately annoys people	___ Never	___ Rarely	_X_ Sometimes	___ Frequently
5)	Blames others for own mistakes	___ Never	_X_ Rarely	___ Sometimes	___ Frequently
6)	Easily annoyed by others	___ Never	___ Rarely	_X_ Sometimes	___ Frequently
7)	Angry/resentful	___ Never	___ Rarely	_X_ Sometimes	___ Frequently
8)	Spiteful/vindictive	___ Never	___ Rarely	_X_ Sometimes	___ Frequently
9)	Defiant	___ Never	___ Rarely	_X_ Sometimes	___ Frequently
10)	Bullies/teases others	___ Never	_X_ Rarely	___ Sometimes	___ Frequently
11)	Initiates fights	_X_ Never	___ Rarely	___ Sometimes	___ Frequently
12)	Uses a weapon	_X_ Never	___ Rarely	___ Sometimes	___ Frequently
13)	Physically cruel to people	_X_ Never	___ Rarely	___ Sometimes	___ Frequently
14)	Physically cruel to animals	_X_ Never	___ Rarely	___ Sometimes	___ Frequently
15)	Stealing	___ Never	_X_ Rarely	___ Sometimes	___ Frequently
16)	Forced sexual activity	_X_ Never	___ Rarely	___ Sometimes	___ Frequently
17)	Intentional arson	_X_ Never	___ Rarely	___ Sometimes	___ Frequently
18)	Burglary	_X_ Never	___ Rarely	___ Sometimes	___ Frequently
19)	"Cons" other people	___ Never	_X_ Rarely	___ Sometimes	___ Frequently
20)	Runs away from home	_X_ Never	___ Rarely	___ Sometimes	___ Frequently
21)	Truant at school	_X_ Never	___ Rarely	___ Sometimes	___ Frequently
22)	Doesn't pay attention to details	___ Never	___ Rarely	_X_ Sometimes	___ Frequently
23)	Several careless mistakes	___ Never	___ Rarely	_X_ Sometimes	___ Frequently
24)	Does not listen when spoken to	___ Never	___ Rarely	_X_ Sometimes	___ Frequently
25)	Doesn't finish chores/homework	___ Never	___ Rarely	_X_ Sometimes	___ Frequently
26)	Difficulty organizing tasks	___ Never	___ Rarely	_X_ Sometimes	___ Frequently
27)	Loses things	___ Never	___ Rarely	_X_ Sometimes	___ Frequently
28)	Easily distracted	___ Never	___ Rarely	_X_ Sometimes	___ Frequently
29)	Forgetful in daily activities	___ Never	___ Rarely	_X_ Sometimes	___ Frequently
30)	Fidgety/squirmy	___ Never	___ Rarely	___ Sometimes	_X_ Frequently
31)	Difficulty remaining seated	___ Never	___ Rarely	___ Sometimes	_X_ Frequently
32)	Runs/climbs around excessively	___ Never	___ Rarely	___ Sometimes	_X_ Frequently
33)	Difficulty playing quietly	___ Never	___ Rarely	___ Sometimes	_X_ Frequently
34)	Hyperactive	___ Never	___ Rarely	___ Sometimes	_X_ Frequently
35)	Difficulty awaiting turn	___ Never	___ Rarely	___ Sometimes	_X_ Frequently
36)	Interrupts others	___ Never	___ Rarely	___ Sometimes	_X_ Frequently
37)	Problems pronouncing words	___ Never	_X_ Rarely	___ Sometimes	___ Frequently

38) Poor grades in school	___ Never	___ Rarely	___ Sometimes	_X_ Frequently
39) Expelled from school	_X_ Never	___ Rarely	___ Sometimes	___ Frequently
40) Drug abuse	_X_ Never	___ Rarely	___ Sometimes	___ Frequently
41) Alcohol consumption	_X_ Never	___ Rarely	___ Sometimes	___ Frequently
42) Depression	_X_ Never	___ Rarely	___ Sometimes	___ Frequently
43) Shy/avoidant/withdrawn	_X_ Never	___ Rarely	___ Sometimes	___ Frequently
44) Suicide threats/attempts	_X_ Never	___ Rarely	___ Sometimes	___ Frequently
45) Fatigued	___ Never	_X_ Rarely	___ Sometimes	___ Frequently
46) Anxious/nervous	___ Never	_X_ Rarely	___ Sometimes	___ Frequently
47) Excessive worrying	_X_ Never	___ Rarely	___ Sometimes	___ Frequently
48) Sleep disturbance	___ Never	___ Rarely	_X_ Sometimes	___ Frequently
49) Panic attacks	_X_ Never	___ Rarely	___ Sometimes	___ Frequently
50) Mood shifts	___ Never	___ Rarely	_X_ Sometimes	___ Frequently

53) For each of the behaviors noted earlier as occurring FREQUENTLY, or if it causes significant impairment, write a brief description of how it impacts the child's or other people's lives. Give examples. Use the back of this page as needed.

Behaviors of concern	Impact on child or others
30) Fidgety/squirmy	Always moving around, constant movement, always shifting in seat.
31) Difficulty remaining seated	Can't sit still long enough in school to learn important material.
32) Runs/climbs excessively	Often climbing on furniture, runs around the house too often.
33) Difficulty playing quietly	When playing she screams, hollers, and makes unusual noises most of the time.
34) Hyperactive	Always on the go, like "climbing the walls."
35) Difficulty awaiting turn	When in line becomes fidgety, impatient, and pushy. People make comments.
36) Interrupts others	When people visit our house we can't get a word in. She won't stop at school either. Several notes sent home from teacher about this problem.
38) Poor school grades	She is intelligent, but does not take in the information because she can't sit still.

54) Briefly describe the child's way of expressing the following emotions or behaviors:

Anger: _Shouts, screams, temper tantrums when very angry. She yells, "I hate you!"_

Happiness: _Active, smiling, sometimes claps hands._

Sadness: _Cries easily when sad. May slam doors for attention._

Anxiety: _May stutter at times._

55) List the child's behaviors that you would like to see change: _To increase her ability to sit still and listen to other people such as teachers and family. To be able to be calm and relax._

56) Additional information you believe would be helpful: _None_

PLEASE RETURN THIS AND OTHER ASSESSMENT MATERIALS TO THIS
OFFICE AT LEAST TWO DAYS BEFORE YOUR NEXT APPOINTMENT.

Form 14   Personal History Form—Adult (18+)

Client's name: _____   Date: _____

Gender: ___ F   ___ M   Date of birth: _____   Age: _____

Form completed by (if someone other than client): _____

Address: _____   City: _____   State: _____   Zip: _____

Phone (home): _____   (work): _____   ext: _____

If you need any more space for any of the questions please use the back of the sheet.

Primary reason(s) for seeking services:

___ Anger management   ___ Anxiety   ___ Coping   ___ Depression

___ Eating disorder   ___ Fear/phobias   ___ Mental confusion   ___ Sexual concerns

___ Sleeping problems   ___ Addictive behaviors   ___ Alcohol/drugs

___ Other mental health concerns (specify): _____

Family Information

Relationship	Name	Age	Living Yes	Living No	Living with you Yes	Living with you No
Mother	_____	_____	___	___	___	___
Father	_____	_____	___	___	___	___
Spouse	_____	_____	___	___	___	___
Children	_____	_____	___	___	___	___
	_____	_____	___	___	___	___
	_____	_____	___	___	___	___

Significant others (brothers, sisters, grandparents, step-relatives, half-relatives. Please specify relationship.)

Relationship	Name	Age	Living Yes	Living No	Living with you Yes	Living with you No
_____	_____	_____	___	___	___	___
_____	_____	_____	___	___	___	___
_____	_____	_____	___	___	___	___
_____	_____	_____	___	___	___	___
_____	_____	_____	___	___	___	___
_____	_____	_____	___	___	___	___

Marital Status (more than one answer may apply)

___ Single   ___ Divorce in process   ___ Unmarried, living together

       Length of time: _____   Length of time: _____

___ Legally married   ___ Separated   ___ Divorced

Length of time: _____   Length of time: _____   Length of time: _____

___ Widowed   ___ Annulment

Length of time: _____   Length of time: _____   Total number of marriages: ___

Assessment of current relationship (if applicable): ___ Good ___ Fair ___ Poor

Parental Information

___ Parents legally married   ___ Mother remarried: Number of times: _____

___ Parents have even been separated   ___ Father remarried: Number of times: _____

___ Parents ever divorced

Special circumstances (e.g., raised by person other than parents, information about spouse/children not living with you, etc.): _____

Development

Are there special, unusual, or traumatic circumstances that affected your development? ___ Yes ___ No

If Yes, please describe: _____

Has there been history of child abuse? ___ Yes ___ No

If Yes, which type(s)? ___ Sexual ___ Physical ___ Verbal

If Yes, the abuse was as a: ___ Victim ___ Perpetrator

Other childhood issues: ___ Neglect ___ Inadequate nutrition ___ Other (please specify): _____

Comments re: childhood development: _____

_____

Social Relationships

Check how you generally get along with other people: (check all that apply)

___ Affectionate   ___ Aggressive   ___ Avoidant   ___ Fight/argue often   ___ Follower

___ Friendly   ___ Leader   ___ Outgoing   ___ Shy/withdrawn   ___ Submissive

___ Other (specify): _____

Sexual orientation: _____   Comments: _____

Sexual dysfunctions? ___ Yes ___ No

If Yes, describe: _____

Any current or history of being as sexual perpetrator? ___ Yes ___ No

If Yes, describe: _____

Cultural/Ethnic

To which cultural or ethnic group, if any, do you belong? _____

Are you experiencing any problems due to cultural or ethnic issues? ___ Yes ___ No

If Yes, describe: _____

Other cultural/ethnic information: _____

Spiritual/Religious

How important to you are spiritual matters? ___ Not   ___ Little   ___ Moderate   ___ Much

Are you affiliated with a spiritual or religious group? ___ Yes   ___ No

If Yes, describe: _____

Were you raised within a spiritual or religious group? ___ Yes   ___ No

If Yes, describe: _____

Would you like your spiritual/religious beliefs incorporated into the counseling? ___ Yes   ___ No

If Yes, describe: _____

Legal

Current Status

Are you involved in any active cases (traffic, civil, criminal)? ___ Yes   ___ No

If Yes, please describe and indicate the court and hearing/trial dates and charges: _____
_____

Are you presently on probation or parole? ___ Yes   ___ No

If Yes, please describe: _____

Past History

Traffic violations: ___ Yes ___ No		DWI, DUI, etc.: ___ Yes ___ No	
Criminal involvement: ___ Yes ___ No		Civil involvement: ___ Yes ___ No	

If you responded Yes to any of the above, please fill in the following information.

Charges	Date	Where (city)	Results
_____	_____	_____	_____
_____	_____	_____	_____
_____	_____	_____	_____

Education

Fill in all that apply: Years of education: _____   Currently enrolled in school? ___ Yes   ___ No

___ High school grad/GED

___ Vocational: Number of years: ___ Graduated: ___ Yes ___ No Major: _____

___ College: Number of years: ___ Graduated: ___ Yes ___ No Major: _____

___ Graduate: Number of years: ___ Graduated: ___ Yes ___ No Major: _____

Other training: _____

Special circumstances (e.g., learning disabilities, gifted): _____

Employment

Begin with most recent job, list job history: _____

Employer	Dates	Title	Reason left the job	How often miss work?
_____	_____	_____	_____	_____
_____	_____	_____	_____	_____
_____	_____	_____	_____	_____
_____	_____	_____	_____	_____

Currently: ___ FT ___ PT ___ Temp ___ Laid-off ___ Disabled ___ Retired
___ Social Security ___ Student ___ Other (describe): _____

Military

Military experience? ___ Yes ___ No   Combat experience? ___ Yes ___ No

Where: _____

Branch: _____   Discharge date: _____

Date drafted: _____   Type of discharge: _____

Date enlisted: _____   Rank at discharge: _____

Leisure/Recreational

Describe special areas of interest or hobbies (e.g., art, books, crafts, physical fitness, sports, outdoor activities, church activities, walking, exercising, diet/health, hunting, fishing, bowling, traveling, etc.)

Activity	How often now?	How often in the past?
_____	_____	_____
_____	_____	_____
_____	_____	_____
_____	_____	_____

Medical/Physical Health

___ AIDS	___ Dizziness	___ Nose bleeds
___ Alcoholism	___ Drug abuse	___ Pneumonia
___ Abdominal pain	___ Epilepsy	___ Rheumatic Fever
___ Abortion	___ Ear infections	___ Sexually transmitted diseases
___ Allergies	___ Eating problems	___ Sleeping disorders
___ Anemia	___ Fainting	___ Sore throat
___ Appendicitis	___ Fatigue	___ Scarlet Fever
___ Arthritis	___ Frequent urination	___ Sinusitis
___ Asthma	___ Headaches	___ Small Pox
___ Bronchitis	___ Hearing problems	___ Stroke
___ Bed wetting	___ Hepatitis	___ Sexual problems
___ Cancer	___ High blood pressure	___ Tonsillitis
___ Chest pain	___ Kidney problems	___ Tuberculosis
___ Chronic pain	___ Measles	___ Toothache
___ Colds/Coughs	___ Mononucleosis	___ Thyroid problems
___ Constipation	___ Mumps	___ Vision problems
___ Chicken Pox	___ Menstrual pain	___ Vomiting
___ Dental problems	___ Miscarriages	___ Whooping cough
___ Diabetes	___ Neurological disorders	___ Other (describe): _____
___ Diarrhea	___ Nausea	_____

List any current health concerns: _____

List any recent health or physical changes: _____

_____

Nutrition

Meal	How often (times per week)	Typical foods eaten	Typical amount eaten
Breakfast	___ / week	_____	___ No ___ Low ___ Med ___ High
Lunch	___ / week	_____	___ No ___ Low ___ Med ___ High
Dinner	___ / week	_____	___ No ___ Low ___ Med ___ High
Snacks	___ / week	_____	___ No ___ Low ___ Med ___ High

Comments: *Some days I have no appetite.* _____

Current prescribed medications	Dose	Dates	Purpose	Side effects
_____	_____	_____	_____	_____
_____	_____	_____	_____	_____
_____	_____	_____	_____	_____
_____	_____	_____	_____	_____

Current over-the-counter meds	Dose	Dates	Purpose	Side effects
_____	_____	_____	_____	_____
_____	_____	_____	_____	_____
_____	_____	_____	_____	_____
_____	_____	_____	_____	_____

Are you allergic to any medications or drugs? ___ Yes ___ No

If Yes, describe: _____

_____

	Date	Reason	Results
Last physical exam	_____	_____	_____
Last doctor's visit	_____	_____	_____
Last dental exam	_____	_____	_____
Most recent surgery	_____	_____	_____
Other surgery	_____	_____	_____
Upcoming surgery	_____	_____	_____

Family history of medical problems: _____

_____

Pleases check if there have been any recent changes in the following:

___ Sleep patterns   ___ Eating patterns   ___ Behavior   ___ Energy level

___ Physical activity level   ___ General disposition   ___ Weight   ___ Nervousness/tension

Describe changes in areas in which you checked above: _____

_____

Chemical Use History

	Method of use and amount	Frequency of use	Age of first use	Age of last use	Used in last 48 hours		Used in last 30 days	
					Yes	No	Yes	No
Alcohol	_____	_____	_____	_____	__	__	__	__
Barbiturates	_____	_____	_____	_____	__	__	__	__
Valium/Librium	_____	_____	_____	_____	__	__	__	__
Cocaine/Crack	_____	_____	_____	_____	__	__	__	__
Heroin/Opiates	_____	_____	_____	_____	__	__	__	__
Marijuana	_____	_____	_____	_____	__	__	__	__
PCP/LSD/Mescaline	_____	_____	_____	_____	__	__	__	__
Inhalants	_____	_____	_____	_____	__	__	__	__
Caffeine	_____	_____	_____	_____	__	__	__	__
Nicotine	_____	_____	_____	_____	__	__	__	__
Over the counter	_____	_____	_____	_____	__	__	__	__
Prescription drugs	_____	_____	_____	_____	__	__	__	__
Other drugs	_____	_____	_____	_____	__	__	__	__

Substance of preference

1. _____   3. _____

2. _____   4. _____

Substance Abuse Questions

Describe when and where you typically uses substances: _____
_____

Describe any changes in your use patterns: _____
_____

Describe how your use has affected your family or friends (include their perceptions of your use): ____
_____

Reason(s) for use:

___ Addicted   ___ Build confidence   ___ Escape   ___ Self-medication

___ Socialization   ___ Taste   ___ Other (specify): _____

How do you believe your substance use affects your life? _____

Who or what has helped you in stopping or limiting your use? _____

Does/Has someone in your family present/past have/had a problem with drugs or alcohol?

___ Yes   ___ No   If Yes, describe: _____

Have you had withdrawal symptoms when trying to stop using drugs or alcohol? ___ Yes   ___ No

If Yes, describe: _____

Have you had adverse reactions or overdose to drugs or alcohol? (describe): _____
_____

2.72

Does your body temperature change when you drink? ___ Yes ___ No

If Yes, describe: _____

Have drugs or alcohol created a problem for your job? ___ Yes ___ No

If Yes, describe: _____

Counseling/Prior Treatment History

Information about client (past and present):

	Yes	No	When	Where	Your reaction to overall experience
Counseling/Psychiatric treatment	___	___	_____	_____	_____
Suicidal thoughts/attempts	___	___	_____	_____	_____
Drug/alcohol treatment	___	___	_____	_____	_____
Hospitalizations	___	___	_____	_____	_____
Involvement with self-help groups (e.g., AA, Al-Anon, NA, Overeaters Anonymous)	___	___	_____	_____	_____

Information about family/significant others (past and present):

	Yes	No	When	Where	Your reaction to overall experience
Counseling/Psychiatric treatment	___	___	_____	_____	_____
Suicidal thoughts/attempts	___	___	_____	_____	_____
Drug/alcohol treatment	___	___	_____	_____	_____
Hospitalizations	___	___	_____	_____	_____
Involvement with self-help groups (e.g., AA, Al-Anon, NA, Overeaters Anonymous)	___	___	_____	_____	_____

Please check behaviors and symptoms that occur to you more often than you would like them to take place:

___ Aggression   ___ Elevated mood   ___ Phobias/fears

___ Alcohol dependence   ___ Fatigue   ___ Recurring thoughts

___ Anger   ___ Gambling   ___ Sexual addiction

___ Antisocial behavior   ___ Hallucinations   ___ Sexual difficulties

___ Anxiety   ___ Heart palpitations   ___ Sick often

___ Avoiding people   ___ High blood pressure   ___ Sleeping problems

___ Chest pain   ___ Hopelessness   ___ Speech problems

___ Cyber addiction   ___ Impulsivity   ___ Suicidal thoughts

___ Depression   ___ Irritability   ___ Thoughts disorganized

___ Disorientation   ___ Judgment errors   ___ Trembling

___ Distractibility   ___ Loneliness   ___ Withdrawing

___ Dizziness   ___ Memory impairment   ___ Worrying

___ Drug dependence   ___ Mood shifts   ___ Other (specify): _____

___ Eating disorder   ___ Panic attacks   _____

Briefly discuss how the above symptoms impair your ability to function effectively: _____
_____
_____
_____
_____
_____
_____
_____
_____
_____

Any additional information that would assist us in understanding your concerns or problems: _____
_____
_____
_____
_____
_____
_____
_____
_____
_____

What are your goals for therapy? _____
_____
_____
_____
_____
_____
_____
_____

Do you feel suicidal at this time? ___ Yes   ___ No
If Yes, explain: _____
_____
_____
_____

For Staff Use

Therapist's signature/credentials: _____   Date: ____/____/_____

Supervisor's comments: _____
_____
_____   Physical exam: ___ Required   ___ Not required

Supervisor's signature/credentials: _____   Date: ____/____/_____
(Certifies case assignment, level of care and need for exam)

Client's name: _Judy Doe_   Date: _3/8/1999_

Gender: _X_ F   ___ M   Date of birth: _7/6/1948_   Age: _50_

Form completed by (if someone other than client): _____same_____

Address: _1234 Main St._   City: _Pleasantville_   State: _NJ_   Zip: _99998_

Phone (home): _201-555-5555_   (work): _201-555-5554_   ext: _281_

If you need any more space for any of the questions please use the back of the sheet.

Primary reason(s) for seeking services:

_X_ Anger management   ___ Anxiety   _X_ Coping   _X_ Depression

___ Eating disorder   ___ Fear/phobias   ___ Mental confusion   ___ Sexual concerns

___ Sleeping problems ___ Addictive behaviors   ___ Alcohol/drugs

___ Other mental health concerns (specify): _____

Family Information

Relationship	Name	Age	Living Yes	Living No	Living with you Yes	Living with you No
Mother	Reana Sims	73	X			X
Father	Roger Sims			X		
Spouse	Bill Doe	51	X		X	
Children	Sally Doe	24	X			X
	James Doe	16	X		X	
	Julie Doe	12	X		X	

Significant others (brothers, sisters, grandparents, step-relatives, half-relatives. Please specify relationship.)

Relationship	Name	Age	Living Yes	Living No	Living with you Yes	Living with you No
Brother	Steven Doe	51	X			X
Sister	Holly Lockery	46	X			X
Sister	Sheila Kropp	44	X			X
Brother	Raymond Doe	42	X			X

Marital Status (more than one answer may apply)

___ Single   ___ Divorce in process   ___ Unmarried, living together

                         Length of time: _____   Length of time: _____

_X_ Legally married   ___ Separated   ___ Divorced

Length of time: __22 years__   Length of time: _____   Length of time: _____

___ Widowed   ___ Annulment

Length of time: _____   Length of time: _____   Total number of marriages: _1_

Assessment of current relationship (if applicable): ___ Good   ___ Fair   _X_ Poor

Parental Information

_X_ Parents legally married   ___ Mother remarried: Number of times: _____

___ Parents have even been separated   ___ Father remarried: Number of times: _____

___ Parents ever divorced

Special circumstances (e.g., raised by person other than parents, information about spouse/children not living with you, etc.): _None_ _____

Development

Are there special, unusual, or traumatic circumstances that affected your development? ___ Yes _X_ No

If Yes, please describe: _____

Has there been history of child abuse? ___ Yes   _X_ No

If Yes, which type(s)? ___ Sexual   ___ Physical   ___Verbal

If Yes, the abuse was as a: ___ Victim   ___ Perpetrator

Other childhood issues: ___ Neglect ___ Inadequate nutrition ___ Other (please specify): _____

Comments re: childhood development: _My mother and older sister seemed to think that they could_ _make all of my decisions. It goes on today!_ _____

Social Relationships

Check how you generally get along with other people: (check all that apply)

___ Affectionate   ___ Aggressive   ___ Avoidant   ___ Fight/argue often   ___ Follower

_X_ Friendly   ___ Leader   _X_ Outgoing   ___ Shy/withdrawn   ___ Submissive

___ Other (specify): _But now I'm withdrawn_ _____

Sexual orientation: _Heterosexual_   Comments: _____

Sexual dysfunctions? ___ Yes _X_ No

If Yes, describe: _____

Any current or history of being as sexual perpetrator? ___ Yes _X_ No

If Yes, describe: _____

Cultural/Ethnic

To which cultural or ethnic group, if any, do you belong? _____ _White, middle class_ _____

Are you experiencing any problems due to cultural or ethnic issues? ___ Yes _X_ No

If Yes, describe: _____

Other cultural/ethnic information: _None_ _____

Spiritual/Religious

How important to you are spiritual matters? ___ Not ___ Little _X_ Moderate ___ Much

Are you affiliated with a spiritual or religious group? ___ Yes _X_ No

If Yes, describe: _____

Were you raised within a spiritual or religious group? _X_ Yes ___ No

If Yes, describe: _Catholic, strict_____

Would you like your spiritual/religious beliefs incorporated into the counseling? ___ Yes _X_ No

If Yes, describe: _____

Legal

Current Status

Are you involved in any active cases (traffic, civil, criminal)? ___ Yes _X_ No

If Yes, please describe and indicate the court and hearing/trial dates and charges: _____

_____

Are you presently on probation or parole? ___ Yes _X_ No

If Yes, please describe: _____

Past History

Traffic violations: _X_ Yes ___ No   DWI, DUI, etc.: ___ Yes _X_ No

Criminal involvement: ___ Yes _X_ No   Civil involvement: ___ Yes _X_ No

If you responded Yes to any of the above, please fill in the following information.

Charges	Date	Where (city)	Results
Speeding ticket	1993	Baneville	$80 fine

Education

Fill in all that apply: Years of education: _16_ Currently enrolled in school? ___ Yes _X_ No

___ High school grad/GED

___ Vocational: Number of years: ___ Graduated: ___ Yes ___ No Major: _____

_X_ College: Number of years: _4_ Graduated: ___ Yes ___ No Major: _____

___ Graduate: Number of years: ___ Graduated: ___ Yes ___ No Major: _____

Other training: _____

Special circumstances (e.g., learning disabilities, gifted): _____None_____

Employment

Begin with most recent job, list job history: _____

Employer	Dates	Title	Reason left the job	How often miss work?
Empire School	1983–present	Teacher		2–4/month
Bently School	1969–1983	Teacher	Moved	Seldom

Currently: _X_ FT ___ PT ___ Temp ___ Laid-off ___ Disabled ___ Retired
___ Social Security ___ Student ___ Other (describe): _____

Military

Military experience? ___ Yes ___ No   Combat experience? ___ Yes ___ No

Where: _____

Branch: _____   Discharge date: _____

Date drafted: _____   Type of discharge: _____

Date enlisted: _____   Rank at discharge: _____

Leisure/Recreational

Describe special areas of interest or hobbies (e.g., art, books, crafts, physical fitness, sports, outdoor activities, church activities, walking, exercising, diet/health, hunting, fishing, bowling, traveling, etc.)

Activity	How often now?	How often in the past?
Bowling	*None*	*3x/month*
Exercising	*None*	*Daily*
Reading	*1 hr/wk*	*2 hr/day*

Medical/Physical Health

___ AIDS	___ Dizziness	___ Nose bleeds
___ Alcoholism	___ Drug abuse	___ Pneumonia
___ Abdominal pain	___ Epilepsy	___ Rheumatic Fever
___ Abortion	___ Ear infections	___ Sexually transmitted diseases
___ Allergies	___ Eating problems	_X_ Sleeping disorders
___ Anemia	___ Fainting	___ Sore throat
___ Appendicitis	_X_ Fatigue	___ Scarlet Fever
___ Arthritis	___ Frequent urination	___ Sinusitis
___ Asthma	_X_ Headaches	___ Small Pox
___ Bronchitis	___ Hearing problems	___ Stroke
___ Bed wetting	___ Hepatitis	_X_ Sexual problems
___ Cancer	___ High blood pressure	___ Tonsillitis
___ Chest pain	___ Kidney problems	___ Tuberculosis
___ Chronic pain	___ Measles	___ Toothache
___ Colds/Coughs	___ Mononucleosis	___ Thyroid problems
___ Constipation	___ Mumps	___ Vision problems
___ Chicken Pox	___ Menstrual pain	___ Vomiting
___ Dental problems	___ Miscarriages	___ Whooping cough
___ Diabetes	___ Neurological disorders	___ Other (describe): _____
___ Diarrhea	___ Nausea	

List any current health concerns: _Usually in good health_ _____

List any recent health or physical changes: _Increasing headaches, fatigue and poor sleep. Have_ _____
   lost 20 pounds in past year. _____

Nutrition

Meal	How often (times per week)	Typical foods eaten	Typical amount eaten
Breakfast	_3_ / week	_Cereal or toast_	___ No ___ Low _X_ Med ___ High
Lunch	_5_ / week	_Sandwich or soup_	___ No ___ Low _X_ Med ___ High
Dinner	_7_ / week	_Meat, potatoe, veg_	___ No _X_ Low ___ Med ___ High
Snacks	_7_ / week	_Candy bar_	___ No ___ Low _X_ Med ___ High

Comments: _Some days I have no appetite._

Current prescribed medications	Dose	Dates	Purpose	Side effects
None				

Current over-the-counter meds	Dose	Dates	Purpose	Side effects
Aspirin	_2 tabs_	_past year_	_headache_	_None_

Are you allergic to any medications or drugs? ___ Yes _X_ No

If Yes, describe: _____

	Date	Reason	Results
Last physical exam	_1994_	_Routine physical_	_Good health_
Last doctor's visit	_1998_	_Headache_	_None_
Last dental exam	_1997_	_Check-up_	_2 cavities filled_
Most recent surgery	_None_		
Other surgery			
Upcoming surgery	_None_		

Family history of medical problems: _No family history of medical problems in family_

Pleases check if there have been any recent changes in the following:

_X_ Sleep patterns   _X_ Eating patterns   _X_ Behavior   _X_ Energy level

_X_ Physical activity level   _X_ General disposition   ___ Weight   ___ Nervousness/tension

Describe changes in areas in which you checked above: _I want to be motivated to teach like I used to. I want to be happy again._

Chemical Use History

	Method of use and amount	Frequency of use	Age of first use	Age of last use	Used in last 48 hours		Used in last 30 days	
					Yes	No	Yes	No
Alcohol	_Wine–1 glass_	_Holidays_	_24_	_present_		_X_	_X_	
Barbiturates								
Valium/Librium								
Cocaine/Crack								
Heroin/Opiates								
Marijuana								
PCP/LSD/Mescaline								
Inhalants								
Caffeine								
Nicotine								
Over the counter	_Aspirin–2 tabs_	_3x/week_	_teen_	_present_	_X_		_X_	
Prescription drugs								
Other drugs								

Substance of preference

1. _____   3. _____

2. _____   4. _____

Substance Abuse Questions

Describe when and where you typically uses substances: _No substance abuse issues_ _____

_____

Describe any changes in your use patterns: _____

_____

Describe how your use has affected your family or friends (include their perceptions of your use): ____

_____ _No effect_ _____

Reason(s) for use:

___ Addicted   ___ Build confidence   ___ Escape   ___ Self-medication

_X_ Socialization   ___ Taste   ___ Other (specify): _____

How do you believe your substance use affects your life? _Not_ _____

Who or what has helped you in stopping or limiting your use? _____

Does/Has someone in your family present/past have/had a problem with drugs or alcohol?

_X_ Yes ___ No   If Yes, describe: _Sometimes my father drank too much._ _____

Have you had withdrawal symptoms when trying to stop using drugs or alcohol? ___ Yes _X_ No

If Yes, describe: _____

Have you had adverse reactions or overdose to drugs or alcohol? (describe):_____

_____

Does your body temperature change when you drink? ___ Yes _X_ No

If Yes, describe: _____

Have drugs or alcohol created a problem for your job? ___ Yes _X_ No

If Yes, describe: _____

Counseling/Prior Treatment History

Information about client (past and present):

	Yes	No	When	Where	Your reaction to overall experience
Counseling/Psychiatric treatment	_X_	___	_1968_	_Lowe Clinic Building_	_Very helpful_
Suicidal thoughts/attempts	_X_	___	_1968 and now_	_____	_Scared because my kids are older now._
Drug/alcohol treatment	___	_X_	_____	_____	_____
Hospitalizations	___	_X_	_____	_____	_____
Involvement with self-help groups (e.g., AA, Al-Anon, NA, Overeaters Anonymous)	___	_X_	_____	_____	_____

Information about family/significant others (past and present):

	Yes	No	When	Where	Your reaction to overall experience
Counseling/Psychiatric treatment	___	_X_	_____	_____	_____
Suicidal thoughts/attempts	___	_X_	_____	_____	_____
Drug/alcohol treatment	___	_X_	_____	_____	_____
Hospitalizations	___	_X_	_____	_____	_____
Involvement with self-help groups (e.g., AA, Al-Anon, NA, Overeaters Anonymous)	___	_X_	_____	_____	_____

Please check behaviors and symptoms that occur to you more often than you would like them to take place:

___ Aggression	___ Elevated mood	___ Phobias/fears
___ Alcohol dependence	_X_ Fatigue	___ Recurring thoughts
_X_ Anger	___ Gambling	___ Sexual addiction
___ Antisocial behavior	___ Hallucinations	_X_ Sexual difficulties
___ Anxiety	___ Heart palpitations	___ Sick often
_X_ Avoiding people	___ High blood pressure	_X_ Sleeping problems
___ Chest pain	_X_ Hopelessness	___ Speech problems
___ Cyber addiction	___ Impulsivity	_X_ Suicidal thoughts
_X_ Depression	_X_ Irritability	___ Thoughts disorganized
___ Disorientation	___ Judgment errors	___ Trembling
___ Distractibility	_X_ Loneliness	_X_ Withdrawing
___ Dizziness	___ Memory impairment	___ Worrying
___ Drug dependence	___ Mood shifts	___ Other (specify): _____
___ Eating disorder	___ Panic attacks	_____

Briefly discuss how the above symptoms impair your ability to function effectively: _I just don't_ _care about anything. I don't want to be around people, go to work or even get up in the morning._ _I'm a loser. I feel like quitting teaching. I am empty inside and just don't care most of the time._

Any additional information that would assist us in understanding your concerns or problems: _What_ _good am I? I'm a poor wife and a poor teacher._

What are your goals for therapy? _Feel alive again._

Do you feel suicidal at this time? _X_ Yes ___ No
If Yes, explain: _But, I won't do it._

For Staff Use

Therapist's signature/credentials: ___Darlene Benton, PhD___ Date: _3 / 8 / 1999_

Supervisor's comments: _Fully assess suicide potential. Consider leave at work. Schedule medical_ _evaluation immediately._

_____ Physical exam: _X_ Required ___ Not required

Supervisor's signature/credentials: _Sharon Bell, PhD_ Date: _3 / 12 / 1999_
(Certifies case assignment, level of care and need for exam)

Form 15   Personal History Form—Child (<18)

Client's name: _____   Date: _____

Gender: ___ F   ___ M   Date of birth: _____   Age: _____   Grade in school: _____

Form completed by (if someone other than client): _____

Address: _____   City: _____   State: _____   Zip: _____

Phone (home): _____   (work): _____   Ext: _____

If you need any more space for any of the following questions please use the back of the sheet.

Primary reason(s) for seeking services:

____ Anger management   ____ Anxiety   ___ Coping   ___ Depression

____ Eating disorder   ____ Fear/phobias   ___ Mental confusion ___ Sexual concerns

____ Sleeping problems   ___ Addictive behaviors ___ Alcohol/drugs   ___ Hyperactivity

___ Other mental health concerns (specify): _____
_____

Family History

Parents

With whom does the child live at this time? _____

Are parent's divorced or separated? _____

If Yes, who has legal custody? _____

Were the child's parents ever married? ___ Yes   ___ No

Is there any significant information about the parents' relationship or treatment toward the child which might be beneficial in counseling? ___ Yes   ___ No

If Yes, describe: _____

Client's Mother

Name: _____   Age: _____   Occupation: _____   ___ FT   ___ PT

Where employed: _____   Work phone: _____

Mother's education: _____

Is the child currently living with mother? ___ Yes   ___ No

___ Natural parent ___ Step-parent ___Adoptive parent ___Foster home ___ Other (specify): _____

Is there anything notable, unusual or stressful about the child's relationship with the mother?

___ Yes   ___ No   If Yes, please explain: _____
_____

How is the child disciplined by the mother? _____

For what reasons is the child disciplined by the mother? _____

Client's Father

Name: _____ Age: _____ Occupation: _____ ___ FT ___ PT

Where employed: _____ Work phone: _____

Father's education: _____

Is the child currently living with father? ___ Yes ___ No

___ Natural parent ___ Step-parent ___Adoptive parent ___Foster home ___ Other (specify): _____

Is there anything notable, unusual or stressful about the child's relationship with the mother?

___ Yes ___ No   If Yes, please explain: _____

_____

How is the child disciplined by the father? _____

For what reasons is the child disciplined by the father? _____

Client's Siblings and Others Who Live in the Household

Names of Siblings	Age	Gender	Lives	Quality of relationship with the client
_____	__	__ F __ M	__ home __ away	__ poor __ average __ good
_____	__	__ F __ M	__ home __ away	__ poor __ average __ good
_____	__	__ F __ M	__ home __ away	__ poor __ average __ good
_____	__	__ F __ M	__ home __ away	__ poor __ average __ good

Others living in the household	Age	Gender	Relationship (e.g., cousin, foster child)	
_____	__	__ F __ M	_____	__ poor __ average __ good
_____	__	__ F __ M	_____	__ poor __ average __ good
_____	__	__ F __ M	_____	__ poor __ average __ good
_____	__	__ F __ M	_____	__ poor __ average __ good

Comments: _____

_____

_____

Family Health History

Have any of the following diseases occurred among the child's blood relatives? (parents, siblings, aunts, uncles or grandparents) Check those which apply:

___ Allergies   ___ Deafness   ___ Muscular Dystrophy

___ Anemia   ___ Diabetes   ___ Nervousness

___ Asthma   ___ Glandular problems   ___ Perceptual motor disorder

___ Bleeding tendency ___ Heart diseases   ___ Mental Retardation

___ Blindness   ___ High blood pressure   ___ Seizures

___ Cancer   ___ Kidney disease   ___ Spinal Bifida

___ Cerebral Palsy   ___ Mental illness   ___ Suicide

___ Cleft lips   ___ Migraines   ___ Other (specify): _____

___ Cleft palate   ___ Multiple sclerosis   _____

Comments re: Family Health: _____

_____

2.84

Childhood/Adolescent History

Pregnancy/Birth

Has the child's mother had any occurances of miscarriages or stillborns? ___ Yes ___ No

If Yes, describe: _____

Was the pregnancy with child planned? ___ Yes ___ No   Length of pregnancy: _____

Mother's age at child's birth: _____   Father's age at child's birth: _____

Child number ___ of ___ total children.

How many pounds did the mother gain during the pregnancy? _____

While pregnant did the mother smoke? ___ Yes ___ No   If Yes, what amount: _____

Did the mother use drugs of alcohol? ___ Yes ___ No   If Yes, type/amount: _____

While pregnant, did the mother have any medical or emotional difficulties? (e.g., surgery, hypertension, medication) ___ Yes ___ No

If Yes, describe: _____

Length of labor: _____   Induced: ___ Yes ___ No   Caesarean? ___ Yes ___ No

Baby's birth weight: _____   Baby's birth length: _____

Describe any physical or emotional complications with the delivery: _____

_____

Describe any complications for the mother or the baby after the birth: _____

_____

Length of hospitalization: Mother: _____   Baby: _____

Infancy/Toddlerhood Check all which apply:

___ Breast fed	___ Milk allergies	___ Vomiting	___ Diarrhea
___ Bottle fed	___ Rashes	___ Colic	___ Constipation
___ Not cuddly	___ Cried often	___ Rarely cried	___ Overactive
___ Resisted solid food	___ Trouble sleeping	___ Irritable when awakened	___ Lethargic

Developmental History Please note the age at which the following behaviors took place:

Sat alone: _____   Dressed self: _____

Took 1st steps: _____   Tied shoe laces: _____

Spoke words: _____   Rode two-wheeled bike: _____

Spoke sentences: _____   Toilet trained: _____

Weaned: _____   Dry during day: _____

Fed self: _____   Dry during night: _____

Compared with others in the family, child's development was: ___ slow ___ average ___ fast

Age for following developments (fill in where applicable)

Began puberty: _____   Menstruation: _____

Voice change: _____   Convulsions: _____

Breast development: _____   Injuries or hospitalization: _____

Issues that affected child's development (e.g., physical/sexual abuse, inadequate nutrition, neglect, etc.)

_____

_____

Education

Current school: _____ School phone number: _____

Type of school: ___ Public ___ Private ___ Home schooled ___ Other (specify): _____

Grade: _____ Teacher: _____ School Counselor: _____

In special education? ___ Yes ___ No   If Yes, describe: _____

In gifted program? ___ Yes ___ No   If Yes, describe: _____

Has child ever been held back in school? ___ Yes ___ No   If Yes, describe: _____

Which subjects does the child enjoy in school? _____

Which subjects does the child dislike in school? _____

What grades does the child usually receive in school? _____

Have there been any recent changes in the child's grades? ___ Yes ___ No

If Yes, describe: _____

Has the child been tested psychologically? ___ Yes ___ No

If Yes, describe: _____

Check the descriptions which specifically relate to your child.

Feelings about School Work:

___ Anxious   ___ Passive   ___ Enthusiastic   ___ Fearful

___ Eager   ___ No expression   ___ Bored   ___ Rebellious

___ Other (describe): _____

Approach to School Work:

___ Organized   ___ Industrious   ___ Responsible   ___ Interested

___ Self-directed   ___ No initiative   ___ Refuses   ___ Does only what is expected

___ Sloppy   ___ Disorganized   ___ Cooperative   ___ Doesn't complete assignments

___ Other (describe): _____

Performance in School (Parent's Opinion):

___ Satisfactory   ___ Underachiever   ___ Overachiever

___ Other (describe): _____

Child's Peer Relationships:

___ Spontaneous   ___ Follower   ___ Leader   ___ Difficulty making friends

___ Makes friends easily   ___ Long-time friends   ___ Shares easily

___ Other (describe): _____

Who handles responsibility for your child in the following areas?

    School: ___ Mother ___ Father ___ Shared ___ Other (specify): _____

    Health: ___ Mother ___ Father ___ Shared ___ Other (specify): _____

    Problem behavior: ___ Mother ___ Father ___ Shared ___ Other (specify): _____

If the child is involved in a vocational program or works a job, please fill in the following:

What is the child's attitude toward work? ___ Poor ___ Average ___ Good ___ Excellent

Current employer: _____ Position: _____ Hours per week: _____

How have the child's grades in school been affected since working? ___ Lower ___ Same ___ Higher

How many previous jobs or placements has the child had? _____

Usual length of employment: _____ Usual reason for leaving: _____

Leisure/Recreational

Describe special areas of interest or hobbies (e.g., art, books, crafts, physical fitness, sports, outdoor activities, church activities, walking, exercising, diet/health, hunting, fishing, bowling, school activities, scouts, etc.)

Activity	How often now?	How often in the past?
_____	_____	_____
_____	_____	_____
_____	_____	_____
_____	_____	_____

Medical/Physical Health

___ Abortion
___ Asthma
___ Blackouts
___ Bronchitis
___ Cerebral Palsy
___ Chicken Pox
___ Congenital problems
___ Croup
___ Diabetes
___ Diphtheria
___ Dizziness
___ Ear aches
___ Ear infections
___ Eczema
___ Encephalitis
___ Fevers

___ Hayfever
___ Heart trouble
___ Hepatitis
___ Hives
___ Influenza
___ Lead poisoning
___ Measles
___ Meningitis
___ Miscarriage
___ Multiple sclerosis
___ Mumps
___ Muscular Dystrophy
___ Nose bleeds
___ Other skin rashes
___ Paralysis
___ Pleurisy

___ Pneumonia
___ Polio
___ Pregnancy
___ Rheumatic Fever
___ Scarlet Fever
___ Seizures
___ Severe colds
___ Severe head injury
___ Sexually transmitted disease
___ Thyroid disorders
___ Vision problems
___ Wearing glasses
___ Whooping cough
___ Other

_____

List any current health concerns: _____

_____

List any recent health or physical changes: _____

_____

Nutrition

Meal	How often (times per week)	Typical foods eaten	Typical amount eaten			
Breakfast	___ / week	_____	___ No	___ Low	___ Med	___ High
Lunch	___ / week	_____	___ No	___ Low	___ Med	___ High
Dinner	___ / week	_____	___ No	___ Low	___ Med	___ High
Snacks	___ / week	_____	___ No	___ Low	___ Med	___ High

Comments: _____

<u>**Most recent examinations**</u>

Type of examination	Date of most recent visit	Results
Physical examination	_____	_____
Dental examination	_____	_____
Vision examination	_____	_____
Hearing examination	_____	_____

Current prescribed medications	Dose	Dates	Purpose	Side effects
_____	_____	_____	_____	_____
_____	_____	_____	_____	_____
_____	_____	_____	_____	_____
_____	_____	_____	_____	_____

Current over-the-counter meds	Dose	Dates	Purpose	Side effects
_____	_____	_____	_____	_____
_____	_____	_____	_____	_____
_____	_____	_____	_____	_____
_____	_____	_____	_____	_____

Immunization record (check immunizations the child/adolescent has received):

	DPT	Polio
2 months	___	___
4 months	___	___
6 months	___	___
18 months	___	___
4–5 years	___	___

15 months ___ MMR (Measles, Mumps, Rubella)

24 months ___ HBPV (Hib)

Prior to school ___ HepB

Chemical Use History

Does the child/adolescent use or have a problem with alcohol or drugs? ___ Yes ___ No

If Yes, describe: _____

_____

Counseling/Prior Treatment History

Information about child/adolescent (past and present):

	Yes	No	When	Where	Reaction or overall experience
Counseling/Psychiatric treatment	___	___	_____	_____	_____
Suicidal thoughts/attempts	___	___	_____	_____	_____
Drug/alcohol treatment	___	___	_____	_____	_____
Hospitalizations	___	___	_____	_____	_____

Behavioral/Emotional

Please check any of the following that are typical for your child:

___ Affectionate	___ Frustrated easily	___ Sad
___ Aggressive	___ Gambling	___ Selfish
___ Alcohol problems	___ Generous	___ Separation anxiety
___ Angry	___ Hallucinations	___ Sets fires
___ Anxiety	___ Head banging	___ Sexual addiction
___ Attachment to dolls	___ Heart problems	___ Sexual acting out
___ Avoids adults	___ Hopelessness	___ Shares
___ Bedwetting	___ Hurts animals	___ Sick often
___ Blinking, jerking	___ Imaginary friends	___ Short attention span
___ Bizarre behavior	___ Impulsive	___ Shy, timid
___ Bullies, threatens	___ Irritable	___ Sleeping problems
___ Careless, reckless	___ Lazy	___ Slow moving
___ Chest pains	___ Learning problems	___ Soiling
___ Clumsy	___ Lies frequently	___ Speech problems
___ Confident	___ Listens to reason	___ Steals
___ Cooperative	___ Loner	___ Stomach aches
___ Cyber addiction	___ Low self-esteem	___ Suicidal threats
___ Defiant	___ Messy	___ Suicidal attempts
___ Depression	___ Moody	___ Talks back
___ Destructive	___ Nightmares	___ Teeth grinding
___ Difficulty speaking	___ Obedient	___ Thumb sucking
___ Dizziness	___ Often sick	___ Tics or twitching
___ Drugs dependence	___ Oppositional	___ Unsafe behaviors
___ Eating disorder	___ Over active	___ Unusual thinking
___ Enthusiastic	___ Over weight	___ Weight loss
___ Excessive masturbation	___ Panic attacks	___ Withdrawn
___ Expects failure	___ Phobias	___ Worries excessively
___ Fatigue	___ Poor appetite	___ Other:
___ Fearful	___ Psychiatric problems	_____
___ Frequent injuries	___ Quarrels	_____

Please describe any of the above (or other) concerns: _____
_____

How are problem behaviors generally handled? _____
_____

What are the family's favorite activities? _____
_____

What does the child/adolescent do with unstructured time? _____
_____

Has the child/adolescent experienced death? (friends, family pets, other) ___ Yes ___ No

At what age? ____ If Yes, describe the child's/adolescent's reaction: _____

_____

Have there been any other significant changes or events in your child's life? (family, moving, fire, etc.)

___ Yes ___ No If Yes, describe: _____

_____

Any additional information that you believe would assist us in understanding your child/adolescent?

_____

_____

_____

Any additional information that would assist us in understanding current concerns or problems?

_____

_____

_____

What are your goals for the child's therapy? _____

_____

What family involvement would you like to see in the therapy? _____

_____

Do you believe the child is suicidal at this time? ___ Yes ___ No

If Yes, explain: _____

_____

For Staff Use

Therapist's comments: _____

_____

_____

_____

_____

Therapist's signature/credentials: _____ Date: ____/____/_____

Supervisor's comments: _____

_____

_____

_____ Physical exam: ___ Required ___ Not required

Supervisor's signature/credentials: _____ Date: ____/____/_____

(Certifies case assignment, level of care and need for exam)

Form 15A   Personal History Form—Child (<18)

(Completed)

Client's name: __William Olden__   Date: __4/4/1999__

Gender: ___ F _X_ M   Date of birth: __3/7/1984__   Age: __15__ Grade in school: __10__

Form completed by (if someone other than client): __Mother: Lanna Olden__

Address: __3257 Brooks Ave # 316__   City: __Provo__   State: __ND__ Zip: __02511__

Phone (home): __555-3742__   (work): _____   Ext: _____

If you need any more space for any of the following questions please use the back of the sheet.

Primary reason(s) for seeking services:

_X_ Anger management   ___ Anxiety   _X_ Coping   _X_ Depression

___ Eating disorder   ___ Fear/phobias   ___ Mental confusion   ___ Sexual concerns

___ Sleeping problems   ___ Addictive behaviors   ___ Alcohol/drugs   ___ Hyperactivity

___ Other mental health concerns (specify): _____

_____

Family History

Parents

With whom does the child live at this time? __Mother__

Are parent's divorced or separated? __Divorced 2 years__

If Yes, who has legal custody? __Mother__

Were the child's parents ever married? _X_ Yes   ___ No

Is there any significant information about the parents' relationship or treatment toward the child which might be beneficial in counseling? _X_ Yes   ___ No

If Yes, describe: __Dysfunctional, violent relationship__

Client's Mother

Name: __Lanna Olden__   Age: __35__ Occupation: __Billing clerk__   _X_ FT   ___ PT

Where employed: __Century Clinic__   Work phone: __555-3373__

Mother's education: __H.S. graduate__

Is the child currently living with mother? _X_ Yes   ___ No

_X_ Natural parent ___ Step-parent ___Adoptive parent ___Foster home ___ Other (specify): _____

Is there anything notable, unusual or stressful about the child's relationship with the mother?

_X_ Yes ___ No   If Yes, please explain: __Very defiant toward me since I remarried.__

_____

How is the child disciplined by the mother? __Time-out__

For what reasons is the child disciplined by the mother? __Sassing, not doing school work.__

Client's Father

Name: _Reno Olden_ Age: _38_ Occupation: _Furnace repair_ _X_ FT ___ PT

Where employed: _Century Furnace_ Work phone: _555-7337_

Father's education: _H.S. graduate + 2 yrs voc. tech_

Is the child currently living with father? ___ Yes _X_ No

_X_ Natural parent ___ Step-parent ___ Adoptive parent ___ Foster home ___ Other (specify): _____

Is there anything notable, unusual or stressful about the child's relationship with the mother?

_X_ Yes ___ No If Yes, please explain: _He idolizes his father, but father seldom phones_ _or visits._

How is the child disciplined by the father? _Spanking, I believe_

For what reasons is the child disciplined by the father? _____

Client's Siblings and Others Who Live in the Household

Names of Siblings	Age	Gender		Lives			Quality of relationship with the client		
Marsha Olden	_12_	_X_ F	___ M	_X_ home	___ away		_X_ poor	___ average	___ good
_____	___	___ F	___ M	___ home	___ away		___ poor	___ average	___ good
_____	___	___ F	___ M	___ home	___ away		___ poor	___ average	___ good
_____	___	___ F	___ M	___ home	___ away		___ poor	___ average	___ good

Others living in the household		Gender		Relationship (e.g., cousin, foster child)		poor	average	good
_____	___	___ F	___ M	_____	___ poor	___ average	___ good	
_____	___	___ F	___ M	_____	___ poor	___ average	___ good	
_____	___	___ F	___ M	_____	___ poor	___ average	___ good	
_____	___	___ F	___ M	_____	___ poor	___ average	___ good	

Comments: _He is increasingly move picking on his sister. Sometimes he hits her or trashes her_ _room. Often teases her._

Family Health History

Have any of the following diseases occurred among the child's blood relatives? (parents, siblings, aunts, uncles or grandparents) Check those which apply:

___ Allergies	___ Deafness	___ Muscular Dystrophy
___ Anemia	___ Diabetes	___ Nervousness
___ Asthma	___ Glandular problems	___ Perceptual motor disorder
___ Bleeding tendency	___ Heart diseases	___ Mental Retardation
___ Blindness	___ High blood pressure	___ Seizures
___ Cancer	___ Kidney disease	___ Spinal Bifida
___ Cerebral Palsy	___ Mental illness	___ Suicide
___ Cleft lips	___ Migraines	___ Other (specify): _____
___ Cleft palate	___ Multiple sclerosis	_____

Comments re: Family Health: _Good health_

Childhood/Adolescent History

Pregnancy/Birth

Has the child's mother had any occurances of miscarriages or stillborns? ___ Yes _X_ No

If Yes, describe: _____

Was the pregnancy with child planned? ___ Yes _X_ No   Length of pregnancy: _Full term_

Mother's age at child's birth: _20_   Father's age at child's birth: _23_

Child number _1_ of _2_ total children.

How many pounds did the mother gain during the pregnancy? _32_

While pregnant did the mother smoke? ___ Yes _X_ No   If Yes, what amount: _____

Did the mother use drugs of alcohol? ___ Yes _X_ No   If Yes, type/amount: _____

While pregnant, did the mother have any medical or emotional difficulties? (e.g., surgery, hypertension, medication) _X_ Yes ___ No

If Yes, describe: _Ongoing physical abuse and stress_

Length of labor: _6 hrs_   Induced? ___ Yes _X_ No   Caesarean? ___ Yes _X_ No

Baby's birth weight: _9lb 1 oz_   Baby's birth length: _average_

Describe any physical or emotional complications with the delivery: _None_

_____

Describe any complications for the mother or the baby after the birth: _None_

_____

Length of hospitalization: Mother: _3 days_   Baby: _3 days_

Infancy/Toddlerhood Check all which apply:

___ Breast fed	___ Milk allergies	___ Vomiting	___ Diarrhea
_X_ Bottle fed	___ Rashes	___ Colic	___ Constipation
___ Not cuddly	_X_ Cried often	___ Rarely cried	___ Overactive
___ Resisted solid food	___ Trouble sleeping	_X_ Irritable when awakened	___ Lethargic

Developmental History Please note the age at which the following behaviors took place:

Sat alone: _6–7m_		Dressed self: _28m_
Took 1st steps: _11m_		Tied shoe laces: _4 1/2y_
Spoke words: _11m_		Rode two-wheeled bike: _5y_
Spoke sentences: _18m_		Toilet trained: _2 1/2y_
Weaned: _14m_		Dry during day: _18m_
Fed self: _16m_		Dry during night: _3y_

Compared with others in the family, child's development was: ___ slow _X_ average ___ fast

Age for following developments (fill in where applicable)

Began puberty: _12–13_   Menstruation: _____

Voice change: _12–13_   Convulsions: _____

Breast development: _____   Injuries or hospitalization: _____

Issues that affected child's development (e.g., physical/sexual abuse, inadequate nutrition, neglect, etc.)

Observed abuse from father to mother

Education

Current school: __*Dalton*__   School phone number: _____*555-2253*_____

Type of school: _X_ Public ___ Private ___ Home schooled ___ Other (specify): _____

Grade: __*10*__   Teacher: _____*Several*_____   School Counselor: _____*Mrs. Keenan*_____

In special education? ___ Yes _X_ No   If Yes, describe: __*Emotional/Behavioral Program*__

In gifted program? ___ Yes ___ No   If Yes, describe: _____

Has child ever been held back in school? ___ Yes _X_ No   If Yes, describe: _____

Which subjects does the child enjoy in school? __*None*_____

Which subjects does the child dislike in school? __*All*_____

What grades does the child usually receive in school? __*C–D–F*_____

Have there been any recent changes in the child's grades? _X_ Yes ___ No

If Yes, describe: __*Decreasing past 2 years*_____

Has the child been tested psychologically? ___ Yes _X_ No

If Yes, describe: __*Except IQ test (115)*_____

Check the descriptions which specifically relate to your child.

Feelings about School Work:

___ Anxious   ___ Passive   ___ Enthusiastic   ___ Fearful

___ Eager   ___ No expression   ___ Bored   ___ Rebellious

___ Other (describe): _____

Approach to School Work:

___ Organized   ___ Industrious   ___ Responsible   ___ Interested

___ Self-directed   _X_ No initiative   _X_ Refuses   ___ Does only what is expected

___ Sloppy   ___ Disorganized   ___ Cooperative   _X_ Doesn't complete assignments

___ Other (describe): _____

Performance in School (Parent's Opinion):

___ Satisfactory   _X_ Underachiever   ___ Overachiever

___ Other (describe): __*Refuses to do work*_____

Child's Peer Relationships:

___ Spontaneous   ___ Follower   ___ Leader   _X_ Difficulty making friends

___ Makes friends easily   ___ Long-time friends   ___ Shares easily

_X_ Other (describe): __*Bullies peers*_____

Who handles responsibility for your child in the following areas?

School: _X_ Mother ___ Father ___ Shared ___ Other (specify): _____

Health: _X_ Mother ___ Father ___ Shared ___ Other (specify): _____

Problem behavior: _X_ Mother ___ Father ___ Shared ___ Other (specify): _____

If the child is involved in a vocational program or works a job, please fill in the following:

What is the child's attitude toward work? ___ Poor ___ Average ___ Good ___ Excellent

Current employer: _____ Position: _____ Hours per week: _____

How have the child's grades in school been affected since working? ___ Lower ___ Same ___ Higher

How many previous jobs or placements has the child had? _____

Usual length of employment: _____ Usual reason for leaving: _____

2.94

Leisure/Recreational

Describe special areas of interest or hobbies (e.g., art, books, crafts, physical fitness, sports, outdoor activities, church activities, walking, exercising, diet/health, hunting, fishing, bowling, school activities, scouts, etc.)

Activity	How often now?	How often in the past?
Baseball team	*None*	*2x/wk*
Exercising	*None*	*Daily*
School activities	*None*	*1x/wk*

Medical/Physical Health

___ Abortion	___ Hayfever	___ Pneumonia
___ Asthma	___ Heart trouble	___ Polio
___ Blackouts	___ Hepatitis	___ Pregnancy
___ Bronchitis	___ Hives	___ Rheumatic Fever
___ Cerebral Palsy	___ Influenza	___ Scarlet Fever
_X_ Chicken Pox	___ Lead poisoning	___ Seizures
___ Congenital problems	_X_ Measles	___ Severe colds
___ Croup	___ Meningitis	___ Severe head injury
___ Diabetes	___ Miscarriage	___ Sexually transmitted disease
___ Diphtheria	___ Multiple sclerosis	___ Thyroid disorders
___ Dizziness	___ Mumps	___ Vision problems
___ Ear aches	___ Muscular Dystrophy	___ Wearing glasses
___ Ear infections	___ Nose bleeds	___ Whooping cough
___ Eczema	___ Other skin rashes	___ Other
___ Encephalitis	___ Paralysis	_____
___ Fevers	___ Pleurisy	

List any current health concerns: *None*
_____

List any recent health or physical changes: *None*
_____

Nutrition

Meal	How often (times per week)	Typical foods eaten	Typical amount eaten			
Breakfast	_7_ / week	*Cereal*	___ No ___ Low	_X_ Med	___ High
Lunch	_7_ / week	*Soup or sandwich*	___ No ___ Low	_X_ Med	___ High
Dinner	_7_ / week	*Hot meal*	___ No ___ Low	_X_ Med	___ High
Snacks	_7_ / week		___ No ___ Low	_X_ Med	___ High

Comments: *No eating problems*

Most recent examinations

Type of examination	Date of most recent visit	Results
Physical examination	_8-97_	_School physical: no problems_
Dental examination	_8-97_	_1 cavity_
Vision examination	_5-96_	_Good vision_
Hearing examination	_OK_	

Current prescribed medications	Dose	Dates	Purpose	Side effects
None				

Current over-the-counter meds	Dose	Dates	Purpose	Side effects
None				

Immunization record (check immunizations the child/adolescent has received):

	DPT	Polio
2 months	_X_	_X_
4 months	_X_	_X_
6 months	_X_	_X_
18 months	_X_	_X_
4–5 years	_X_	_X_

15 months _X_ MMR (Measles, Mumps, Rubella)

24 months _X_ HBPV (Hib)

Prior to school _X_ HepB

Chemical Use History

Does the child/adolescent use or have a problem with alcohol or drugs? ___ Yes _X_ No

If Yes, describe: _____

Counseling/Prior Treatment History

Information about child/adolescent (past and present):

	Yes	No	When	Where	Reaction or overall experience
Counseling/Psychiatric treatment	___	_X_			
Suicidal thoughts/attempts	___	_X_			
Drug/alcohol treatment	___	_X_			
Hospitalizations	___	_X_			

Behavioral/Emotional

Please check any of the following that are typical for your child:

___ Affectionate	_X_ Frustrated easily	___ Sad
_X_ Aggressive	___ Gambling	___ Selfish
___ Alcohol problems	___ Generous	___ Separation anxiety
_X_ Angry	___ Hallucinations	___ Sets fires
___ Anxiety	___ Head banging	___ Sexual addiction
___ Attachment to dolls	___ Heart problems	___ Sexual acting out
___ Avoids adults	___ Hopelessness	___ Shares
___ Bedwetting	___ Hurts animals	___ Sick often
___ Blinking, jerking	___ Imaginary friends	___ Short attention span
___ Bizarre behavior	___ Impulsive	___ Shy, timid
_X_ Bullies, threatens	_X_ Irritable	___ Sleeping problems
___ Careless, reckless	___ Lazy	___ Slow moving
___ Chest pains	___ Learning problems	___ Soiling
___ Clumsy	___ Lies frequently	___ Speech problems
___ Confident	___ Listens to reason	___ Steals
___ Cooperative	___ Loner	___ Stomach aches
___ Cyber addiction	_?_ Low self-esteem	___ Suicidal threats
_X_ Defiant	___ Messy	___ Suicidal attempts
___ Depression	_X_ Moody	_X_ Talks back
___ Destructive	___ Nightmares	___ Teeth grinding
___ Difficulty speaking	___ Obedient	___ Thumb sucking
___ Dizziness	___ Often sick	___ Tics or twitching
___ Drugs dependence	_X_ Oppositional	___ Unsafe behaviors
___ Eating disorder	___ Over active	___ Unusual thinking
___ Enthusiastic	___ Over weight	___ Weight loss
___ Excessive masturbation	___ Panic attacks	___ Withdrawn
___ Expects failure	___ Phobias	___ Worries excessively
___ Fatigue	___ Poor appetite	___ Other:
___ Fearful	___ Psychiatric problems	_____
___ Frequent injuries	_X_ Quarrels	_____

Please describe any of the above (or other) concerns: __The problem is his attitude and the way he treats people. No criminal behaviors. He used to be good.__

How are problem behaviors generally handled? __Time out, discussion, sometime yell or threaten him.__

What are the family's favorite activities? __Picnics, movies, go to mall, visit zoo.__

What does the child/adolescent do with unstructured time? __TV or agitate sister__

2.97

Has the child/adolescent experienced death? (friends, family pets, other) ___ Yes _X_ No

At what age? _____   If Yes, describe the child's/adolescent's reaction: _____

_____

Have there been any other significant changes or events in your child's life? (family, moving, fire, etc.)

_X_ Yes   ___ No   If Yes, describe: _My divorce and soon remarriage._____

_____

Any additional information that you believe would assist us in understanding your child/adolescent?

_Since I remarried he has been uncontrollable. I believe that he saw his father bully me, and he___

_wants to be like his father. His step-father isn't that way._____

_____

Any additional information that would assist us in understanding current concerns or problems?

_His behavior is now causing marriage problems for me._____

_____

_____

What are your goals for the child's therapy? ___Calm down—respect adults, make friends,_____

_be cooperative._____

What family involvement would you like to see in the therapy? ___We are willing to do anything!___

_____

Do you believe the child is suicidal at this time? ___ Yes _X_ No

If Yes, explain: _____

_____

For Staff Use

Therapist's comments: ___R/O ODD, conduct, ADHD, Adjustment Disorder, Dysthymia_____

_____

_____

_____

_____

Therapist's signature/credentials: ___Charles W. Wollat, MSW_____   Date: _4_ / _8_ / _1999_

Supervisor's comments: ___Suggest individual and family counseling. Seems like O.D.D. secondary___

_to Adjustment Disorder._____

_____

_____

_____ Physical exam: ___ Required _X_ Not required

Supervisor's signature/credentials: _Samuel Jones, LICSW_____   Date: _4_ / _8_ / _1999_

(Certifies case assignment, level of care and need for exam)

Form 16   Emotional/Behavioral Assessment

Name (answers apply to): _____   Date: _____

Residence: _____   DOB: _____   Age: _____

Address: _____   City: _____   State: _____   Zip: _____

Respondent's name: _____   Relationship: _____

Please use the back of any sheet of more space if needed.

1. Check the following behaviors or skills that describe positive characteristics of the client. (Add others that apply.)

___ Accepts praise	___ Friendly	___ Polite
___ Affectionate	___ Gregarious	___ Reading/writing
___ Apologizes	___ Grooming/hygiene	___ Respects others
___ Assertive	___ Helpful	___ Responsible
___ Cleanliness (household)	___ Hobbies/crafts	___ Safety skills
___ Community skills	___ Honesty	___ Sense of humor
___ Cooperative	___ Independent	___ Shares
___ Courteous	___ Insightful	___ Survival skills
___ Daily living skills	___ Listening skills	___ Verbal expression
___ Dependable	___ Money management skills	___ Works hard
___ Emotional	___ Motivated	___ _____
___ Eye contact	___ Organized	___ _____
___ _____	___ _____	___ _____

Comments on any of the above: _____

_____

2. Which of the following normal emotions or responses do you recognize as at least sometimes taking place with the client? (Add others that apply.)

___ Anger	___ Embarrassment	___ Grief
___ Anxiety	___ Envy	___ Happiness
___ Boredom	___ Fear	___ Loneliness
___ Depression	___ Frustration	___ Stress
___ _____	___ _____	___ _____

3. List any concerns you have regarding any of the above emotions or responses. _____

_____

_____

_____

4. How does s/he express (verbally and nonverbally) the following emotions?

Happiness: _____

_____

Sadness: _____

_____

Anger: _____

_____

Frustration: _____

_____

5. Briefly describe any self-injurious behaviors (SIBs) and/or inappropriate self-stimulation behaviors (SSBs).

Behavior: (describe the problem behavior)
Antecedents: (describe what usually takes place before the behavior occurs)
Consequences: (describe what actions are taken after the behavior occurs)
Frequency/duration: (describe how often and for how long it occurs)

Behavior: _____
Antecedents: _____
Consequences: _____
Frequency/duration: _____

Behavior: _____
Antecedents: _____
Consequences: _____
Frequency/duration: _____

Behavior: _____
Antecedents: _____
Consequences: _____
Frequency/duration: _____

6. Briefly describe aggressive acts (to people or property).

Behavior: _____
Antecedents: _____
Consequences: _____
Frequency/duration: _____

Behavior: _____
Antecedents: _____
Consequences: _____
Frequency/duration: _____

Behavior: _____
Antecedents: _____
Consequences: _____
Frequency/duration: _____

7. Describe any inappropriate sexual behavior. ___ None known

_____

_____

_____

8. Describe any inappropriate social behaviors. ___ None known

_____

_____

_____

9. How would you rate his/her listening skills?

Low		Average		High	___ NA
1	2	3	4	5	

Comments: _____

10. How would you rate his/her ability to cope with problems?

Low		Average		High	___ NA
1	2	3	4	5	

Comments: _____

11. How would you rate his/her respect for other people?

Low		Average		High	___ NA
1	2	3	4	5	

Comments: _____

12. How would you rate his/her ability to manage anger?

Low		Average		High	___ NA
1	2	3	4	5	

Comments: _____

13. How would you rate his/her motivation to change negative behaviors?

Low		Average		High	___ NA
1	2	3	4	5	

Comments: _____

14. How would you rate his/her ability to accept constructive criticism?

Low		Average		High	___ NA
1	2	3	4	5	

Comments: _____

15. How would you rate his/her potential for increased independent living?

Low		Average		High	___ NA
1	2	3	4	5	

Comments: _____

16. Please list any significant stressful events or major changes in his/her life in the past six months (e.g., loss of loved one, significant others moving, change in residence, new roommate or housemate, new sibling, major illness, etc.). ___ None known

_____
_____
_____

If applicable, what behavioral/emotional effects may this have had? ___ None known

_____
_____
_____

17. Check any of the following which apply to him/her. (Add others that apply.)

___ Anxiety	___ Explosive behaviors	___ Schizophrenia
___ Auditory hallucinations	___ Impulse control concerns	___ Sexual concerns
___ Chemical dependency	___ Mood shifts	___ Social withdrawal
___ Conduct problems	___ Obsessive/compulsive	___ Suicidal threats
___ Depression	___ Paranoid	___ Thought disorder
___ Eating disorder	___ Phobias/fears	___ Visual hallucinations
___ _____	___ _____	___ _____

Describe behavioral effects or incidents of each of the above items.

_____
_____
_____
_____
_____
_____
_____
_____
_____

18. Briefly describe any past events that may be difficult for him/her to handle at this time (e.g., abuse, injuries).

_____
_____
_____

19. Briefly describe any past events that were particularly encouraging or led to positive life changes for him/her.

_____
_____
_____

20. Please list any other information about him/her (e.g., important background information, special strengths/weaknesses, concerns with other people, problems on the job).

_____
_____
_____

Form 16A   Emotional/Behavioral Assessment
(Completed)

Name (answers apply to): ___Christine Watters___   Date: ___4/6/1999___

Residence: ___(family residence)___   DOB: ___3/6/1993___ Age: ___6___

Address: ___45678 Hayward St.___   City: ___Tacoma___   State: ___WA___ Zip: ___99889___

Respondent's name: ___Lisa Watters___   Relationship: ___Mother___

Please use the back of any sheet of more space if needed.

1. Check the following behaviors or skills that describe positive characteristics of the client. (Add others that apply.)

   _X_ Accepts praise   ___ Friendly   ___ Polite
   _X_ Affectionate   ___ Gregarious   ___ Reading/writing
   ___ Apologizes   _X_ Grooming/hygiene   ___ Respects others
   _X_ Assertive   ___ Helpful   ___ Responsible
   ___ Cleanliness (household) _X_ Hobbies/crafts   ___ Safety skills
   _X_ Community skills   ___ Honesty   _X_ Sense of humor
   ___ Cooperative   _X_ Independent   ___ Shares
   _X_ Courteous   ___ Insightful   ___ Survival skills
   _X_ Daily living skills   ___ Listening skills   ___ Verbal expression
   ___ Dependable   ___ Money management skills ___ Works hard
   ___ Emotional   ___ Motivated   ___ _____
   ___ Eye contact   ___ Organized   ___ _____
   ___ _____   ___ _____   ___ _____

   Comments on any of the above: ___She is a good girl, but just can't stay with any one activity___
   ___for very long. She tries to be helpful, but goes on to something else.___

2. Which of the following normal emotions or responses do you recognize as at least sometimes taking place with the client? (Add others that apply.)

   _X_ Anger   _X_ Embarrassment   ___ Grief
   _X_ Anxiety   ___ Envy   _X_ Happiness
   _X_ Boredom   ___ Fear   ___ Loneliness
   ___ Depression   _X_ Frustration   _X_ Stress
   ___ _____   ___ _____   ___ _____

3. List any concerns you have regarding any of the above emotions or responses. ___She gets___
   ___angry and frustrated too easily. This makes her more hyperactive.___
   _____
   _____
   _____

4. How does s/he express (verbally and nonverbally) the following emotions?

Happiness: _When Christine is happy she is much more helpful around the house. She smiles and might sing. She doesn't directly say she is happy._

Sadness: _She initially will be mopey and withdrawn. After a while she might act like she is mad at everybody. She cries very easily, but doesn't seem to recognize depression._

Anger: _Temper tantrums. It doesn't take much for her to hit people or throw things in her room. At times she will verbally abuse others._

Frustration: _Same as anger._

5. Briefly describe any self-injurious behaviors (SIBs) and/or inappropriate self-stimulation behaviors (SSBs).

Behavior: (describe the problem behavior)
Antecedents: (describe what usually takes place before the behavior occurs)
Consequences: (describe what actions are taken after the behavior occurs)
Frequency/duration: (describe how often and for how long it occurs)

Behavior: _None_
Antecedents: _____
Consequences: _____
Frequency/duration: _____

Behavior: _____
Antecedents: _____
Consequences: _____
Frequency/duration: _____

Behavior: _____
Antecedents: _____
Consequences: _____
Frequency/duration: _____

6. Briefly describe aggressive acts (to people or property).

Behavior: _Temper tantrums_
Antecedents: _When she does not get her way_
Consequences: _Time out in her room, lose upcoming privileges_
Frequency/duration: _4–5 times per week/15–30 minutes_

Behavior: _Inappropriate yelling at family members_
Antecedents: _When she is frustrated or not able to get things immediately_
Consequences: _Time out, lose privileges_
Frequency/duration: _3–4 times per week/varies_

Behavior: _Throw toys against wall_
Antecedents: _When she is mad at her sister_
Consequences: _Must apologize, time out_
Frequency/duration: _1 time per week_

7. Describe any inappropriate sexual behavior. _X_ None known

_____
_____
_____

8. Describe any inappropriate social behaviors. ___ None known

   Children at school tease her because of her hyperactivity and immaturity. She then acts even
   more immature and may cry and receive more teasing. She is beginning to lash out
   physically at her classmates.

9. How would you rate his/her listening skills?

Low		Average		High	___ NA
1	(2)	3	4	5	

   Comments: _She hears but rarely listens. She is too active to have time for listening._

10. How would you rate his/her ability to cope with problems?

Low		Average		High	___ NA
(1)	2	3	4	5	

   Comments: _Very poor_

11. How would you rate his/her respect for other people?

Low		Average		High	___ NA
1	(2)	3	4	5	

   Comments: _____

12. How would you rate his/her ability to manage anger?

Low		Average		High	___ NA
(1)	2	3	4	5	

   Comments: _____

13. How would you rate his/her motivation to change negative behaviors?

Low		Average		High	___ NA
1	(2)	3	4	5	

   Comments: _____

14. How would you rate his/her ability to accept constructive criticism?

Low		Average		High	___ NA
1	2	(3)	4	5	

   Comments: _____

15. How would you rate his/her potential for increased independent living?

Low		Average		High	___ NA
1	2	(3)	4	5	

   Comments: _____

16. Please list any significant stressful events or major changes in his/her life in the past six months (e.g., loss of loved one, significant others moving, change in residence, new roommate or housemate, new sibling, major illness, etc.). ___ None known

Her grandmother died about four months ago.

If applicable, what behavioral/emotional effects may this have had? ___ None known

She spend every Saturday at her grandmother's home. They were very close. Although Christine was hyperactive before her grandmother died, she has been much more defiant in the past few months.

17. Check any of the following which apply to him/her. (Add others that apply.)

___ Anxiety   _X_ Explosive behaviors   ___ Schizophrenia

___ Auditory hallucinations   _X_ Impulse control concerns   ___ Sexual concerns

___ Chemical dependency   ___ Mood shifts   ___ Social withdrawal

_X_ Conduct problems   ___ Obsessive/compulsive   ___ Suicidal threats

___ Depression   ___ Paranoid   ___ Thought disorder

___ Eating disorder   ___ Phobias/fears   ___ Visual hallucinations

___ _____   ___ _____   ___ _____

Describe behavioral effects or incidents of each of the above items.

Conduct problems and explosive behaviors: When she does not get her way she gets very frustrated and, at times, will lash out at anything or anyone in her way. It does not take much to set her off. She has never hurt anyone. She usually has a tantrum, then cools off after about 1/2 hour, especially if she gets no attention for the tantrum.

Impulse control: She can't wait for anything. She often gets into trouble at school for cutting in line. She always wants things before it is the right time. She gets edgy when she has to wait.

18. Briefly describe any past events that may be difficult for him/her to handle at this time (e.g., abuse, injuries).

None known

19. Briefly describe any past events that were particularly encouraging or led to positive life changes for him/her.

20. Please list any other information about him/her (e.g., important background information, special strengths/weaknesses, concerns with other people, problems on the job).

Form 17   Emotional/Behavioral Update

Client's name: _____   Date: _____

Describe any stressful events in the client's life which have taken place recently (e.g., friend moved away, sickness): _____

_____

_____

_____

_____

_____

Describe any positive events in the client's life which have taken place recently (e.g., vacation, earned an award): _____

_____

_____

_____

_____

_____

Positive behaviors since last session (emotional, behavioral, social, etc.)

Date(s)	Behavior	How was it reinforced or rewarded?
_____	_____	_____
_____	_____	_____
_____	_____	_____

Problem areas since last session (emotional, behavioral, social, etc.)

Date(s)	Behavior	What were the consequences?
_____	_____	_____
_____	_____	_____
_____	_____	_____

Caregiver's comments: _____

_____

_____

Caregiver's signature: _____   Date: _____/_____/_____

Form 17A   Emotional/Behavioral Update

(Completed)

Client's name: _William Olden_   Date: ___6/10/1999___

Describe any stressful events in the client's life which have taken place recently (e.g., friend moved away, sickness): _Had argument with the friend he met last month. Has not talked to him in_ _four days._

Describe any positive events in the client's life which have taken place recently (e.g., vacation, earned an award): _____

Positive behaviors since last session (emotional, behavioral, social, etc.)

Date(s)	Behavior	How was it reinforced or rewarded?
6/4/1998	Did homework as per plan	Choice of weekend activity
6/8/1998	Discussed his anger without verbal abuse	Later bedtime on weekend
6/9/1998	Apologized to teacher for past behaviors	Allowed extensions on late homework

Problem areas since last session (emotional, behavioral, social, etc.)

Date(s)	Behavior	What were the consequences?
6/3/1998	Started argument with friend, bullied him	Written apology
6/7/1998	Temper tantrum	Discussion

Caregiver's comments: _He continues to struggle but there are improvements, family counseling_ _helps him get along with step-father._

Caregiver's signature: _Lanna Olden_   Date: _6_ / _10_ / _1999_

Form 18 Biopsychosocial Report

Client's name: _____ Case number: _____ Date: _____

Age: _____ Gender: ___ F ___ M Race: _____ Marital status: _____

1. **Current Family and Significant Relationships**   (See Personal History Form)
   (Include strengths, stressors, problems, recent changes, changes desired and comments on family and relationship circumstances)

   _____

   _____

   _____

2. **Childhood/Adolescent History**   (See Personal History Form)
   (Developmental milestones, past behavioral concerns, environment, abuse, school, social, mental health)

   _____

   _____

   _____

3. **Social Relationships**   (See Personal History Form)
   (Include strengths, stressors, problems, recent changes, changes desired and comments on current circumstances)

   _____

   _____

   _____

4. **Cultural/Ethnic**   (See Personal History Form)
   (Include strengths, stressors, problems, recent changes, changes desired and beliefs/practices to incorporate into therapy)

   _____

   _____

   _____

5. **Spiritual/Religious**   (See Personal History Form)
   (Include strengths, stressors, problems, recent changes, changes desired and beliefs/practices to incorporate into therapy)

   _____

   _____

   _____

6. **Legal**   (See Personal History Form)
   (Include current and previous legal concerns and their impact on behavior, affect and relationship)

   _____

   _____

   _____

7. Education   (See Personal History Form)
(Include strengths, stressors, problems, recent changes, changes desired and comments on current circumstances)

_____
_____
_____

8. Employment/Vocational   (See Personal History Form)
(Include strengths, stressors, problems, recent changes, changes desired and comments on current circumstances)

_____
_____
_____

9. Military   (See Personal History Form)
(Include current impact on affect and behavior)

_____
_____
_____

10. Leisure/Recreational   (See Personal History Form)
(Include strengths, stressors, problems, recent changes, changes desired)

_____
_____
_____

11. Medical/Physical Health   (See Personal History Form)
(Include speech, language and hearing, visual impairment, sensorimotor dysfunctions, immunization status for children and physical factors affecting medical condition and/or medical factors affecting physical condition)

_____
_____
_____

12. Chemical Use History   (See Personal History Form)
(When relevant, include information such as previous and current use patterns, impact on functioning, drugs of choice, last use, relapse dynamics, motivation to recover, overdose history, and patient's perception of the problem)

_____
_____
_____

13. Counseling/Psychiatric History   (See Personal History Form)
(Include benefits and setbacks of previous treatment, reasons for admission, termination, and cycles)

_____
_____
_____

Integrated Summary

Clinical Assessment/Diagnostic Summary

(Evaluate, integrate and summarize the following information: Background, medical, social, presenting problem, signs and symptoms and impairments. Tie these in with the patient's strengths and needs. Integration of data is more important than specific details.)

_____
_____
_____
_____
_____
_____
_____
_____
_____
_____
_____
_____
_____
_____
_____
_____
_____
_____
_____
_____
_____
_____
_____
_____
_____
_____
_____
_____

	Diagnosis	Code
Axis I	_____	_____
Axis II	_____	_____
Axis III	_____	_____
Axis IV	_____	
Axis V	Current GAF = _____	

Therapist's signature/credentials: _____ Date: ____/____/_____

Form 18A   Biopsychosocial Report

(Completed)

Client's name: _Judy Doe_   Case number: _DJ030899_   Date: _5/3/1999_

Age: _50_   Gender: _X_ F ___ M   Race: _Caucasian_   Marital status: _Married_

1. **Current Family and Significant Relationships**   (See Personal History Form)

   (Include strengths, stressors, problems, recent changes, changes desired and comments on family and relationship circumstances)

   Supportive family of origin, but intrusive. Able to vent feelings with Mother. Avoiding
   other relatives. High marital conflict, possible divorce. Seldom asserts self to spouse,
   child, or family of origin.

2. **Childhood/Adolescent History**   (See Personal History Form)

   (Developmental milestones, past behavioral concerns, environment, abuse, school, social, mental health)

   History of usually being a follower. Did well in school academically, but considered self as
   "homely and unpopular." Viewed self as being in "shadow of older sister."
   No developmental delays physically. No counseling as a child.

3. **Social Relationships**   (See Personal History Form)

   (Include strengths, stressors, problems, recent changes, changes desired and comments on current circumstances)

   Has had a few close friends since adolescence, but has turned down their invitations. Now
   no contact in several months. Feels rejected about it. Not initiating any social interactions.

4. **Cultural/Ethnic**   (See Personal History Form)

   (Include strengths, stressors, problems, recent changes, changes desired and beliefs/practices to incorporate into therapy)

   Mainstream, middle class values/beliefs, no changes or unusual circumstances

5. **Spiritual/Religious**   (See Personal History Form)

   (Include strengths, stressors, problems, recent changes, changes desired and beliefs/practices to incorporate into therapy)

   History of strong religious convictions. Went to church "religiously" until past year.
   Feels guilty. Will not consider suicide due to "hell." Misses singing in church but
   can't get herself to go.

6. **Legal**   (See Personal History Form)

   (Include current and previous legal concerns and their impact on behavior, affect and relationship)

   No legal history

7. **Education** (See Personal History Form)

(Include strengths, stressors, problems, recent changes, changes desired and comments on current circumstances)

Did well in high school academically. Always on honor roll. Didn't feel challenged.

College was more competitive but earned GPA of 2.9. Earned teaching certificate.

8. **Employment/Vocational** (See Personal History Form)

(Include strengths, stressors, problems, recent changes, changes desired and comments on current circumstances)

Very stable work history. But lately "no motivation" to teach or oversee students. Views

students as demanding. Used to believe teaching is rewarding. Gets along "neutrally"

with other teachers. Tries to hide depression at school.

9. **Military** (See Personal History Form)

(Include current impact on affect and behavior)

N/A

10. **Leisure/Recreational** (See Personal History Form)

(Include strengths, stressors, problems, recent changes, changes desired)

No current activities. Used to enjoy relaxing, exercising, and various sports; feels "too

tired and worn out." Wants to resume activities some day.

11. **Medical/Physical Health** (See Personal History Form)

(Include speech, language and hearing, visual impairment, sensorimotor dysfunctions, immunization status for children and physical factors affecting medical condition and/or medical factors affecting physical condition)

No physical problems in the past. Over past year experiencing weight loss, headaches,

fatigue, low libido, poor sleep. "Feels like 100 years old," symptoms concordant with

depression.

12. **Chemical Use History** (See Personal History Form)

(When relevant, include information such as previous and current use patterns, impact on functioning, drugs of choice, last use, relapse dynamics, motivation to recover, overdose history, and patient's perception of the problem)

Rare, light social drinking. No history of drunkeness, drug abuse or any negative

consequences.

13. **Counseling/Psychiatric History** (See Personal History Form)

(Include benefits and setbacks of previous treatment, reasons for admission, termination, and cycles)

Relationship break-up in college led to diagnosis of depression. Counseling was successful,

learned coping skills, set goals, and increased pleasurable activities. Has had a few minor

bouts of depression since then but it was manageable. No psychiatric hospitalizations.

Integrated Summary

Clinical Assessment/Diagnostic Summary

(Evaluate, integrate and summarize the following information: Background, medical, social, presenting problem, signs and symptoms and impairments. Tie these in with the patient's strengths and needs. Integration of data is more important than specific details.)

Judy Doe presents with significant depression and marital conflict. She was treated previously for depression 20 years ago due to relationship issues. Counseling was successful. She describes herself as always being in good health, but currently several signs of depression are endorsed. She appears dysphoric and makes several self-depricating statements. She views her family of origin as her only support system. She has a history of academic achievement, and graduated teacher's college. Her employment history is remarkably stable. Increased marital conflict over the past year has coincided with a relapse of Major Depression. Divorce threats exacerbate her symptoms. Major concerns at this time are occupational affective, and social impairment. She is considering taking a leave of absence from work due to inability to concentrate adequately on teaching and formulating lesson plans. She states that she wants to "get better again" but "needs direction," as in her previous counseling.

	Diagnosis	Code
Axis I	*Major Depression, recurrent moderate*	*296.32*
Axis II	*Deferred*	
Axis III	*Defer to physician*	
Axis IV	*Marital Discord, social and occupational problems*	
Axis V	Current GAF = *55*	

Therapist's signature/credentials: *Darlene Benton, PhD*   Date: *5 / 3 / 1999*

Form 19   Diagnostic Assessment Report

Name: _____   Therapist: _____

Intake/Assessment date(s): _____   Report date: _____

1. **Purpose of Visit/Current Life Situation** (Include duration/frequency of symptoms)

_____
_____
_____
_____
_____
_____
_____
_____
_____
_____
_____

2. **History of Current Problem/Developmental Incidents/Treatment History/ Medications, etc.**

_____
_____
_____
_____
_____
_____
_____
_____
_____
_____
_____

3. **Current Functioning, Symptoms, and Impairments** (e.g., occupational, social, emotional)

_____
_____
_____
_____
_____
_____
_____

Strengths: _____
Weaknesses: _____

4. Family Mental Health History

_____
_____
_____
_____
_____
_____
_____
_____
_____
_____
_____

5. Other (Substance abuse, suicidal ideations, court referral, etc.)

_____
_____
_____
_____
_____
_____
_____
_____
_____
_____
_____
_____

Mental Status Exam

	Normal	Slight		Moderate		Severe	
	0	1	2	3	4	5	6
Appearance							
Unkempt, unclean, disheveled	(__)	(__)	(__)	(__)	(__)	(__)	(__)
Clothing and/or grooming atypical	(__)	(__)	(__)	(__)	(__)	(__)	(__)
Unusual physical characteristics	(__)	(__)	(__)	(__)	(__)	(__)	(__)

Comments re: Appearance: _____
_____

	Normal	Slight		Moderate		Severe	
	0	1	2	3	4	5	6
Posture							
Slumped	(__)	(__)	(__)	(__)	(__)	(__)	(__)
Rigid, tense	(__)	(__)	(__)	(__)	(__)	(__)	(__)

	Normal	Slight		Moderate		Severe	
	0	1	2	3	4	5	6
Facial Expressions Suggest							
Anxiety	(__)	(__)	(__)	(__)	(__)	(__)	(__)
Depression, sadness	(__)	(__)	(__)	(__)	(__)	(__)	(__)
Absence of feeling, blandness	(__)	(__)	(__)	(__)	(__)	(__)	(__)
Atypical, unusual	(__)	(__)	(__)	(__)	(__)	(__)	(__)

	Normal	Slight		Moderate			Severe
	0	1	2	3	4	5	6

General Body Movements

	0	1	2	3	4	5	6
Accelerated, increased speed	(__)	(__)	(__)	(__)	(__)	(__)	(__)
Decreased, slowed	(__)	(__)	(__)	(__)	(__)	(__)	(__)
Atypical, unusual	(__)	(__)	(__)	(__)	(__)	(__)	(__)
Restless, fidgety	(__)	(__)	(__)	(__)	(__)	(__)	(__)

	Normal	Slight		Moderate			Severe
	0	1	2	3	4	5	6

Speech

	0	1	2	3	4	5	6
Rapid speech	(__)	(__)	(__)	(__)	(__)	(__)	(__)
Slowed speech	(__)	(__)	(__)	(__)	(__)	(__)	(__)
Loud speech	(__)	(__)	(__)	(__)	(__)	(__)	(__)
Soft speech	(__)	(__)	(__)	(__)	(__)	(__)	(__)
Mute	(__)	(__)	(__)	(__)	(__)	(__)	(__)
Atypical quality (e.g., slurring)	(__)	(__)	(__)	(__)	(__)	(__)	(__)

	Normal	Slight		Moderate			Severe
	0	1	2	3	4	5	6

Therapist/Client Relationship

	0	1	2	3	4	5	6
Domineering, controlling	(__)	(__)	(__)	(__)	(__)	(__)	(__)
Submissive, compliant, dependent	(__)	(__)	(__)	(__)	(__)	(__)	(__)
Provocative, hostile, challenging	(__)	(__)	(__)	(__)	(__)	(__)	(__)
Suspicious, guarded, evasive	(__)	(__)	(__)	(__)	(__)	(__)	(__)
Uncooperative, noncompliant	(__)	(__)	(__)	(__)	(__)	(__)	(__)

Comments re: Behavior: _____

_____

_____

	Normal	Slight		Moderate			Severe
	0	1	2	3	4	5	6

Affect/Mood

	0	1	2	3	4	5	6
Inappropriate to thought content	(__)	(__)	(__)	(__)	(__)	(__)	(__)
Increased liability of affect	(__)	(__)	(__)	(__)	(__)	(__)	(__)
Blunted, dulled, bland	(__)	(__)	(__)	(__)	(__)	(__)	(__)
Euphoria, elation	(__)	(__)	(__)	(__)	(__)	(__)	(__)
Anger, hostility	(__)	(__)	(__)	(__)	(__)	(__)	(__)
Anxiety, fear, apprehension	(__)	(__)	(__)	(__)	(__)	(__)	(__)
Depression, sadness	(__)	(__)	(__)	(__)	(__)	(__)	(__)

Comments re: Affect: _____

_____

_____

	Normal	Slight		Moderate			Severe
	0	1	2	3	4	5	6

Perception

	Normal 0	Slight 1	2	Moderate 3	4	5	Severe 6
Illusions	(__)	(__)	(__)	(__)	(__)	(__)	(__)
Auditory hallucinations	(__)	(__)	(__)	(__)	(__)	(__)	(__)
Visual hallucinations	(__)	(__)	(__)	(__)	(__)	(__)	(__)
Other hallucinations	(__)	(__)	(__)	(__)	(__)	(__)	(__)

Comments re: Perception: _____

_____

_____

Intellectual Functioning Impairments

	Normal 0	Slight 1	2	Moderate 3	4	5	Severe 6
Level of consciousness	(__)	(__)	(__)	(__)	(__)	(__)	(__)
Attention span, distractible	(__)	(__)	(__)	(__)	(__)	(__)	(__)
Abstract thinking	(__)	(__)	(__)	(__)	(__)	(__)	(__)
Calculation ability	(__)	(__)	(__)	(__)	(__)	(__)	(__)
Intelligence	(__)	(__)	(__)	(__)	(__)	(__)	(__)

Orientation

	Normal 0	Slight 1	2	Moderate 3	4	5	Severe 6
Time	(__)	(__)	(__)	(__)	(__)	(__)	(__)
Place	(__)	(__)	(__)	(__)	(__)	(__)	(__)
Person	(__)	(__)	(__)	(__)	(__)	(__)	(__)

Memory Impairment

	Normal 0	Slight 1	2	Moderate 3	4	5	Severe 6
Recent	(__)	(__)	(__)	(__)	(__)	(__)	(__)
Remote	(__)	(__)	(__)	(__)	(__)	(__)	(__)

Insight

	Normal 0	Slight 1	2	Moderate 3	4	5	Severe 6
Denies psych problems	(__)	(__)	(__)	(__)	(__)	(__)	(__)
Blames others	(__)	(__)	(__)	(__)	(__)	(__)	(__)

Judgment Impairments

	Normal 0	Slight 1	2	Moderate 3	4	5	Severe 6
Decision making	(__)	(__)	(__)	(__)	(__)	(__)	(__)
Impulse control	(__)	(__)	(__)	(__)	(__)	(__)	(__)

	Normal	Slight		Moderate			Severe
	0	1	2	3	4	5	6

Thought Content

	0	1	2	3	4	5	6
Obsessions	(__)	(__)	(__)	(__)	(__)	(__)	(__)
Compulsions	(__)	(__)	(__)	(__)	(__)	(__)	(__)
Phobias	(__)	(__)	(__)	(__)	(__)	(__)	(__)
Depersonalization	(__)	(__)	(__)	(__)	(__)	(__)	(__)
Suicidal ideation	(__)	(__)	(__)	(__)	(__)	(__)	(__)
Homicidal ideation	(__)	(__)	(__)	(__)	(__)	(__)	(__)
Delusions	(__)	(__)	(__)	(__)	(__)	(__)	(__)

Comments re: Thinking: _____

_____

_____

Diagnosis Validation

Primary diagnosis: _____

Name of test	Results
_____	_____
_____	_____
_____	_____
_____	_____
_____	_____

Biographical Information (Specific BIF references)

_____

_____

_____

_____

_____

Collateral Information

_____

_____

_____

_____

_____

Case/Intake Notes, MSE References (Include brief descriptions, dates, and line numbers)

_____

_____

_____

_____

_____

Diagnosis 2: _____   (Make copies for additional Dx's)

Name of test   Results

_____   _____
_____   _____
_____   _____
_____   _____
_____   _____

Biographical Information (Specific BIF references)

_____
_____
_____
_____
_____

Case/Intake Notes, MSE References (Include brief descriptions, dates, and line numbers)

_____
_____
_____
_____
_____

Diagnostic Impressions

Axis I   _____
Axis II   _____
Axis III _____
Axis IV   _____
Axis V   _____

Needed Mental Health Services

___ Further assessment (specify): _____

___ Individual   ___ Group   ___ Family   ___ Other (specify): _____

Other Needed Services

___ Psychiatric consultation   ___ Physical exam   ___ Neurological consultation

___ CD evaluation   ___ Other (specify): _____

Did client/guardian sign the treatment plan? ___ No   ___ Yes

Was Dx explained to client? ___ No   ___ Yes

Therapist's signature: _____   Date: ____/____/_____

Supervisor's signature: _____   Date: ____/____/_____

Form 19A   Diagnostic Assessment Report

(Completed)

Name: _____ *Judy Doe* _____   Therapist: _____ *DLB* _____

Intake/Assessment date(s): ___ *3/8/1999 & 3/15/1999* ___   Report date: _____ *3/16/1999* _____

1. **Purpose of Visit/Current Life Situation** (Include duration/frequency of symptoms)

   Self-referred. Has felt increasingly sad for past year (average 3 of 4 days). Usually fatigued. Increased withdrawal has led to loss of two friends (with whom she use to be close) in past month. Now avoids them. Spouse threatening to leave soon due to her anger outbursts and lack of sexual activity. Describes marriage as "on the rocks." May desire marital counseling at a later date. Quite dissatisfied with teaching career, home life, and self. Little/no motivation to "get things done." Missed 2–4 days of work per month in past year due to "boredom/frustration with job." Currently finds no pleasures in life.

2. **History of Current Problem/Developmental Incidents/Treatment History/ Medications, etc.**

   Prior counseling for depression in 1967–1968 due to depression after breaking up with a college boyfriend. Does not remember the focus of the sessions, but believes that depression was alleviated until approximately the past year or so. Now feeling "depressed, like when in college." No meds at that time. Increased marital conflict developing, little time spent together; generally shouting, blaming, no sex or intimacy. Markedly decreased satisfaction as schoolteacher. Several self-deprecating statements regarding teaching and parenting effectiveness. Past two years insomnia. Wakes up 3–4x/night. No mania. Past year lost 20#. Views life as "monotonous, uneventful, boring." Exercises 3x/week, but not fun. Wants to "start feeling human again."

3. **Current Functioning, Symptoms, and Impairments** (e.g., occupational, social, emotional)

   1) Impaired social functioning (previously spent 1–2 evenings per week with friends, now is rarely with others). Has lost friends, initiates little/no social interactions. 2) Marital conflict leading to increased anxiety level. Avoiding family/friends. 3) Occupational impairment; missing 2–4 days/month (1 year ago rarely missed work), views teaching performance as poor at this time. 4) Emotional impairment; sad most of time, fatigued, anhedonia, low ego strength.

   Strengths: _____ *Moderately motivated to change. Religious reasons vs. suicidality.*
   Weaknesses: _____ *Seems to blame others for past failures. Level of insight.*

2.121

4. Family Mental Health History

Describes family of origin as functional. 2nd of 5 children. Left home at age 18 (college).
No known family Hx of depression or other mental health concerns. Historically good
communication with family. Hx of mother and older sibling helping/making several of her
decisions. Family generally provides positive social support, but often viewed as intrusive
by client.

5. Other (Substance abuse, suicidal ideations, court referral, etc.)

Does not view self as chemically dependent. No suicidal plan; ideations when stressed.
Signed Limits of Confidentiality. Contracted for actions to be taken when experiencing
suicidal thoughts; given phone numbers for Therapist, Crisis Hotline, and Mental Health
Intake.

Mental Status Exam

	Normal 0	Slight 1	2	Moderate 3	4	Severe 5	6
Appearance							
Unkempt, unclean, disheveled	(_)	(_)	(_)	(_X_)	(_)	(_)	(_)
Clothing and/or grooming atypical	(_X_)	(_)	(_)	(_)	(_)	(_)	(_)
Unusual physical characteristics	(_X_)	(_)	(_)	(_)	(_)	(_)	(_)

Comments re: Appearance: *T-shirt and jogging pants, moderately groomed, hair somewhat*
disheveled.

	Normal 0	Slight 1	2	Moderate 3	4	Severe 5	6
Posture							
Slumped	(_)	(_)	(_)	(_)	(_X_)	(_)	(_)
Rigid, tense	(_)	(_)	(_)	(_X_)	(_)	(_)	(_)

	Normal 0	Slight 1	2	Moderate 3	4	Severe 5	6
Facial Expressions Suggest							
Anxiety	(_)	(_X_)	(_)	(_)	(_)	(_)	(_)
Depression, sadness	(_)	(_)	(_)	(_)	(_)	(_X_)	(_)
Absence of feeling, blandness	(_)	(_)	(_)	(_)	(_X_)	(_)	(_)
Atypical, unusual	(_X_)	(_)	(_)	(_)	(_)	(_)	(_)

General Body Movements

	Normal 0	Slight 1	2	Moderate 3	4	5	Severe 6
Accelerated, increased speed	(X)	(_)	(_)	(_)	(_)	(_)	(_)
Decreased, slowed	(_)	(_)	(_)	(_)	(X)	(_)	(_)
Atypical, unusual	(X)	(_)	(_)	(_)	(_)	(_)	(_)
Restless, fidgety	(_)	(X)	(_)	(_)	(_)	(_)	(_)

Speech

	Normal 0	Slight 1	2	Moderate 3	4	5	Severe 6
Rapid speech	(X)	(_)	(_)	(_)	(_)	(_)	(_)
Slowed speech	(_)	(_)	(_)	(_)	(X)	(_)	(_)
Loud speech	(X)	(_)	(_)	(_)	(_)	(_)	(_)
Soft speech	(_)	(_)	(_)	(X)	(_)	(_)	(_)
Mute	(X)	(_)	(_)	(_)	(_)	(_)	(_)
Atypical quality (e.g., slurring)	(_)	(X)	(_)	(_)	(_)	(_)	(_)

Therapist/Client Relationship

	Normal 0	Slight 1	2	Moderate 3	4	5	Severe 6
Domineering, controlling	(X)	(_)	(_)	(_)	(_)	(_)	(_)
Submissive, compliant, dependent	(_)	(_)	(_)	(_)	(X)	(_)	(_)
Provocative, hostile, challenging	(X)	(_)	(_)	(_)	(_)	(_)	(_)
Suspicious, guarded, evasive	(X)	(_)	(_)	(_)	(_)	(_)	(_)
Uncooperative, noncompliant	(X)	(_)	(_)	(_)	(_)	(_)	(_)

Comments re: Behavior: *Low eye contact*

Affect/Mood

	Normal 0	Slight 1	2	Moderate 3	4	5	Severe 6
Inappropriate to thought content	(X)	(_)	(_)	(_)	(_)	(_)	(_)
Increased liability of affect	(X)	(_)	(_)	(_)	(_)	(_)	(_)
Blunted, dulled, bland	(_)	(_)	(_)	(X)	(_)	(_)	(_)
Euphoria, elation	(X)	(_)	(_)	(_)	(_)	(_)	(_)
Anger, hostility	(_)	(_)	(X)	(_)	(_)	(_)	(_)
Anxiety, fear, apprehension	(_)	(X)	(_)	(_)	(_)	(_)	(_)
Depression, sadness	(_)	(_)	(_)	(_)	(X)	(_)	(_)

Comments re: Affect: *Behavior, speech, and affect concordant. Onset of most recent episode of depression in past year. Depressed 3 or 4 days, most of day. Daily crying spells, cries when alone. Easily annoyed, but does not express frustration.*

	Normal	Slight		Moderate			Severe
	0	1	2	3	4	5	6

Perception

	Normal 0	Slight 1	2	Moderate 3	4	5	Severe 6
Illusions	(X)	(__)	(__)	(__)	(__)	(__)	(__)
Auditory hallucinations	(X)	(__)	(__)	(__)	(__)	(__)	(__)
Visual hallucinations	(X)	(__)	(__)	(__)	(__)	(__)	(__)
Other hallucinations	(X)	(__)	(__)	(__)	(__)	(__)	(__)

Comments re: Perception: _None_ _____

_____

_____

Intellectual Functioning Impairments

	Normal 0	Slight 1	2	Moderate 3	4	5	Severe 6
Level of consciousness	(X)	(__)	(__)	(__)	(__)	(__)	(__)
Attention span, distractible	(__)	(__)	(X)	(__)	(__)	(__)	(__)
Abstract thinking	(X)	(__)	(__)	(__)	(__)	(__)	(__)
Calculation ability	(X)	(__)	(__)	(__)	(__)	(__)	(__)
Intelligence	(X)	(__)	(__)	(__)	(__)	(__)	(__)

Orientation

	Normal 0	Slight 1	2	Moderate 3	4	5	Severe 6
Time	(X)	(__)	(__)	(__)	(__)	(__)	(__)
Place	(X)	(__)	(__)	(__)	(__)	(__)	(__)
Person	(X)	(__)	(__)	(__)	(__)	(__)	(__)

Memory Impairment

	Normal 0	Slight 1	2	Moderate 3	4	5	Severe 6
Recent	(__)	(X)	(__)	(__)	(__)	(__)	(__)
Remote	(X)	(__)	(__)	(__)	(__)	(__)	(__)

Insight

	Normal 0	Slight 1	2	Moderate 3	4	5	Severe 6
Denies psych problems	(__)	(__)	(X)	(__)	(__)	(__)	(__)
Blames others	(__)	(X)	(__)	(__)	(__)	(__)	(__)

Judgment Impairments

	Normal 0	Slight 1	2	Moderate 3	4	5	Severe 6
Decision making	(__)	(__)	(__)	(X)	(__)	(__)	(__)
Impulse control	(__)	(__)	(__)	(__)	(X)	(__)	(__)

	Normal	Slight		Moderate			Severe
	0	1	2	3	4	5	6

Thought Content

Obsessions (X) (_) (_) (_) (_) (_) (_)
Compulsions (X) (_) (_) (_) (_) (_) (_)
Phobias (X) (_) (_) (_) (_) (_) (_)
Depersonalization (X) (_) (_) (_) (_) (_) (_)
Suicidal ideation (_) (_) (_) (X) (_) (_) (_)
Homicidal ideation (X) (_) (_) (_) (_) (_) (_)
Delusions (X) (_) (_) (_) (_) (_) (_)

Comments re: Thinking: _Historical incidents of poor judgment and impulsivity with subsequent_
depression. At times will withdraw or miss work when frustrated. Denies suicidal attempts.
Ideations at times. Blames self for not motivating spouse, children, and students.

Diagnosis Validation

Primary diagnosis: _296.32 Major depression, recurrent, moderate, w/o psychotic features_

Name of test	Results
Minnesota Multiphasic	_Elevated 2–4–7 Depression, anxiety, CD potential_
Personality Inventory—2	_Profile typical of cycles of acting out, guilt, depression_
(MMPI–2)	_Raw score 32—Severe_
Beck Depression	
Inventory (BDI)	

Biographical Information (Specific BIF references)

Frequent feelings of hopelessness, loneliness, no one caring, failure, disappointment, can't do
anything right, difficulties concentrating, depression, and having no emotions. Unwanted Sx of
avoiding people, depression, fatigue, hopelessness, loneliness, loss of sexual interest, frequent
sickness, sleeping difficulties, suicidal thoughts, withdrawal, and worrying. Experiences little/no
pleasure.

Collateral Information

Have requested records from previous therapist.

Case/Intake Notes, MSE References (Include brief descriptions, dates, and line numbers)

3/8/1997, Intake Notes. Section 8; poor appetite: 13: Crying spells daily, fatigued, low ego
strength, social withdrawal increasing; 14: psychomotor retardation, blunted affect, difficulty
making decisions, suicidal ideation, appeared depressed; 15: usually feels depressed guilt feelings,
insomnia.

Diagnosis 2: _Deferred 799.9_ _____ (Make copies for additional Dx's)

Name of test   Results

_____   _____
_____   _____
_____   _____
_____   _____
_____   _____

Biographical Information (Specific BIF references)

_____
_____
_____
_____
_____

Case/Intake Notes, MSE References (Include brief descriptions, dates, and line numbers)

_____
_____
_____
_____
_____

Diagnostic Impressions

Axis I _____ _296.32 Major depression, recurrent, moderate, w/o psychotic features_ _____

Axis II _____ _Deferred_ _____

Axis III _____ _Defer to physician_ _____

Axis IV _____ _Spousal discord, loss of friends_ _____

Axis V _____ _Global Assessment of Functioning (GAF): Current: 58   Past year: 78_ _____

Needed Mental Health Services

___ Further assessment (specify): _____

_X_ Individual ___ Group ___ Family ___ Other (specify): _____

Other Needed Services

_X_ Psychiatric consultation   _X_ Physical exam   ___ Neurological consultation

___ CD evaluation   ___ Other (specify): _____

Did client/guardian sign the treatment plan? ___ No _X_ Yes

Was Dx explained to client? ___ No _X_ Yes

Therapist's signature: _____ _Darlene L. Benton, PhD_ _____ Date: __3_ / _16_ / _1999_

Supervisor's signature: _____ _Sharon Bell, PhD_ _____ Date: __3_ / _16_ / _1999_

Form 20   Diagnostic Assessment—Lower Functioning

Name: _____   Date: _____

Gender: ___ F ___ M   Race: _____   DOB: _____   Age: _____

Residence: _____   Contact person(s):
           _____
           _____   Phone: _____

Date entered residence: _____

Employment: _____   Contact person(s):
            _____
            _____   Phone: _____

Day program: _____   Contact person(s):
             _____
             _____   Phone: _____

County case manager: _____   Phone: _____

Guardianship: _____   Comments: _____

Guardian's name and address if not client or case manager: _____

Address: _____   City: _____   State: _____   Zip: _____

SS number: _____

Insurance company: _____

Address: _____   City: _____   State: _____   Zip: _____

Policy number: _____   Group number: _____

Purpose of evaluation: _____

Referred by: _____   Title: _____

Family member to contact: _____

Address: _____   City: _____   State: _____   Zip: _____

1. Background Information

Place of birth: _____   Complications: _____

Intellectual development: _____

_____

Social development: _____

_____

Emotional development: _____

_____

Schooling: _____

_____

Employment/Vocational history: _____

_____

Residential history:

        Name of residence   From   To

_____   _____   _____

_____   _____   _____

_____   _____   _____

Mother: _____

_____

Father: _____

_____

Siblings: Number _____ of _____ siblings. Their ages, sex, comments: _____

_____

Sexual concerns: _____

_____

2. Medical Concerns

Present physical concerns: _____

_____

Behavioral/emotional effects of physical concerns: _____

_____

Past physical concerns: _____

_____

Past suicidal attempts? ___ No   ___ Yes

If Yes, explain: _____

_____

Medications: _____

_____

Currently under physician's care? ___ No   ___ Yes

If Yes, for what purpose(s): _____

_____

Currently in psychological therapy? ___ No   ___ Yes

If Yes, explain: _____

_____

3. Present Behaviors

From staff (oral interview): Positive: _____

_____

Negative: _____

_____

From written sources: Positive: _____

_____

Negative: _____

_____

Observations/Interview: _____

_____

4. Emotional Issues

From staff (oral interview): _____

_____

From written sources: _____

_____

Observations/Interview: _____

_____

Comments: _____

_____

5. Observations

_____

_____

Appearance: _____

Gestures/Mannerisms: _____

Attention span: _____

Level of interest: _____

Speech: _____

Level of conversation: _____

Affect: _____

Eye contact: _____

Cooperation: _____

Understanding of why being interviewed: _____

6. Adaptive Functioning

_____

_____

_____

_____

_____

_____

7. Previous Testing

By whom: _____ Purpose: _____ Date: _____

Results: _____

_____

8. Present Testing (list below, plus see test profiles)

_____

_____

_____

_____

9. Clinical Diagnosis

Axis I: _____

Axis II: _____

Axis III: _____

Axis IV: _____

Axis V: _____

Comments: _____

_____

10. Recommendations

Appropriateness of residential services: _____

_____

Appropriateness of day program/employment: _____

_____

Guardianship: _____

_____

Current/Future mental health/behavioral services: _____

_____

Strategies for caregivers: _____

_____

_____

Additional information needed: _____

_____

11. Summary

_____

_____

_____

_____

_____

_____

_____

_____

Therapist's signature: _____ Date: ____/____/_____

Form 20A   Diagnostic Assessment—Lower Functioning

(Completed)

Name: _Peter Fowler_   Date: _3/17/1999_

Gender: ___ F _X_ M   Race: _African-Amer._   DOB: _8/12/1974_   Age: _24_

Residence: _Alternatives_   Contact person(s):
             3001 10th Ave N   _Rod Collins_
             Miami, ME 71111   Phone: _555-1778_

Date entered residence: _4/7/1994_

Employment: _Sullivan's Market_   Contact person(s):
              108 Hagar Rd   _Jan Wente_
              Miami, ME 71112   Phone: _555-2841_

Day program: _DAC_   Contact person(s):
               400 8th Ave S   _Pat O'Brien_
               Miami, ME 71113   Phone: _555-9426_

County case manager: _Ron Bolton_   Phone: _555-8522_

Guardianship: _State_   Comments: _____

Guardian's name and address if not client or case manager: _Joseph Fowler_

Address: _4126 'J' Street_   City: _Miami_   State: _ME_   Zip: _71112_

SS number: _987-65-4321_

Insurance company: _State Insurance Fund_

Address: _1418 Capitol Blvd_   City: _Miami_   State: _ME_   Zip: _71115_

Policy number: _987-65-4321-F_   Group number: _N/A_

Purpose of evaluation: _Periodic psychological update_

Referred by: _Ron Bolton_   Title: _County Social Worker_

Family member to contact: _Same as guardian_

Address: _____   City: _____   State: ____   Zip: _____

1. Background Information

Place of birth: _Miami, ME_   Complications: _Oxygen deprived_

Intellectual development: _Diagnosis of MR at birth. Developmental delays in all areas._

Social development: _History of no close friendships. Very intrusive in other's personal space. Friendly._

Emotional development: _Life-long issues in anger management when stressed with environmental changes._

Schooling: _State Hospital age 3–12 in Myer Program. Special education while in foster care age 13–19. No mainstreaming._

Employment/Vocational history: _No history of competitive employment. Always in supervised setting with minimal tasks._

Residential history:

Name of residence	From	To
State Hospital	Birth	1984
Hanna Foster Home	1984	1994
Alternatives Group Home	1994	Present

Mother: _Gave up to state custody at birth. No contact since birth._

Father: _Unknown_

Siblings: Number _DK_ of _____ siblings. Their ages, sex, comments: _____

Sexual concerns: _No issues. Expresses interest in nude photos in magazines. No history of relationships._

2. Medical Concerns

Present physical concerns: _Tires easily, frequent respiratory problems_

Behavioral/emotional effects of physical concerns: _Frustrated when he cannot keep up with others._

Past physical concerns: _Several operations as child (no records available, though). Seizures until age 8._

Past suicidal attempts? _X_ No ___ Yes
If Yes, explain: _____

Medications: _None—Previous Tegretol–dose unknown_

Currently under physician's care? ___ No _X_ Yes
If Yes, for what purpose(s): _Monitor respiratory concerns_

Currently in psychological therapy? _X_ No ___ Yes
If Yes, explain: _____

3. Present Behaviors

From staff (oral interview): Positive: _Helpful when praised. Always on time. Keeps room very clean._

Negative: _Behavioral outbursts when frustrated. Will aggress verbally and physically toward staff average 1x/week._

From written sources: Positive: _Staff records indicate 85% compliance in behavioral programming._

Negative: _Staff records indicate spuratic anger outbursts. Property damage 3x last month._

Observations/Interview: _He spoke only a few words during interview. He cooperates with all staff requests._

4. Emotional Issues

From staff (oral interview): _Staff report that he is usually happy but, changes in environment lead to much frustration and poor coping strategies._

From written sources: _Staff records indicate no behavioral issues._

Observations/Interview: _Neutral affect. Did not appear to be depressed, anxious, irritable, or angry._

Comments: _Very little affective expression._

5. Observations

Sat still during entire interview. Did not appear to be stressed. No unusual mannerisms. Laughed at appropriate times. Interrupted staff 4x during staff interview.

Appearance: _Neatly dressed, but 2 buttons undone_

Gestures/Mannerisms: _At times rocked back and forth_

Attention span: _Stared into space a few times. Moderate_

Level of interest: _Seemed interested when his name was mentioned_

Speech: _Spoke very little. 3–4 word sentences. 85% understandable_

Level of conversation: _Poor_

Affect: _Neutral_

Eye contact: _Poor most of the time_

Cooperation: _Moderate_

Understanding of why being interviewed: _No_

6. Adaptive Functioning

Staff report that he requires 24 hour staffing. Never left in home alone. Is able to dress self, perform personal hygiene, and help with household chores. Not able to cook, shop, or use phone independently. History of being vulnerable to strangers. Does not seem to understand the function of money.

7. Previous Testing

By whom: _Jill Cheng, MS_   Purpose: _Periodic Eval_   Date: _3/10/1994_

Results: _Full-scale IQ = 51   Adaptive functioning score = 54   Does not read or perform any math.   Axis I = No diagnosis   Axis II = Moderate MR_

8. Present Testing (list below, plus see test profiles)

Full-scale IQ = 50   Adaptive functioning score = 55

9. Clinical Diagnosis

Axis I: _No diagnosis   V71.09_

Axis II: _Moderate MR   318_

Axis III: _Records indicate respiratory problems_

Axis IV: _Social problems_

Axis V: _SD_

Comments: _No significant differences in test scores or adaptive functioning._

10. Recommendations

Appropriateness of residential services: _Current services are appropriate and in his best interest at this time._

Appropriateness of day program/employment: _Suggest continuing present services_

Guardianship: _Not able to be own guardian. Suggest state remain as guardian._

Current/Future mental health/behavioral services: _No counseling suggested. Consider behavioral programming dealing with rewarding constructive coping mechanisms._

Strategies for caregivers: _Reinforce adaptive behaviors by providing increased choices. Do not give any attention to attention seeking behaviors. Visibly chart his progress and praise him for it._

Additional information needed: _Reports from day program and job placement regarding any behavioral issues._

11. Summary

Peter Fowler was referred for a periodic psychological evaluation as required by the state. He was quiet and calm during the entire interview. Staff report no significant emotional issues except temper outbursts when stressed. At times he will hit staff members. Intellectual and adaptive functioning indicates moderate MR. He is not able to function independently. Adaptive functioning is similar to a person approximately age 8. No changes in functioning are noted since his previous evaluation. Suggest keeping present residence, day program, employment and state guardianship.

Therapist's signature: _Sarah Bloom, PhD_   Date: _3 / 12 / 1999_

Chapter 3

Evaluation Forms
and Procedures

Generally much more information is needed when a psychological evaluation has been requested, compared to the information required for a client entering a few sessions of therapy. But the following psychological evaluation forms may also be used prior to therapy when needed.

Although the examples of psychological evaluation forms for adults and children are similar, several differences exist, such as the use of collateral information provided by parents, developmental issues, diagnostic categories, and the Mental Status Exam. Each may be used for general purposes and formal evaluations such as Social Security Disability evaluations. A structured interview format is employed from which the final report may be easily dictated. A sample of both an adult and child evaluation are included.

FORMS 21 and 22
Adult and Child
Psychological Evaluations

The psychological evaluation is a structured interview designed to provide symptoms, history, daily activities, ability to relate to others, substance abuse, and an extensive mental status evaluation. The form is also designed to help evaluate thought, affective, personality, and somatoform disorders, plus memory and concentration.

These forms are not ends in themselves; rather, they provide structure for an interview and subsequent data for a psychological report or treatment plan. The requested information in each section is self-explanatory for those trained in diagnostic interviewing and mental status evaluations.

The psychological evaluation forms cover several areas of functioning in the client's life. Information such as a typical daily schedule is useful when conducting the evaluation for assessing mental and physical disabilities. The *Clinical Documentation Primer* (Wiger, 1999) provides detailed explanations as to how to conduct a psychological evaluation.

Form 21   Psychological Evaluation—Adult

Client's name: _____

Phone (home): _____ ID#: _____ Date: _____

Address: _____ City: _____ State: _____ Zip: _____

Transportation to interview: _____ ___ Alone ___ With others ___ Drove ___ Driven

Collateral information by: _____ Relationship: _____

Physical Description

Identification given: _____ Race: _____ Gender: ___ F ___ M

Age: _____ Height: _____ Weight: _____ Eyes: _____ Hair: _____

Clothing: _____ Hygiene: _____ Other: _____

History

1. **Signs and Symptoms** Client's statement of problem and impairments (e.g., social, occupational, affective, cognitive, memory, physical)

   Symptoms or disability(ies)   Resulting impairment(s)

   _____   _____
   _____   _____
   _____   _____
   _____   _____
   _____   _____
   _____   _____

   As seen by professional: _____

   _____

2. **History of Present Illness**

   Events or incidents leading to need for services/benefits: _____

   _____

   _____

   Family Hx of Sx's: _____

   Onset/Frequency/Duration/Intensity/Cycling of symptoms: _____

   _____

   _____

   Was there a clear time when Sx's worsened? _____

   Previous diagnosis (include by whom): _____

   Course of illness: ___ Improving ___ Stable ___ Deteriorating ___ Varies

   Current status of past diagnoses? _____

   Precipitating factors/events (e.g., emotional, environmental, social): _____

   _____

E = Employment   V= Volunteering

Currently: ___ Yes ___ No   Hours: _____   (Describe below. Include longest position)

	Positions	Dates	FT/PT/Temp	Problems?	Reason left
___ E ___ V	_____	_____	____	_____	_____
___ E ___ V	_____	_____	____	_____	_____

Usual length of employment: _____   Usual reason(s) for leaving: _____

Usual reasons for missing work or leaving early: _____   Frequency: _____

Military: ___ N ___ Y   Dates: _____   Branch: _____

Highest rank: _____   Discharge: _____

Problems in military: _____

Medications   C = Current   P = Previous   (attempt to obtain at least 5 years history)

1. ___ C ___ P   Name: _____   Purpose: _____
   Dr. _____ of _____
   Dose: ___ mg X ___ /day   Dates: _____   Compliance: _____
   Last taken: _____   Effectiveness: _____
   Side effects: _____   Effect without the med: _____

2. ___ C ___ P   Name: _____   Purpose: _____
   Dr. _____ of _____
   Dose: ___ mg X ___ /day   Dates: _____   Compliance: _____
   Last taken: _____   Effectiveness: _____
   Side effects: _____   Effect without the med: _____

3. ___ C ___ P   Name: _____   Purpose: _____
   Dr. _____ of _____
   Dose: ___ mg X ___ /day   Dates: _____   Compliance: _____
   Last taken: _____   Effectiveness: _____
   Side effects: _____   Effect without the med: _____

4. ___ C ___ P   Name: _____   Purpose: _____
   Dr. _____ of _____
   Dose: ___ mg X ___ /day   Dates: _____   Compliance: _____
   Last taken: _____   Effectiveness: _____
   Side effects: _____   Effect without the med: _____

Mental Health Treatment History ___ Currently in Tx   (attempt to obtain at least 5 years history)

Dates	Purpose	In/Out pt.	Response to Tx	Professional
_____	_____	___ I ___ O	_____	_____
_____	_____	___ I ___ O	_____	_____

___ Check if continued on back

History of suicidality (___ ideations, ___threats, ___ attempts): _____

Physical Health Treatment History   (attempt to obtain at least 5 years history)

Primary physician: _____ of _____ since _____ frequency _____

Dates	Purpose	In/Out pt.	Response to Tx	Professional
_____	_____	___ I ___ O	_____	_____
_____	_____	___ I ___ O	_____	_____

___ Check if continued on back

Current special services (___ social ___ educational ___ legal): _____

Note and resolve any discrepancies between stated information and records: _____

BEGIN 5/30 MINUTE MEMORY CHECK

Current Level of Daily Functioning

1. **Current Hobbies, Interests and Activities**

Hobby/interest (How persistently is it followed?)   Frequency   Duration

_____   _____   _____

_____   _____   _____

_____   _____   _____

_____   _____   _____

_____   _____   _____

Realistic, appropriate, compare to previous functioning: _____

_____

2. **Activities**

___ Rent   ___ Own: ___ house   ___ apartment   ___ townhouse   ___ duplex

                              ___ condo   ___ mobile home   ___ other: _____

Who else lives there? (relationships, ages): _____

What kind of things do you usually make for: Frequency   Problems

Breakfast: _____   _____   _____

Lunch: _____   _____   _____

Dinner: _____   _____   _____

Physical challenges in bathing/grooming? _____   Need reminders? _____

Daily Schedule Include chores, shopping, meals, meds, yard work, repairs, hobbies, employment, school. In time order, in and out of the house. What the client can do independently. Note persistence, pace.

Time   Activity

_____   _____

_____   _____

_____   _____

_____   _____

_____   _____

_____   _____

_____   _____

_____   _____

_____   _____

_____   _____

_____   _____

_____   _____

_____   _____

_____   _____

5 MINUTE MEMORY CHECK _____ = ___ / 3

Activities performed in the home (e.g., write letters, crafts, physical exercise, gardening, house repairs, cooking, drawing, painting, take care of pets, lifting, sewing, auto repairs, reading)

Activity	Frequency	Duration	Effects	Independent
_____	_____	_____	_____	_____
_____	_____	_____	_____	_____
_____	_____	_____	_____	_____
_____	_____	_____	_____	_____

Activities outside the home (e.g., movies, eat out, meetings, dancing, go for walks, shopping, hunting, fishing, sports, bars, biking, bowling, volunteering, clubs, organizations, religious services, AA, classes, babysitting, travel)

Activity	Frequency	Duration	Effects	Independent
_____	_____	_____	_____	_____
_____	_____	_____	_____	_____
_____	_____	_____	_____	_____
_____	_____	_____	_____	_____

Ability to focus/concentrate on these activities (in and out of house): _____
_____

When Sx's increase how are these followed? _____
___ Drive   ___ Run errands   ___ Use public transportation (___ bus,   ___ taxi)
___ Go shopping? How often? _____   Problems? _____   Independently? ___ N ___ Y
___ Walk places? How far? _____   How often? _____   Other: _____
How do you financially care for basic needs? _____
Who pays the bills? _____   Who handles the finances? _____
___ Savings account   ___ Checking account   ___ Money orders
___ Others pay/write checks   ___ Figure change

3. **Living Situation**

Living conditions: (___ family, ___ alone, ___ group home; ___ crowded, ___dysfunctional; ability to follow rules/procedures)
_____

4. **Ability to Relate to Others** (e.g., ___ aggressive, ___ dependent, ___ defiant, ___ avoidant, ___ oppositional, ___ normal)
_____

Adults: _____   Authority figures: _____
Peers: _____   Police: _____
Family: _____   Children: _____
Neighbors: _____   Other: _____
Have best friend? _____   Group of friends? _____
Activities with friends (include frequency, duration, and problems): _____
_____
How well did client relate (examiner, office personnel) during office visit? _____
_____

5. Substance Abuse (if applicable)

Detailed history and current information regarding substance abuse patterns.

Last drink and/or use of drugs: _____

Age of onset: _____   Substances used historically: _____

History of usage: _____

_____

_____

_____

_____

_____

_____

	A	B	C
Current substances used	_____	_____	_____
Level of usage (how much?)	_____	_____	_____
Frequency (how often?)	_____	_____	_____
Duration (length of episodes)	_____	_____	_____

Effects on functioning (impact on activities, interests, ability to relate, persistence/pace): _____

_____

Reason(s) for usage: ___ taste ___ escape ___ self-medicate ___ addiction ___ other: _____

___ Weekdays? What time(s) of day? _____

___ Weekends? What time(s) of day? _____

___ Alone ___ Home ___ With others ___ Bars ___ Other: _____

How often do you drink to the point of intoxication (or get high) in a given week? _____

How many binges in a given year? _____   Frequency/duration of binges? _____

Describe treatment history and medical/social consequences of the abuse (e.g., DWIs, DTs and tremors, blackouts, job loss, divorce, etc.): _____

_____

_____

Level of functioning when not drinking or using drugs (e.g., during periods of sobriety or Tx):

_____

_____

6. History of Arrests/Incarcerations

_____

_____

Mental Status Exam

1. Clinical Observations (Entire page: Leave blank if normal. Check and comment if remarkable.)

Appearance

___ Appears age, +/-	___ Grooming	___ Hair	___ Odor
___ Posture	___ Health	___ Nails	___ Demeanor

_____

_____

Activity Level

___ Mannerisms	___ Gestures	___ Alert	___ Lethargic	___ Limp
___ Rigid	___ Relaxed	___ Combative	___ Hyperactive	___ Bored
___ Gait	___ Eye contact	___ Distracted	___ Preoccupied	___ Vigilance

_____

_____

Speech

___ Vocabulary	___ Details	___ Volume
___ Pace	___ Reaction time	___ Pitch
___ Pressured	___ Hesitant	___ Monotonous
___ Slurred	___ Stuttering	___ Mumbled
___Echolalia	___ Neologisms	___ Repetitions
___ Pronunciation	___ % Understood: _____	

_____

_____

Attitude Toward Examiner

___ Attentive	___ Distracted	___ Cooperative	___ Friendly	___ Interested
___ Frank	___ Hostile	___ Defiant	___ Guarded	___ Defensive
___ Evasive	___ Hesitant	___ Manipulative	___ Humorous	___ Historian +/-

_____

_____

2. Stream of Consciousness

Speech

___ Spontaneous	___ Inhibited	___ Blocked	___ Illogical	___ Vague
___ Pressured	___ Slowed	___ Disorganized	___ Rambling	___ Derailment
___ Coherent	___ Cause/effect	___ Neologisms		

Thinking

___ Relevant	___ Coherent	___ Goal directed	___ Loose & Rambling

Thought Processes

___ Number of ideas	___ Flight of ideas	___ Hesitance

_____

3. Thought Content

Preoccupations

___ Obsessions	___ Compulsions	___ Phobias	___ Homicide	___ Antisocial

Suicidal, Current

___ Threats	___ Ideas	___ Plan

History

___ Attempts	___ Threats	___ Ideas

Hallucinations

___ Voices	___ Visions	___ Content	___ Setting	___ Sensory system

Illusions: _____

Delusions

___ Persecutory	___ Somatic	___ Grandeur

Ideas of Reference

___ Controlled	___ Broadcasting	___ Antisocial	___ Validity
___ Content	___ Mood	___ Bizarre	

_____

4. Affect/Mood

Affective Observations

Range	___ Normal	___ Expansive	___ Restricted	___ Blunted	___ Flat
Appropriateness	___ Concordant		___ Discordant (with speech/ideas)		
Mobility	___ Normal	___ Decreased (constricted, fixed)	___ Increased (labile)		
Intensity	___ Normal	___ Mild	___ Strong		
Psychomotor	___ Normal	___ Retardation	___ Agitation		
Predominant mood	___ Neutral	___ Euthymic	___ Dysphoric	___ Euphoric	___ Manic
Level of anxiety	___ Normal	___ High (describe): _____			
Irritability	___ Normal	___ High (describe): _____			
Anger expression	___ Normal	___ High (describe): _____			

Mood (Rule in and rule out signs and symptoms)

Frequency/Intensity in Daily Life (give specific examples or impairments/strengths, frequency, duration.)

Clearly Validate with DSM-IV Criteria

Affection toward others: _____

Anger: ___ anger mng't issues   ___ property destruction

        ___ explosive behaviors   ___ assaultive behaviors

How does the client act on anger?

Onset: _____   Frequency: _____

Duration: _____   Severity: _____

Examples: _____

_____

Panic Attacks: 4+, Abrupt development of:

___ palpitations	___ sweating	___ trembling
___ shortness of breath	___ feeling of choking	___ chest pain
___ nausea	___ dizziness	___ light-headed
___ derealization	___ fear of losing control	___ fear of dying
___ numbness	___ chills	___ hot flashes
___ Other: _____		

Onset: _____   Frequency: _____

Duration: _____   Severity: _____

Anxiety: GAD: 3+, most of time, 6 months:

___ restlessness	___ easily fatigued	___ concentration
___ irritability	___ muscle tension	___ sleep disturbance
___ Other: _____		

Onset: _____   Frequency: _____

Duration: _____   Severity: _____

Depression: MDE: 2+ wks, 5+:

___ usually depressed   ___ anhedonia

___ wght +/- 5%/month   ___ appetite +/-

___ sleep +/-   ___ fatigue

___ psychomotor +/-   ___ worthlessness/guilt

___ concentration   ___ other: ___ crying spells   ___ withdrawal

___ death/suicidal ideation

___ Other: _____

_____

Onset: _____   Frequency: _____

Duration: _____   Severity: _____

Dysthymia: ___ depressed most of time   ___ onset; adult 2+ child/adolescent 1+ yrs, 2+ of:

___ +/- appetite or eating   ___ in/hypersomnia   ___ low energy/fatigue

___ low self-esteem   ___ low concentration/decisions   ___ hopelessness

___ Other: _____

_____

Onset: _____   Frequency: _____

Duration: _____   Severity: _____

Mania: 3+:

___ grandiosity   ___ low sleep   ___ talkative   ___ flight of ideas

___ distractibility   ___ goals/agitation   ___ excessive pleasure

___ Other: _____

_____

Onset: _____   Frequency: _____

Duration: _____   Severity: _____

PTSD: Traumatic event with intense response: 1+:

Distressing:

___ recollections   ___ dreams   ___ reliving

___ cues   ___ physiological reactivity with cues

3+:

___ avoid thoughts   ___ avoid environmental   ___ poor recall of events

___ low interest   ___ detachment   ___ restricted range of affect

___ foreshortened future

2+:

___ sleep   ___ anger   ___ concentration

___ hypervigilance   ___ startle response

___ Other: _____

_____

Onset: _____   Frequency: _____

Duration: _____   Severity: _____

5. **Sensorium/Cognition**

   A) Reality Contact (How in touch with reality is the client?): _____

   Able to hold normal conversation? ___ Yes ___ No Notes: _____

   B) Orientation X3: ___ Time ___ Place ___ Person Notes: _____

   C) Concentration:

   Attention to tasks/conversation; distractability: _____

   Count to 40 by 3s beginning at 1.

   (___ 1, ___ 4, ___ 7, ____, 10, ____, 13, ____, 16, ____, 19, ____, 22, ____, 25, ____, 28, ____, 31, ____, 34, ____, 37, ____, 40)

   Number of errors: ____ Time between digits: _____ Other: _____

   Count backward by 7s.

   (___ 100, ___ 93, ____, 86, ____, 79, ____, 72, ____, 65, ___, 58, ___, 51, ____, 44, ____, 37, ____, 30, ____, 23, ____, 16, ____, 9, ____, 2) _____

   Number of errors: ____ Time between digits: _____ Other: _____

   5 + 8 = ____ 7 x 4 = ____ 12 x 6 = ____ 65/5 = ____ Timing: _____

   Digits forward and backward (Average adult: FWD = 5–7 BWD – 4–6)

   FWD: ___ 42 ___ 318 ___ 6385 ___ 96725 ___ 864972 ___ 5739481 ___ 31749852

   BWD: ___ 75 ___ 582 ___ 9147 ___ 74812 ___ 839427 ___ 7392641 ___ 49521863

   FWD = ___ BWD = ___ Evaluation: ___ L ___ M ___ H

   Spell WORLD ___ FWD _____ BWD Months of year backward: _____

   Spell EARTH ___ FWD _____ BWD Concentration evaluation: ___ L ___ M ___ H

   D) Memory:

   30 MINUTE MEMORY CHECK (5 = ___ / 3) 30 = _____ = ___ / 3

   Remote Memory

   Childhood data: ___ Schools attended ___ Teacher's names/faces ___ Street grew up on

   Historical events: Kennedy ___ Event ___ Activities

   M L King ___ Event ___ Activities

   Space Shuttle Challenger ___ Event ___ Activities

   Other: _____

   Recent Memory (Y = Yes N = No V = Vague)

   ___ Activities past few months ___ Past few days ___ Past weekend

   ___ Yesterday (events, meals, etc.) ___ Today (events, meals, etc.)

   ___ Activities of past holiday ___ Other: _____

   Client's statements re: memory functioning: _____

   Specific examples of memory problems: _____

   _____

   Compared to previous functioning: _____

   _____

Evaluation of memory: _____

Long-term: ___ L ___ M ___ H   Short-term: ___ L ___ M ___ H

Immediate: ___ L ___ M ___ H

E) Information: (knowledge of current events)

Does the client: ___ read newspaper?   How often? _____

       ___ TV/radio news?   How often? _____

Name current: ___ local ___ national news event: _____

President's name: ___   Past 3 Presidents: ___   3 large cities: ___

F) Abstractive Capacity

Interpretation of various proverbs   Interpretation Given

"Rolling stone gathers no moss": _____

"Early bird catches the worm": _____

"Strike while the iron is hot": _____

"Don't cry over spilled milk": _____

Interpretations: ___ "DK"   ___ Would not try   ___ Abstract

           ___ Concrete   ___ Age-appropriate   ___ Unusual: _____

G) Judgment

"First one in theatre to see smoke and fire": _____

"Find stamped envelope in street": _____

Any history of problems in judgment? _____

H) Insight (awareness of issues: what level?)

___ Complete denial   ___ Slight awareness

___ Awareness, but blames others   ___ Intellectual insight, but few changes likely

___ Emotional insight, understanding, changes can occur

Client's statement regarding actions needed to get better: _____

_____

Comment on client's level of insight to problems: _____

I) Intellectual Level/Education/IQ Estimate

Education level: Formal: _____   Informal: _____

Military training: _____   Career training: _____

Intelligence: As per client: _____   Observed: _____

General knowledge: _____   School grades: _____

Career background: _____   Estimated IQ: _____

6. Somatoform & Personality Disorders

Somatoform Disorder: 4 pain Sx's:

___ head   ___ abdomen   ___ back   ___ joints   ___ extremities

___ chest   ___ rectum   ___ menstruation   ___ sexual intercourse   ___ urination

2 gastrointestinal Sx's:

___ nausea   ___ bloating   ___ vomiting   ___ diarrhea   ___ fool intolerance

1 pseudoneurological Sx:

___ conversion Sx	___ impaired coordination	___ aphonia
___ urinary retention	___ hallucinations	___ loss of touch or pain sensation
___ double vision	___ blindness	___ deafness
___ seizures	___ dissociative Sx	___ loss of consciousness

___ Other: _____

_____

History of problem: _____

_____

Primary/secondary gain: _____

_____

Family response: _____

_____

Selective nature of Sx: _____

_____

Observations (pain, fatigue, gait, dizziness): _____

_____

Personality Disorder (Fully describe any evidence of a personality disorder):

A. Any personality disorder must result in deviation in two or more of the following enduring patterns of inner experience and behavior differing markedly from cultural expectations:

    ___ 1) cognition ___ 2) affectivity ___ 3) interpersonal functioning ___ 4) impulse control

B. The pattern is inflexible across a wide range of experiences.

C. The pattern leads to clinically significant distress or functional impairment.

D. The pattern is stable, long duration and can be traced to at least adolescence or early adulthood.

E. The pattern is not secondary to Axis I.

F. The pattern is not due to a substance or medical condition.

Cluster A

Paranoid (4+)	Schizoid (4+)	Schizotypal (5+)
___ Suspicious	___ Undesirous of friendships	___ Ideas of reference
___ Unjustified distrust	___ Solitary activities	___ Odd beliefs
___ Reluctant to confide	___ Low sexual interest	___ Unusual perceptions
___ Hidden meanings	___ Few pleasures	___ Odd thinking/speech
___ Grudges, unforgiving	___ Lacks close friends	___ Suspicious/paranoid ideation
___ Perceived character attacks	___ Indifferent to praise/criticism	___ Inappropriate/constricted affect
___ Sexual suspicious of partner	___ Emotional coldness/ detachment	___ Odd appearance/behavior
		___ Lacks close friends
		___ Excessive, social anxiety which does not diminish with familiarity

Cluster B

Antisocial (3+ since age 15)

___ Unlawful behaviors

___ Deceitfulness

___ Impulsivity

___ Irritability. Aggressiveness, fights

___ Disregard for safety; self/others

___ Irresponsibility

___ Lack of remorse

___ Is at least 18 years old

Borderline (5+)

___ High efforts to avoid abandonment

___ Unstable intense relationships

___ Unstable identity/self-image

___ Impulsivity (2+ areas)

___ Recurrent suicidal behaviors

___ Affective instability

___ Chronic feeling of emptiness

___ Inappropriate, intense anger

___ Stress related paranoid ideations or severe dissociative symptoms

Histrionic (5+)

___ Needs center of attention

___ Interacts seductively

___ Shifting, shallow emotions

___ Appearance to draw attn.

___ Speech: impressionistic, but lacks detail

___ Self-dramatization

___ Easily suggestible

___ Considers relationships as more important than they are

Narcissistic (5+)

___ Grandiose sense of self-importance

___ Preoccupied with fantasies of success, power

___ "Special" and understood only by similar people

___ Requires excessive admiration

___ Sense of entitlement

(Narcissistic con't)

___ Interpersonally exploitive

___ Lacks empathy

___ Often envious or believes others envious of him/her

___ Arrogant, hauty

Cluster C

Avoidant (4+)

___ Avoids occupational activities due to fear of criticism

___ Unwilling to get involved unless certain of being liked

___ Restraint in personal relationships due to fear of ridicule

___ Preoccupied with being criticized or rejected in social situations

___ Inhibited in new situations

___ Views self as socially inept/ inferior

___ Reluctant to take risks due to embarrassment

Dependent (5+)

___ Difficulty with decisions

___ Excessive advice seeking

___ Needs others to assume responsibility in major areas

___ Difficulty expressing disagreement

___ Difficulty initiating projects

___ Excessively seeks nuturance and support from others

___ Feels uncomfortable when alone

OCD (4+)

___ Preoccupied with details, lists, order

___ Perfectionism interferes with task completion

___ Excessive devotion to work

___ Overconscientious, inflexible about morality

___ Unable to discard items

___ Reluctant to delegate tasks

___ Miserly spending, hoarding

___ Rigidity, stubbornness

_____

_____

_____

_____

Additional information provided by client: _____

_____

Signs of malingering: _____

_____

8. Assessment

Summary and Diagnostic Findings (Tie together history and mental status findings and relate to diagnosis. Include onset of current Sx of the condition and how far back it goes. Include evaluation of presenting problem vs. stated limitations vs. signs and symptoms. Include prognosis. Integrate collateral information.

This psychologist's confidence in the exam findings is ___ Poor ___ Average ___ High

. . . test findings is ___ Poor ___ Average ___ High

The claimant's ability to understand, retain, and follow instructions is:

___ Poor ___ Average ___ High

Axis I   1: _____

            2: _____

            3: _____

Axis II   1: _____

            2: _____

Axis III   _____

Axis IV Current Stressors: _____

Axis V Current GAF = _____   Highest past year GAF = _____

9. Capacity Statement

Based on your findings:

1) ___ P ___ L ___ M ___ G ___ E   The client's ability to concentrate on and understand directions,

2) ___ P ___ L ___ M ___ G ___ E   Carry out tasks with reasonable persistence and pace,

3) ___ P ___ L ___ M ___ G ___ E   Respond appropriately to ___ co-workers, and ___ supervisors, and

4) ___ P ___ L ___ M ___ G ___ E   Tolerate the stresses in the workplace.

Prognosis: ___ Poor ___ Marginal ___ Guarded ___ Moderate ___ Good ___ Excellent

Qualifiers to prognosis:

___ Med compliance   ___ Tx compliance   ___ Home environment

___ Activity changes   ___ Behavioral changes   ___ Attitudinal changes

___ Education/training   ___ Other: _____

Comments: _____

_____

_____

_____

Form 21A   Psychological Evaluation—Adult

(Completed)

Client's name: _George Wallington_

Phone (home): _123-8976_   ID#: _100498WD_   Date: _10/4/1998_

Address: _3579 Eddington Court_   City: _Standford_   State: _CA_   Zip: _12345_

Transportation to interview: _Car_   _X_ Alone ___ With others   _X_ Drove ___ Driven

Collateral information by: _None_   Relationship: _____

Physical Description

Identification given: _State drivers license_   Race: _Caucasian_   Gender: ___ F _X_ M

Age: _43_   Height: _5–11_   Weight: _195_   Eyes: _Brown_   Hair: _Brown_

Clothing: _Clean, casual_   Hygiene: _Normal_   Other: _Wore glasses_

History

1. **Signs and Symptoms** Client's statement of problem and impairments (e.g., social, occupational, affective, cognitive, memory, physical)

Symptoms or disability(ies)	Resulting impairment(s)
Increase anxiety in social situations, poor concentration, difficulty coping in new situations.	_Occupational: fired from job he held for 12 years due to excessive errors. Missed work 50% of time due to anxious mood._
	Social: Avoiding most people due to emerging panic symptoms. Will not go in crowds.

As seen by professional: _Appeared confused and anxious. Some stuttering and word finding problems._

2. **History of Present Illness**

Events or incidents leading to need for services/benefits: _Auto accident on 3/8/1998, Closed head injury left side. Since then increased symptoms. No previous history of similar impairments._

Family Hx of Sx's: _Negative_

Onset/Frequency/Duration/Intensity/Cycling of symptoms: _Gradual development of anxiety since auto accident. Immediate concerns in concentration. Panic symptoms since returning to work, lasting 30 minutes, moderate severity._

Was there a clear time when Sx's worsened? _Upon returning to work on 7/7/1998_

Previous diagnosis (include by whom): _None_

Course of illness: ___ Improving   ___ Stable   _X_ Deteriorating   ___ Varies

Current status of past diagnoses? _No previous mental health issues_

Precipitating factors/events (e.g., emotional, environmental, social): _Any new situation or crowds of people increase anxiety and confusion._

E = Employment   V = Volunteering

Currently: ___ Yes _X_ No   Hours: _____   (Describe below. Include longest position)

	Positions	Dates	FT/PT/Temp	Problems?	Reason left
_X_ E ___ V	_Computer programmer_	_6/86–9/98_	_FT_	_None until end_	_Terminated_
_X_ E ___ V	_Computer programmer_	_5/74–6/86_	_FT_	_None_	_New position_

Usual length of employment: _12 years_   Usual reason(s) for leaving: _Advance in career_

Usual reasons for missing work or leaving early: _____   Frequency: _____

Military: _X_ N ___ Y   Dates: _____   Branch: _____

Highest rank: _____   Discharge: _____

Problems in military: _____

Medications C = Current P = Previous   (attempt to obtain at least 5 years history)

1. ___ C ___ P Name: _None_ Purpose: _____
   Dr. _____ of _____
   Dose: ___ mg X ___ /day Dates: _____ Compliance: _____
   Last taken: _____ Effectiveness: _____
   Side effects: _____ Effect without the med: _____

2. ___ C ___ P Name: _____ Purpose: _____
   Dr. _____ of _____
   Dose: ___ mg X ___ /day Dates: _____ Compliance: _____
   Last taken: _____ Effectiveness: _____
   Side effects: _____ Effect without the med: _____

3. ___ C ___ P Name: _____ Purpose: _____
   Dr. _____ of _____
   Dose: ___ mg X ___ /day Dates: _____ Compliance: _____
   Last taken: _____ Effectiveness: _____
   Side effects: _____ Effect without the med: _____

4. ___ C ___ P Name: _____ Purpose: _____
   Dr. _____ of _____
   Dose: ___ mg X ___ /day Dates: _____ Compliance: _____
   Last taken: _____ Effectiveness: _____
   Side effects: _____ Effect without the med: _____

Mental Health Treatment History ___ Currently in Tx (attempt to obtain at least 5 years history)

Dates	Purpose	In/Out pt.	Response to Tx	Professional
_____	_No history_	___ I ___ O	_____	_____
_____	_____	___ I ___ O	_____	_____

___ Check if continued on back

History of suicidality (___ ideations, ___ threats, ___ attempts): _No_

Physical Health Treatment History   (attempt to obtain at least 5 years history)

Primary physician: _Betty Relberg_ of _Unity_ since _1978_ frequency _as needed_

Dates	Purpose	In/Out pt.	Response to Tx	Professional
_3/8/98–5/7/98_	_Closed head injury_	_X_ I ___ O	_Marginal_	_Jolder_
5/98–present	_Occup. therapy 2x/wk_	___ I _X_ O	_Gradual increases_	_Denlan_

___ Check if continued on back

Current special services (___ social ___ educational ___ legal): _No_

Note and resolve any discrepancies between stated information and records: _No_

BEGIN 5/30 MINUTE MEMORY CHECK

Current Level of Daily Functioning

1. **Current Hobbies, Interests and Activities**

Hobby/interest (How persistently is it followed?)	Frequency	Duration
Fishing relaxing–as per weather	_1x/week_	_2–3 hrs_
Yard work enjoyable, finds something to do	_daily_	_1 hr_
Crossword puzzles (as per MD) "boring"	_daily_	_1/2 hr_

Realistic, appropriate, compare to previous functioning: _Realistic during time of recovery but significantly lower than pre-morbid functioning._

2. **Activities**

___ Rent   _X_ Own: _X_ house   ___ apartment   ___ townhouse   ___ duplex
___ condo   ___ mobile home   ___ other: _____

Who else lives there? (relationships, ages): _Spouse, 2 daughters (4, 12), 1 son (10)_

What kind of things do you usually make for:	Frequency	Problems
Breakfast: _Cereal, toast_	_daily_	_no_
Lunch: _Sandwich_	_daily_	_no_
Dinner: _Heat up leftovers in microwave_	_1–2x/wk_	_no_

Physical challenges in bathing/grooming? _No_   Need reminders? _No_

Daily Schedule Include chores, shopping, meals, meds, yard work, repairs, hobbies, employment, school. In time order, in and out of the house. What the client can do independently. Note persistence, pace.

Time	Activity
7:00	_Get up, hygiene, bath, dressed, children off to school, spouse to work_
8:00	_Make breakfast independently_
9:00	_Go for walk, about 1/2 mile_
10:00	_Look at newspaper, difficulty reading/concentrating—must often reread_
10:30	_Crossword puzzles, very difficult to concentrate_
11:00	_Yard work–good job if well known task_
12:00	_Lunch independently_
1:00	_Nap (or therapy 2x/week, drives 1/2 mile)_
3:30	_Children home from school, watch TV_
5:00	_Spouse home from work, sometimes help her with dishes_
6:00	_TV with family_
8:00	_Sit on porch_
10:00	_Watch news "confusing"_
11:00	_Bed—wake up 2–3x/night. Before accident, woke up 0–1x/night._

5 MINUTE MEMORY CHECK _____"Car"_____ = _1_ / _3_

Activities performed in the home (e.g., write letters, crafts, physical exercise, gardening, house repairs, cooking, drawing, painting, take care of pets, lifting, sewing, auto repairs, reading)

Activity	Frequency	Duration	Effects	Independent
Physical exercise	_daily_	_1/2 hr_	_"feel less stiff"_	_yes_
Reading	_daily_	_1/2–1 hr_	_confusing_	_yes_
Lite chores	_3–4x/week_	_1 hr_	_ok, if well known_	_sometimes_
Crossword puzzles	_daily_	_1/2 hr_	_confusing_	_yes_

Activities outside the home (e.g., movies, eat out, meetings, dancing, go for walks, shopping, hunting, fishing, sports, bars, biking, bowling, volunteering, clubs, organizations, religious services, AA, classes, babysitting, travel)

Activity	Frequency	Duration	Effects	Independent
Go for walk	_daily_	_1/2–1 hr_	_relaxing if alone_	_yes_
Fishing	_1x/wk_	_2–3 hrs_	_relaxing if alone_	_yes_

Ability to focus/concentrate on these activities (in and out of house): __If the task is simple he does well. If new or complex, very anxiety provoking.__

When Sx's increase how are these followed? __Poorly__

_X_ Drive _____ Run errands _____ Use public transportation (___ bus, ___ taxi)

_X_ Go shopping? How often? _Rarely_ Problems? _Anxiety_ Independently? _X_ N ___ Y

_X_ Walk places? How far? _1/2 mile_ How often? _daily_ Other: _____

How do you financially care for basic needs? __Disability income__

Who pays the bills? _____Spouse_____ Who handles the finances? _____Spouse_____

_X_ Savings account _X_ Checking account ___ Money orders

_X_ Others pay/write checks _X_ Figure change

3. **Living Situation**

Living conditions: (_X_ family, ___ alone, ___ group home; ___ crowded, ___dysfunctional; ability to follow rules/procedures)

__Supportive family, difficult for spouse to take on increased responsibilities__

4. **Ability to Relate to Others** (e.g., ___ aggressive, ___ dependent, ___ defiant, ___ avoidant, ___ oppositional, ___ normal)

_____

Adults: _____Avoids_____ Authority figures: _____+_____

Peers: _____+_____ Police: _____+_____

Family: _____+_____ Children: _____+_____

Neighbors: _____Neutral_____ Other: _____

Have best friend? _Yes, lifelong_ Group of friends? _Yes, little recent contact_

Activities with friends (include frequency, duration, and problems): __Currently some phone calls. Previously saw friends regularly, went to sporting events.__

How well did client relate (examiner, office personnel) during office visit? __Anxious, cooperative.__

5. Substance Abuse (if applicable)

Detailed history and current information regarding substance abuse patterns.

Last drink and/or use of drugs: ___*"last night"*_____

Age of onset: __*16*__   Substances used historically: __*Beer, vodka*_____

History of usage: __*Teenager, occasional usage due to peer pressure. Increased usage in*__
___*college, especially at exam time. During a few times of unemployment has noted periods of*__
___*drunkenness to escape guilt feelings. Recently "a slight buzz" has helped him "feel more*__
___*sociable." Increased use of alcohol three months after accident. "I must drink if I go out in*__
___*public." Drinks when his family is not home. Usually able to hide his drinking. No desire*__
___*to quit.*_____

	A	B	C
Current substances used	*Vodka*	*Beer*	*(No illegal*
Level of usage (how much?)	*Up to 3 fifths/wk*	*12 pk/wk*	*substances)*
Frequency (how often?)	*Daily*	*Daily*	
Duration (length of episodes)	*2–3 hours*	*2–3 hours*	

Effects on functioning (impact on activities, interests, ability to relate, persistence/pace): _*Notes*_
___*effects in positive terms such as "less nervous."*_____

Reason(s) for usage: ___ taste _*X*_ escape ___ self-medicate ___ addiction ___ other: _____

___ Weekdays? What time(s) of day? __*When family is not home*_____

___ Weekends? What time(s) of day? _____

_*X*_ Alone _*X*_ Home ___ With others ___ Bars ___ Other: _____

How often do you drink to the point of intoxication (or get high) in a given week? _*1x/week*__

How many binges in a given year? ___*0*___   Frequency/duration of binges? ___*0*___

Describe treatment history and medical/social consequences of the abuse (e.g., DWIs, DTs and tremors, blackouts, job loss, divorce, etc.): __*No negative consequences to date, but has*__
___*increasing desire/need to drink. Beginning to feel physical need for alcohol, especially on*__
___*weekends, or when with his family in social situations.*_____

Level of functioning when not drinking or using drugs (e.g., during periods of sobriety or Tx):
__*Increased anxiety*_____
_____

6. History of Arrests/Incarcerations

_____*No*_____
_____

Mental Status Exam

1. Clinical Observations (Entire page: Leave blank if normal. Check and comment if remarkable.)

Appearance

___ Appears age, +/-	___ Grooming	___ Hair	___ Odor
___ Posture	___ Health	___ Nails	___ Demeanor

_*Normal physical appearance*_____
_____

3.20

Activity Level

___ Mannerisms	___ Gestures	___ Alert	___ Lethargic	___ Limp
_X_ Rigid	___ Relaxed	___ Combative	___ Hyperactive	___ Bored
___ Gait	___ Eye contact	___ Distracted	___ Preoccupied	___ Vigilance

Somewhat rigid and agitated

Speech

_X_ Vocabulary	_X_ Details	___ Volume
___ Pace	_X_ Reaction time	___ Pitch
_X_ Pressured	___ Hesitant	___ Monotonous
___ Slurred	_X_ Stuttering	___ Mumbled
___Echolalia	___ Neologisms	___ Repetitions
___ Pronunciation	___ % Understood: _100_	

When anxious he began to stutter at times. Delayed reaction time some issues in word
finding. Brief sentences.

Attitude Toward Examiner

_X_ Attentive	___ Distracted	___ Cooperative	___ Friendly	___ Interested
___ Frank	___ Hostile	___ Defiant	___ Guarded	___ Defensive
___ Evasive	___ Hesitant	___ Manipulative	___ Humorous	___ Historian +/-

Attention span swindled at times. Initially anxious, but as rapport developed he seemed
more relaxed.

2. **Stream of Consciousness**

Speech

___ Spontaneous	___ Inhibited	___ Blocked	___ Illogical	___ Vague
___ Pressured	___ Slowed	___ Disorganized	___ Rambling	___ Derailment
___ Coherent	___ Cause/effect	___ Neologisms		

Thinking

___ Relevant	___ Coherent	___ Goal directed	___ Loose & Rambling

Thought Processes

___ Number of ideas	___ Flight of ideas	___ Hesitance

All within normal limits

3. **Thought Content**

Preoccupations

___ Obsessions	___ Compulsions	___ Phobias	___ Homicide	___ Antisocial

Suicidal, Current

___ Threats	___ Ideas	___ Plan

History

___ Attempts	___ Threats	___ Ideas

Hallucinations

___ Voices	___ Visions	___ Content	___ Setting	___ Sensory system

Illusions: _____

Delusions

___ Persecutory	___ Somatic	___ Grandeur

Ideas of Reference

___ Controlled	___ Broadcasting	___ Antisocial	___ Validity
___ Content	___ Mood	___ Bizarre	

No evidence of thought disorder

4. Affect/Mood

Affective Observations

Range	___ Normal	___ Expansive	_X_ Restricted	___ Blunted ___ Flat
Appropriateness	_X_ Concordant		___ Discordant (with speech/ideas)	
Mobility	___ Normal	_X_ Decreased (constricted, fixed)	___ Increased (labile)	
Intensity	___ Normal	_X_ Mild	___ Strong	
Psychomotor	_X_ Normal	___ Retardation	___ Agitation	
Predominant mood	_X_ Neutral	___ Euthymic ___ Dysphoric	___ Euphoric	___ Manic
Level of anxiety	___ Normal	_X_ High (describe): _body/facial expression_		
Irritability	_X_ Normal	___ High (describe): _____		
Anger expression	_X_ Normal	___ High (describe): _____		

Mood (Rule in and rule out signs and symptoms)

Frequency/Intensity in Daily Life (give specific examples or impairments/strengths, frequency, duration.)

Clearly Validate with *DSM-IV* Criteria

Affection toward others: ___*Family only*_____

Anger: ___ anger mng't issues   ___ property destruction

        ___ explosive behaviors   ___ assaultive behaviors

How does the client act on anger?

Onset: _____   Frequency: _____

Duration: _____   Severity: _____

Examples: ___*No anger management problems.*_____

_____

Panic Attacks: 4+, Abrupt development of:

_X_ palpitations	_X_ sweating	___ trembling
_X_ shortness of breath	___ feeling of choking	___ chest pain
___ nausea	___ dizziness	___ light-headed
___ derealization	___ fear of losing control	___ fear of dying
___ numbness	___ chills	___ hot flashes

___ Other: _Increasing symptoms since returning to work after accident._

_____

Onset: ___*2–3 months ago*_____   Frequency: ___*2x/wk*_____

Duration: ___*5–30 min*_____   Severity: ___*Mild/moderate*___

Anxiety: GAD: 3+, most of time, 6 months:

___ restlessness	___ easily fatigued	___ concentration
___ irritability	___ muscle tension	___ sleep disturbance

___ Other: _Anxious only in unfamiliar situations (since head injury). No pre-morbid history_
   of anxiety problems.

Onset: _____   Frequency: _____

Duration: _____   Severity: _____

Depression: MDE: 2+ wks, 5+:

___ usually depressed

___ wght +/- 5%/month

___ sleep +/-

___ psychomotor +/-

___ concentration

___ death/suicidal ideation

___ anhedonia

___ appetite +/-

___ fatigue

___ worthlessness/guilt

___ other: ___ crying spells   ___ withdrawal

___ Other: _Denies clinical depression. Did not appear depressed._

_____

Onset: _____   Frequency: _____

Duration: _____   Severity: _____

Dysthymia: ___ depressed most of time   ___ onset; adult 2+ child/adolescent 1+ yrs, 2+ of:

___ +/- appetite or eating   ___ in/hypersomnia   ___ low energy/fatigue

___ low self-esteem   ___ low concentration/decisions   ___ hopelessness

___ Other: _Denies_

_____

Onset: _____   Frequency: _____

Duration: _____   Severity: _____

Mania: 3+:

___ grandiosity   ___ low sleep   ___ talkative   ___ flight of ideas

___ distractibility ___ goals/agitation ___ excessive pleasure

___ Other: _Denies_

_____

Onset: _____   Frequency: _____

Duration: _____   Severity: _____

PTSD: Traumatic event with intense response: 1+:

Distressing:

___ recollections   ___ dreams   ___ reliving

___ cues   ___ physiological reactivity with cues

3+:

___ avoid thoughts   ___ avoid environmental   ___ poor recall of events

___ low interest   ___ detachment   ___ restricted range of affect

___ foreshortened future

2+:

___ sleep   ___ anger   ___ concentration

___ hypervigilance   ___ startle response

___ Other: _Denies_

_____

Onset: _____   Frequency: _____

Duration: _____   Severity: _____

5. Sensorium/Cognition

A) Reality Contact (How in touch with reality is the client?): _Normal range_

Able to hold normal conversation? _X_ Yes ___ No Notes: _____

B) Orientation X3: _X_ Time _X_ Place _X_ Person Notes: _x 3_

C) Concentration:

Attention to tasks/conversation; distractability: _Asked to have a few questions repeated_

Count to 40 by 3s beginning at 1.

(_X_ 1, _X_ 4, _X_ 7, _11_, 10, _14_, 13, _18_, 16, _22_, 19, _25_, 22, _29_, 25, _32_, 28,

_36_, 31, _39_, 34, _43_, 37, _46_, 40)

Number of errors: _6_ Time between digits: _6–10 sec_ Other: _____

Count backward by 7s.

(_X_ 100, _X_ 93, _84_, 86, _78_, 79, _70_, 72, _63_, 65, _59_, 58, _50_, 51, _43_, 44, _36_,

37, ____, 30, ____, 23, ____, 16, ____, 9, ____, 2)   _Gave up after 37_

Number of errors: _20_ Time between digits: _15+ sec_ Other: _Very difficult for him_

5 + 8 = _13_   7 x 4 = _28_   12 x 6 = _72_   65/5 = _(15)_   Timing: _Slow_

Digits forward and backward (Average adult: FWD = 5–7 BWD = 4–6)

FWD: _X_ 42 _X_ 318 _X_ 6385 _no_ 96725 ___ 864972 ___ 5739481 ___ 31749852

BWD: _X_ 75 _X_ 582 _no_ 9147 ____ 74812 ___ 839427 ___ 7392641 ___ 49521863

FWD = _4_ BWD = _3_   Evaluation: _X_ L ___ M ___ H

Spell WORLD _X_ FWD _DLORW_ BWD Months of year backward: _No_

Spell EARTH _X_ FWD _HTARE_ BWD Concentration evaluation: _X_ L ___ M ___ H

D) Memory:

30 MINUTE MEMORY CHECK (5 = _1_ / 3) 30 = _"Car"_ = _1_ / 3

Remote Memory

Childhood data: _X_ Schools attended _X_ Teacher's names/faces _X_ Street grew up on

Historical events: Kennedy   _X_ Event _X_ Activities

M L King   _X_ Event _X_ Activities

Space Shuttle Challenger   _X_ Event _X_ Activities

Other: _____

Recent Memory (Y = Yes N = No V = Vague)

___ Activities past few months   _V_ Past few days   _N_ Past weekend

___ Yesterday (events, meals, etc.)   _V_ Today (events, meals, etc.)

_N_ Activities of past holiday   ___ Other: _____

Client's statements re: memory functioning: _"Poor . . . frustrating"_

Specific examples of memory problems: _(1) Must make lists or will forget what tasks to do_

during day. (2) Hard to learn new things.

Compared to previous functioning: _Previously no memory issues, did well on challenging_

job, learned well.

3.24

Evaluation of memory: _Long term intact, problems with short-term and immediate_

Long–term: ___ L _X_ M ___ H   Short-term: _X_ L ___ M ___ H

Immediate: _X_ L ___ M ___ H

E) Information: (knowledge of current events)

Does the client: _X_ read newspaper?   How often? _Sundays 1/2 hr_

                  _X_ TV/radio news?   How often? _Daily news on TV_

Name current: _X_ local _X_ national news event: _Vague "politics, weather, crime"_

President's name: _X_   Past 3 Presidents: _No_   3 large cities: _Ok_

F) Abstractive Capacity

Interpretation of various proverbs   Interpretation Given

"Rolling stone gathers no moss": _"Keep busy"_

"Early bird catches the worm": _"First one up gets the best"_

"Strike while the iron is hot": _"Go for it"_

"Don't cry over spilled milk": _____

Interpretations: ___ "DK"   ___ Would not try   _X_ Abstract

                 ___ Concrete   _X_ Age-appropriate   ___ Unusual: _____

G) Judgment

"First one in theatre to see smoke and fire": _"Get out then yell fire"_

"Find stamped envelope in street": _"Mail"_

Any history of problems in judgment? _No_

H) Insight (awareness of issues: what level?)

___ Complete denial   ___ Slight awareness

___ Awareness, but blames others   _X_ Intellectual insight, but few changes likely

___ Emotional insight, understanding, changes can occur

Client's statement regarding actions needed to get better: _"Stay in therapy." "Get out more."_

_____

Comment on client's level of insight to problems: _Adequate_

I) Intellectual Level/Education/IQ Estimate

Education level: Formal: _16 yrs   B. A._   Informal: _Course work_

Military training: _No_   Career training: _____

Intelligence: As per client: _Above average (history)_   Observed: _____

General knowledge: _____   School grades: _"Above average"_

Career background: _Computer programming_   Estimated IQ: _110_

6. Somatoform & Personality Disorders

Somatoform Disorder: 4 pain Sx's:

___ head   ___ abdomen   ___ back   ___ joints   ___ extremities

___ chest   ___ rectum   ___ menstruation   ___ sexual intercourse   ___ urination

2 gastrointestinal Sx's:

___ nausea   ___ bloating   ___ vomiting   ___ diarrhea   ___ fool intolerance

1 pseudoneurological Sx:

___ conversion Sx   ___ impaired coordination   ___ aphonia

___ urinary retention   ___ hallucinations   ___ loss of touch or pain sensation

___ double vision   ___ blindness   ___ deafness

___ seizures   ___ dissociative Sx   ___ loss of consciousness

___ Other: _____

_____

History of problem: *Denies symptoms—History of good health* _____

_____

Primary/secondary gain: _____

_____

Family response: _____

_____

Selective nature of Sx: _____

_____

Observations (pain, fatigue, gait, dizziness): _____

_____

Personality Disorder (Fully describe any evidence of a personality disorder):

A. Any personality disorder must result in deviation in two or more of the following enduring patterns of inner experience and behavior differing markedly from cultural expectations:

    ___ 1) cognition ___ 2) affectivity ___ 3) interpersonal functioning ___ 4) impulse control

B. The pattern is inflexible across a wide range of experiences.

C. The pattern leads to clinically significant distress or functional impairment.

D. The pattern is stable, long duration and can be traced to at least adolescence or early adulthood.

E. The pattern is not secondary to Axis I.

F. The pattern is not due to a substance or medical condition.

Cluster A

Paranoid (4+)	Schizoid (4+)	Schizotypal (5+)
___ Suspicious	___ Undesirous of friendships	___ Ideas of reference
___ Unjustified distrust	___ Solitary activities	___ Odd beliefs
___ Reluctant to confide	___ Low sexual interest	___ Unusual perceptions
___ Hidden meanings	___ Few pleasures	___ Odd thinking/speech
___ Grudges, unforgiving	___ Lacks close friends	___ Suspicious/paranoid ideation
___ Perceived character attacks	___ Indifferent to praise/criticism	___ Inappropriate/constricted affect
___ Sexual suspicious of partner	___ Emotional coldness/ detachment	___ Odd appearance/behavior
		___ Lacks close friends
		___ Excessive, social anxiety which does not diminish with familiarity

Cluster B

Antisocial (3+ since age 15)

___ Unlawful behaviors

___ Deceitfulness

___ Impulsivity

___ Irritability. Aggressiveness, fights

___ Disregard for safety; self/others

___ Irresponsibility

___ Lack of remorse

___ Is at least 18 years old

Borderline (5+)

___ High efforts to avoid abandonment

___ Unstable intense relationships

___ Unstable identity/self-image

___ Impulsivity (2+ areas)

___ Recurrent suicidal behaviors

___ Affective instability

___ Chronic feeling of emptiness

___ Inappropriate, intense anger

___ Stress related paranoid ideations or severe dissociative symptoms

Histrionic (5+)

___ Needs center of attention

___ Interacts seductively

___ Shifting, shallow emotions

___ Appearance to draw attn.

___ Speech: impressionistic, but lacks detail

___ Self-dramatization

___ Easily suggestible

___ Considers relationships as more important than they are

Narcissistic (5+)

___ Grandiose sense of self-importance

___ Preoccupied with fantasies of success, power

___ "Special" and understood only by similar people

___ Requires excessive admiration

___ Sense of entitlement

(Narcissistic con't)

___ Interpersonally exploitive

___ Lacks empathy

___ Often envious or believes others envious of him/her

___ Arrogant, hauty

Cluster C

Avoidant (4+)

___ Avoids occupational activities due to fear of criticism

___ Unwilling to get involved unless certain of being liked

___ Restraint in personal relationships due to fear of ridicule

___ Preoccupied with being criticized or rejected in social situations

___ Inhibited in new situations

___ Views self as socially inept/ inferior

___ Reluctant to take risks due to embarrassment

Dependent (5+)

___ Difficulty with decisions

___ Excessive advice seeking

___ Needs others to assume responsibility in major areas

___ Difficulty expressing disagreement

___ Difficulty initiating projects

___ Excessively seeks nurturance and support from others

___ Feels uncomfortable when alone

OCD (4+)

___ Preoccupied with details, lists, order

___ Perfectionism interferes with task completion

___ Excessive devotion to work

___ Overconscientious, inflexible about morality

___ Unable to discard items

___ Reluctant to delegate tasks

___ Miserly spending, hoarding

___ Rigidity, stubbornness

No evidence of Personality Disorder _____

_____

_____

_____

Additional information provided by client: __None__

__Testing: See protocol: WAIS-III: high average   WAIS- III: low average__

Signs of malingering: __No__

8. Assessment

Summary and Diagnostic Findings (Tie together history and mental status findings and relate to diagnosis. Include onset of current Sx of the condition and how far back it goes. Include evaluation of presenting problem vs. stated limitations vs. signs and symptoms. Include prognosis. Integrate collateral information.

This psychologist's confidence in the exam findings is ___ Poor ___ Average _X_ High

. . . test findings is ___ Poor ___ Average _X_ High

The claimant's ability to understand, retain, and follow instructions is:

_X_ Poor ___ Average ___ High

Axis I   1: __294.0 Amnestic Disorder due to closed head injury__

                2: __300.22 Panic attacks w/agora phobia__

                3: __303.9 Alcohol dependence, early onset, Hx of above__

Axis II   1: __799.9 No Dx__

                2: _____

Axis III   __Defer to physician__

Axis IV Current Stressors: __Unemployment, social problems, changes in home functioning.__

Axis V Current GAF = __50__   Highest past year GAF = __80__

9. Capacity Statement

Based on your findings:

1) ___ P _X_ L ___ M ___ G ___ E   The client's ability to concentrate on and understand directions,

2) ___ P _X_ L ___ M ___ G ___ E   Carry out tasks with reasonable persistence and pace,

3) ___ P _X_ L ___ M ___ G ___ E   Respond appropriately to ___ co-workers, and ___ supervisors, and

4) ___ P _X_ L ___ M ___ G ___ E   Tolerate the stresses in the workplace.

Prognosis: ___ Poor ___ Marginal _X_ Guarded ___ Moderate ___ Good ___ Excellent

Qualifiers to prognosis:

___ Med compliance   _X_ Tx compliance   ___ Home environment

___ Activity changes   ___ Behavioral changes   ___ Attitudinal changes

_X_ Education/training   ___ Other: _____

Comments: __Suggest: (1) med evaluation; (2) group therapy for those with closed head injuries.__

Form 22   Psychological Evaluation—Child

Client's name: _____

Phone (home): _____   ID#: _____   Date: _____

Address: _____   City: _____   State: _____   Zip: _____

Collateral information by: _____   Relationship: _____

Physical Description

Identification given: _____   Race: _____   Gender: ___ F ___ M

Age: _____   Height: _____   Weight: _____   Eyes: _____   Hair: _____

Clothing: _____   Hygiene: _____   Other: _____

History

1. **Signs and Symptoms** Client's/Caregiver's statement of problems and impairments (e.g., social, academic, affective, cognitive, memory, physical)

    Symptoms or disability(ies)   Resulting impairment(s)

    _____   _____

    _____   _____

    _____   _____

    _____   _____

    _____   _____

    _____   _____

2. **History of Present Illness**

    Events or incidents leading to disabilities: _____

    _____

    Family Hx of Sx's: _____

    Onset of impairment: _____

    Was there a clear time when Sx's worsened? _____

    Previous diagnosis (by whom): _____

    Course of illness: ___ Improving   ___ Stable   ___ Deteriorating   ___ Varies

    Current status of past diagnoses? _____

    Frequency/Duration/Intensity/Cycling of symptoms: _____

    _____

    Precipitating factors (environmental, social): _____

    _____

    Currently working/volunteering? ___ Y   ___ N   If Yes, describe: _____

    _____

    Previous employment/school/volunteering/other activities: _____

Medications   C = Current   P = Previous   (attempt to obtain at least 5 years history)

1. ___ C   ___ P   Name: _____   Purpose: _____

Dr. _____ of _____

Dose: ___ mg X ___ /day   Dates: _____   Compliance: _____

Last taken: _____   Effectiveness: _____

Side effects: _____   Effect without the med: _____

2. ___ C   ___ P   Name: _____   Purpose: _____

Dr. _____ of _____

Dose: ___ mg X ___ /day   Dates: _____   Compliance: _____

Last taken: _____   Effectiveness: _____

Side effects: _____   Effect without the med: _____

3. ___ C   ___ P   Name: _____   Purpose: _____

Dr. _____ of _____

Dose: ___ mg X ___ /day   Dates: _____   Compliance: _____

Last taken: _____   Effectiveness: _____

Side effects: _____   Effect without the med: _____

4. ___ C   ___ P   Name: _____   Purpose: _____

Dr. _____ of _____

Dose: ___ mg X ___ /day   Dates: _____   Compliance: _____

Last taken: _____   Effectiveness: _____

Side effects: _____   Effect without the med: _____

Mental Health Treatment History ___ Currently in Tx   (attempt to obtain at least 5 years history)

Dates	Purpose	In/Out pt.	Response to Tx	Professional
_____	_____	__ I __ O	_____	_____
_____	_____	__ I __ O	_____	_____
_____	_____	__ I __ O	_____	_____

___ Check if continued on back

History of suicidality (___ ideations, ___ threats, ___ attempts): _____

_____

Physical Health Treatment History   (attempt to obtain at least 5 years history)

Primary physician: _____ of _____ since _____ frequency _____

Dates	Purpose	In/Out pt.	Response to Tx	Professional
_____	_____	__ I __ O	_____	_____
_____	_____	__ I __ O	_____	_____
_____	_____	__ I __ O	_____	_____

___ Check if continued on back

Current special services (___ social, ___ educational, ___ legal, ___ physical): _____

_____

Note and resolve any discrepancies between stated information and records: _____

_____

BEGIN 5/30 MINUTE MEMORY CHECK

Current Level of Daily Functioning

1. Current Hobbies, Interests and Activities

Hobby/interest (How persistently is it followed?)	Frequency	Duration
_____	_____	_____
_____	_____	_____
_____	_____	_____
_____	_____	_____

Realistic, appropriate, compare to previous functioning: _____
_____

2. Activities

___ Rent ___ Own: ___ house ___ apartment ___ townhouse ___ duplex
___ condo ___ mobile home ___ other: _____

Who else lives there? (relationships, ages): _____
_____

What kind of things do you usually eat for:	Frequency	Problems
Breakfast: _____	_____	_____
Lunch: _____	_____	_____
Dinner: _____	_____	_____

Physical challenges in bathing/grooming? _____ Need reminders? _____

Daily Schedule Include chores, shopping, meals, meds, yard work, repairs, hobbies, employment, school. In time order, in and out of the house. What the client can do independently? Note persistence, pace, problems.

Time	Activity
_____	_____
_____	_____
_____	_____
_____	_____
_____	_____
_____	_____
_____	_____
_____	_____
_____	_____
_____	_____
_____	_____
_____	_____
_____	_____
_____	_____

5 MINUTE MEMORY CHECK _____ = ___ / 3

Activities performed in the home (write letters, crafts, physical exercise, gardening, house repairs, cooking, drawing, painting, take care of pets, lifting, sewing, auto repairs, reading)

Activity	Frequency	Duration	Effects	Independent
_____	_____	_____	_____	_____
_____	_____	_____	_____	_____
_____	_____	_____	_____	_____

Activities outside the home (e.g., movies, eat out, meetings, dancing, go for walks, shopping, hunting, fishing, sports, bars, biking, bowling, volunteering, religious services, AA, classes, babysitting, travel)

Activity	Frequency	Duration	Effects	Independent
_____	_____	_____	_____	_____
_____	_____	_____	_____	_____
_____	_____	_____	_____	_____

Ability to focus/concentrate on these activities (in and out of house): _____
_____

When Sx's increase how are these followed? _____

___ Drive   ___ Run errands   ___ Use public transportation (___ bus, ___ taxi)

___ Go shopping? How often? _____   Problems? _____   Independently? ___ N ___ Y

___ Walk places? How far? _____   How often? _____   Other: _____

How do you financially care for basic needs? _____

Who pays the bills? _____   Who handles the finances? _____

___ Savings account   ___ Checking account   ___ Money orders

___ Others pay/write checks   ___ Figure change

3. Living Situation

Living conditions: (___ family, ___ alone, ___ group home; ___ crowded, ___dysfunctional; ability to follow rules/procedures)

_____

4. Ability to Relate to Others (e.g., ___ aggressive, ___ dependent, ___ defiant, ___ avoidant, ___ oppositional, ___ normal)

_____

Adults: _____	Authority figures: _____
Peers: _____	Police: _____
Family: _____	Children: _____
Neighbors: _____	Other: _____
Have best friend? _____	Group of friends? _____

Activities with friends (include frequency, duration, and problems): _____
_____

How well did client relate (examiner, office personnel) during office visit? _____
_____

5. **Substance Abuse** (if applicable)

Detailed history and current information regarding substance abuse patterns.

Age of onset: _____   Substances used historically: _____

History of usage: _____

_____

_____

6. **Self-help Skills** (Describe child's ability and assistance needed in the following)

Dressing: _____

Grooming: _____

Feeding self: _____

Avoiding dangers: _____

Independent activities outside the home: _____

Making change($): _____

Taking the bus: _____

7. **Concentration, Persistence and Pace** (age 3–18)

(Describe ability to concentrate, attend, persist and complete tasks in a timely manner.)

_____

_____

_____

Development

Pregnancy: _____   Adverse factors? _____

Delivery: _____   On time? _____

Early development: _____

Walked: _____   Talked: _____   Toilet trained: _____

(Provide specific information on how the child's symptoms impact performance of age appropriate developmental tasks and functional capacity.)

Age Group of Child (fill in appropriate age group)

A. Birth to 3 Years

Locomotion (e.g., crawling, walking, sitting up, pulling oneself into an upright position, etc.):

_____

_____

Language (e.g., vocalization, imitative sounds, talking, receptive skills, ability to follow commands, etc.): _____

_____

_____

Gross motor competence (e.g., reaching, throwing, jumping, grasping, pedaling a tricycle, etc.):

_____

_____

Fine motor competence (pincer grip, grasp, colors, uses pencils, reaches for objects, etc.):
_____
_____

Behavioral/social (e.g., excessive crying, hyperactivity, fear response to separation, aggressiveness, temper outbursts, lethargic, inability to bond, autistic features, efforts at toilet training, ability to relate to peers, siblings, parents, etc.): _____
_____
_____

B. 3 to 6 Years

Locomotion (describe any abnormalities as listed above, describe development of competency):
_____
_____

Communications (speech development, ability to form sentences, clarity of speech, expressive skills, receptive skills, ability to communicate needs, ability to respond to commands, ability to follow simple directions): _____
_____
_____

Motor (describe any abnormalities in fine or gross motor activity, can child use scissors, color within lines, copy simple designs [circle, square] Include observations of any impairments in coordination and/or balance): _____
_____
_____

Social/emotional (toilet training, aggressiveness, hyperactivity, ability to play with others, to share with others, to separate from caregivers, competency in feeding, dressing and grooming skills, temper outbursts, night terrors, manifestations of anxiety, phobias, fear response to separation, observations of bizarre or aberrant behavior): _____
_____
_____

Ability to concentrate, attend, persist, and complete tasks in a timely manner: _____
_____
_____

C. 6 to 16 Years

Locomotion (describe any abnormalities in walking, running, mobility): _____
_____
_____

Communication (reading, writing receptive and expressive language skills, speech): _____
_____
_____

Motor skills (coordination, balance, perceptual motor skills, complex-integrated motor responses):
_____
_____

Ability to concentrate, attend, persist, and complete tasks in a timely manner: _____

_____

_____

D. 16 to 18 Years

Locomotion (describe any abnormalities in mobility): _____

_____

_____

Communications (any abnormalities noted): _____

_____

_____

Social/emotional (relationships to peer group, to school authority figures). Any evidence of oppositional, rebellious, antisocial, aggressive behavior, withdrawal. Assess stress tolerance, potential employment, potential for substance abuse, impairment in reality testing. Comment on identity issues and developing of body awareness: _____

_____

_____

Ability to concentrate, attend, persist, and complete tasks in a timely manner: _____

_____

_____

Other (Comment on any volunteer of after school work, vocational training, jobs associated with the school program in terms of work, ability to persist, complete tasks, and respond appropriately to supervision.): _____

_____

_____

Parents or Caregivers Leave Interview Room at This Time

Mental Status Exam

1. **Clinical Observations** (Entire page: Leave blank if normal. Check and comment if remarkable.)

Appearance

___ Appears age, +/-	___ Grooming	___ Hair	___ Odor
___ Posture	___ Health	___ Nails	___ Demeanor

_____

_____

Activity Level

___ Mannerisms	___ Gestures	___ Alert	___ Lethargic	___ Limp
___ Rigid	___ Relaxed	___ Combative	___ Hyperactive	___ Bored
___ Gait	___ Eye contact	___ Distracted	___ Preoccupied	___ Vigilance

_____

_____

Speech

___ Vocabulary   ___ Details   ___ Volume   ___ Pace

___ Reaction time   ___ Pitch   ___ Pressured   ___ Hesitant

___ Monotonous   ___ Slurred   ___ Stuttering   ___ Mumbled

___ Echolalia   ___ Neologisms   ___ Repetitions   ___ Pronunciation

___ % Understood: _____

_____

_____

Attitude Toward Examiner

___ Attentive   ___ Distracted   ___ Cooperative   ___ Friendly   ___ Interested

___ Frank   ___ Hostile   ___ Defiant   ___ Guarded   ___ Defensive

___ Evasive   ___ Hesitant   ___ Manipulative   ___ Humorous   ___ Historian +/-

_____

_____

2. Stream of Consciousness

Re: Speech:

___ Spontaneous   ___ Inhibited   ___ Blocked   ___ Illogical

___ Vague   ___ Pressured   ___ Slowed   ___ Disorganized

___ Rambling   ___ Derailment   ___ Coherent   ___ Cause/effect

___ Neologisms

Re: Thinking:

___ Relevant   ___ Coherent   ___ Goal directed   ___ Loose & rambling

Re: Thought processes:

___ Number of ideas   ___ Flight of ideas   ___ Hesitance

_____

_____

3. Thought Content

Preoccupations:

___ Obsessions   ___ Compulsions   ___ Phobias   ___ Homicide   ___ Antisocial

Suicidal:

Current: ___ Threats   ___ Ideas   ___ Plan

History: ___ Attempts   ___ Threats   ___ Ideas

Hallucinations:

___ Voices   ___ Visions   ___ Content   ___ Setting   ___ Sensory system

Illusions: _____

Delusions:

___ Persecutory   ___ Somatic   ___ Grandeur

Ideas of reference:

___ Controlled   ___ Broadcasting   ___ Antisocial   ___ Validity

___ Content   ___ Mood   ___ Bizarre

_____

_____

4. Affect/Mood

Affective Observations

Range	___ Normal	___ Expansive	___ Restricted	___ Blunted	___ Flat
Appropriateness	___ Concordant		___ Discordant (with speech/ideas)		
Mobility	___ Normal	___ Decreased (constricted, fixed)	___ Increased (labile)		
Intensity	___ Normal	___ Mild	___ Strong		
Psychomotor	___ Normal	___ Retardation	___ Agitation		
Predominant mood	___ Neutral	___ Euthymic	___ Dysphoric	___ Euphoric	___ Manic
Level of anxiety	___ Normal	___ High (describe): _____			
Irritability	___ Normal	___ High (describe): _____			
Anger expression	___ Normal	___ High (describe): _____			

Mood (Rule in and rule out signs and symptoms)

Frequency/Intensity in Daily Life (give specific examples of impairments/strengths, frequency, duration.)

Clearly Validate with *DSM-IV* Criteria

Affection toward others: _____

Anger: ___ anger mng't issues   ___ property destruction
         ___ explosive behaviors   ___ assaultive behaviors

How does the client act on anger?

Onset: _____   Frequency: _____

Duration: _____   Severity: _____

Examples: _____

_____

Panic Attacks: 4+, Abrupt development of:

___ palpitations	___ sweating	___ trembling
___ shortness of breath	___ feeling of choking	chest pain
___ nausea	___ dizziness	___ light-headed
___ derealization	___ fear of losing control	___ fear of dying
___ numbness	___ chills	___ hot flashes

___ Other: _____

_____

Onset: _____   Frequency: _____

Duration: _____   Severity: _____

Anxiety: GAD: 3+, most of time, 6 months:

___ restlessness	___ easily fatigued	___ concentration
___ irritability	___ muscle tension	___ sleep disturbance

___ Other: _____

_____

Onset: _____   Frequency: _____

Duration: _____   Severity: _____

Depression: MDE: 2+ wks, 5+:

___ usually depressed   ___ anhedonia

___ wght +/- 5%/month   ___ appetite +/-

___ sleep +/-   ___ fatigue

___ psychomotor +/-   ___ worthlessness/guilt

___ concentration   ___ other: ___ crying spells   ___ withdrawal

___ death/suicidal ideation

___ Other: _____

_____

Onset: _____   Frequency: _____

Duration: _____   Severity: _____

Dysthymia: ___ depressed most of time   ___ onset; adult 2+ child/adolescent 1+ yrs, 2+ of:

___ +/- appetite or eating   ___ in/hypersomnia   ___ low energy/fatigue

___ low self-esteem   ___ low concentration/decisions   ___ hopelessness

___ Other: _____

_____

Onset: _____   Frequency: _____

Duration: _____   Severity: _____

Mania: 3+:

___ grandiosity   ___ low sleep   ___ talkative   ___ flight of ideas

___ distractibility   ___ goals/agitation   ___ excessive pleasure

___ Other: _____

_____

Onset: _____   Frequency: _____

Duration: _____   Severity: _____

PTSD: Traumatic event with intense response: 1+:

Distressing:

___ recollections   ___ dreams   ___ reliving

___ cues   ___ physiological reactivity with cues

3+:

___ avoid thoughts   ___ avoid environmental   ___ poor recall of events

___ low interest   ___ detachment   ___ restricted range of affect

___ foreshortened future

2+:

___ sleep   ___ anger   ___ concentration

___ hypervigilance   ___ startle response

___ Other: _____

_____

Onset: _____   Frequency: _____

Duration: _____   Severity: _____

ODD: Pattern of negativistic, hostile and defiant behaviors > 6 months: 4+ of the following:

___ loses temper   ___ argues with adults

___ actively defies adults' requests   ___ deliberately annoys people

___ blames others for own mistakes or misbehavior ___ touchy/easily annoyed

___ angry/resentful   ___ spiteful/vindictive

1+ impairment:

___ social   ___ academic   ___ occupational

_____

_____

Conduct: Repetitive/persistent behaviors violating rights of others. 3+ (past 12 month, 1 in past 6 months)

___ Aggression to people/animals:

___ bullies, threatens, intimidates ___ initiates physical fights

___ has used harmful weapon   ___ physically cruel to: ___ people ___ animals

___ stolen while confronting victim ___ forces sexual activity

Destruction of property:

___ deliberate fire setting (intended damage) ___ deliberate property destruction

Deceitfulness or theft:

___ broken into someone's property ___ often lies/cons ___ has stolen without confrontation

Serious violation of rules:

___ stays out at night against parents' rules before age 13

___ has run away 2+ or one extended   ___ often truant before age 13

1+ impairment:

___ social   ___ academic   ___ occupational

_____

_____

ADHD: Inattention; 6+ Sx, 6+ months:

___ poor attn/careless mistakes ___ difficult sustaining attn. ___ forgetful

___ not listen when spoken to ___ not follow through

___ loses thing   ___ easily distracted

___ difficult organizing, avoids tasks requiring sustained mental effort

AND/OR Hyperactivity/impulsivity, 6+, Hyperactivity:

___ fidgety   ___ leaves seat often ___ runs/climbs

___ difficult being quiet ___ "on the go"   ___ talks excessively

Impulsivity:

___ blurts out answers ___ difficulty awaiting turn ___ interrupts

___ Some Sx < age 7. 1+ impairment:

___ social   ___ academic   ___ occupational

_____

_____

Attention Span During Interview

___ Fidgety   ___ Remained seated   ___ Distracted

___ Blurted answers   ___ Followed directions   ___ Shifted focus

___ Talked excessively   ___ Interrupted   ___ Listened

___ Impulsivity   ___ Understood questions   ___ Attended to questions

___ Other: _____

Rule Out Clinical Syndromes

Pervasive developmental disorders, autistic disorders, specific developmental disabilities, learning disorders, incipient psychotic process, etc.: _____

_____

_____

_____

5. **Sensorium/Cognition**

   Younger Children: Provide a basic assessment of the following:

   A) **Consciousness** (ability to concentrate, confusion, attending): _____

   _____

   B) **Orientation:** ___ Time   ___ Place   ___ Person   Notes: _____

   _____

   C) **Memory:** (recent, long-term, simple facts): _____

   _____

   D) **Estimated Intellectual Functioning:** _____

   _____

   Older Children:

   A) **Reality Contact** (How in touch with reality is client?): _____

   Able to hold normal conversation? ___ Yes   ___ No   Notes: _____

   B) **Orientation X3:** ___ Time   ___ Place   ___ Person   Notes: _____

   C) **Concentration** (age-appropriate measures):

   Count by 1s: _____   Count by 2s: _____   Count by 3s: _____

   Errors: ___ Time: _____   Errors: ___ Time: _____   Errors: ___ Time: _____

   Count to 40 by 3s beginning at 1.

   (___ 1, ___ 4, ___ 7, ___, 10, ___, 13, ___, 16, ___, 19, ___, 22, ___, 25, ___, 28, ___, 31, ___, 34, ___, 37, ___, 40)

   Number of errors: _____   Time between digits: _____   Other: _____

   Count backward by 7s from 100.

   (100, 93, 86, 79, 72, 65, 58, 51, 44, 37, 30, 23, 16, 9, 2.) Errors: ___ Time: _____

   $1 + 2 =$ ___ $2 + 3 =$ ___ $3 - 2 =$ ___ $4 + 8 =$ ___

   $9 + 12 =$ ___ $2 \times 3 =$ ___ $4 \times 4 =$ ___ $7 \times 4 =$ ___

   $12 \times 6 =$ ___ $65/5 =$ ___

Digits forward and backward (for ages 6+)

FWD: ___ 42 ___ 394 ___ 6385 ___ 96725 ___ 864972 ___ 5739481 ___ 31749852

BWD: ___ 73 ___ 582 ___ 9147 ___ 74812 ___ 839427 ___ 7392641 ___ 49521863

FWD = ___ BWD = ___ Evaluation: ___ Below average ___ Average ___ Above average

Spell words: WORLD ___ FWD ___ BWD

STOP ___ FWD ___ BWD

CAT ___ FWD ___ BWD

D) Memory:

Remote Memory

Childhood data: ___ Schools attended ___ Teacher's names/faces ___ Events of past holiday

___ Street grew up on ___ Mother's maiden name

Recent Memory

___ Activities past few months ___ Past few days ___ Activities past weekend

___ Yesterday (events, meals, etc.) ___ Today (events, meals, etc.)

___ Phone number ___ Address

30 MINUTE MEMORY CHECK (5 = ___ / 3) 30 = _____ = ___ / 3

Client's statements re: memory functioning: _____

Long-term: ___ L ___ M ___ H   Short-term: ___ L ___ M ___ H

Immediate: ___ L ___ M ___ H

E) Information: (knowledge of current events)

Does the client: ___ read newspaper?   How often? _____

___ TV/radio news?   How often? _____

Name current local/national news: _____   President's name: _____   3 large cities: ___

F) Judgment

"Find someone's purse in store": _____

"First one in theatre to see smoke and fire": _____

G) Abstractive Capacity

Interpretation of various proverbs   Interpretation Given

"Early bird catches the worm": _____

"Strike while the iron is hot": _____

"Don't cry over spilled milk": _____

Interpretations: ___ "DK" ___ Would not try ___ Abstract

___ Concrete ___ Age-appropriate ___ Unusual: _____

H) Insight (awareness of issues: what level?)

___ Complete denial ___ Slight awareness

___ Awareness, but blames others ___ Intellectual insight, but few changes likely

___ Emotional insight, understanding, changes can occur

Client's statement regarding actions needed to get better: _____

_____

Comment on client's level of insight to problems: _____

I) Intellectual Level/Education/IQ Estimate

Grade in school: _____   Ever repeat a grade? _____   Grades/Progress: _____

Special education classes: _____   Estimated IQ: _____

General knowledge: _____   Selective nature of Sx: _____

J) Adverse Factors Affecting the Child's Ability to Function

(e.g., pain, side effects of meds, dysfunctional family, abuse, physical impairments, teasing, etc.)

_____

_____

_____

_____

Additional comments by caregiver of child: _____

_____

_____

_____

_____

6. **Assessment**

Summary and Diagnostic Findings (Tie together history and mental status findings and relate to diagnosis. Include onset of current Sx of the condition and how far back it goes. Include evaluation of presenting problem vs. stated limitations vs. signs and symptoms. Include prognosis. Integrate collateral information.

This psychologist's confidence in the exam findings is ___ Poor   ___ Average   ___ High

. . . test findings is ___ Poor   ___ Average   ___ High

The claimant's ability to understand, retain, and follow instructions is:

___ Poor   ___ Average   ___ High

Axis I   1: _____

2: _____

3: _____

Axis II   1: _____

2: _____

Axis III Defer to physician

Axis IV Current Stressors: _____

Axis V Current GAF = _____   Highest past year GAF = _____

Prognosis: ___ Poor   ___ Marginal   ___ Guarded   ___ Moderate   ___ Good   ___ Excellent

Qualifiers to prognosis:

___ Med compliance   ___ Tx compliance   ___ Home environment

___ Activity changes   ___ Behavioral changes   ___ Attitudinal changes

___ Education/training   ___ Other: _____

Form 22A Psychological Evaluation—Child

(Completed)

Client's name: _Christine Watters_

Phone (home): _555-0001_ ID#: _040698WC_ Date: _4/6/1998_

Address: _595959 5th Ave_ City: _Moline_ State: _MD_ Zip: _26118_

Collateral information by: _Lisa Watters_ Relationship: _Mother_

Physical Description

Identification given: _None_ Race: _Afr.-Am._ Gender: _X_ F ___ M

Age: _6y-1m_ Height: _4-4_ Weight: _64_ Eyes: _Br_ Hair: _Bl_

Clothing: _Clean, school clothes_ Hygiene: _Normal_ Other: _____

History

1. **Signs and Symptoms** Client's/Caregiver's statement of problems and impairments (e.g., social, academic, affective, cognitive, memory, physical)

Symptoms or disability(ies)	Resulting impairment(s)
Low attention span, disruptive in school,	_Academic: 3 failing grades this term, often_
poor academic performance, needs	_disrupts entire class. School is considering_
constant reminders to stay on task.	_(EBD) special education for emotion/_
	behavioral disturbance. Social: few/no
	friends due to disruptive behaviors. Often
	teased by classmates for immaturity.

2. **History of Present Illness**

Events or incidents leading to disabilities: _Parents noticed hyperactivity at age 3. Several comments from pre-school teachers re: "not focusing" and "always on the go." Parents thought she would "grow out of it."_

Family Hx of Sx's: _Father was hyperactive as child. Older sister diagnosed with ADHD._

Onset of impairment: _Noticed at age 3, but continued increases in symptoms._

Was there a clear time when Sx's worsened? _Beginning of kindergarten: structure._

Previous diagnosis (by whom): _None–no previous evaluations._

Course of illness: ___ Improving ___ Stable _X_ Deteriorating ___ Varies

Current status of past diagnoses? _N/A_

Frequency/Duration/Intensity/Cycling of symptoms: _Parents describe hyperactivity as "constant." They call her "the tornado."_

Precipitating factors (environmental, social): _When not receiving 1–1 attention._

Currently working/volunteering? ___ Y _X_ N If Yes, describe: _____

Previous employment/school/volunteering/other activities: _None_

Medications   C = Current   P = Previous   (attempt to obtain at least 5 years history)

1. ___ C ___ P   Name: _____*None*_____   Purpose: _____
   Dr. _____ of _____
   Dose: ___ mg X ___ /day   Dates: _____   Compliance: _____
   Last taken: _____   Effectiveness: _____
   Side effects: _____   Effect without the med: _____

2. ___ C ___ P   Name: _____   Purpose: _____
   Dr. _____ of _____
   Dose: ___ mg X ___ /day   Dates: _____   Compliance: _____
   Last taken: _____   Effectiveness: _____
   Side effects: _____   Effect without the med: _____

3. ___ C ___ P   Name: _____   Purpose: _____
   Dr. _____ of _____
   Dose: ___ mg X ___ /day   Dates: _____   Compliance: _____
   Last taken: _____   Effectiveness: _____
   Side effects: _____   Effect without the med: _____

4. ___ C ___ P   Name: _____   Purpose: _____
   Dr. _____ of _____
   Dose: ___ mg X ___ /day   Dates: _____   Compliance: _____
   Last taken: _____   Effectiveness: _____
   Side effects: _____   Effect without the med: _____

Mental Health Treatment History ___ Currently in Tx   (attempt to obtain at least 5 years history)

Dates	Purpose	In/Out pt.	Response to Tx	Professional
_____	*No history*	__ I __ O	_____	_____
_____		__ I __ O	_____	_____
_____		__ I __ O	_____	_____

___ Check if continued on back

History of suicidality (___ ideations, ___ threats, ___ attempts): _____*No*_____

_____

Physical Health Treatment History   (attempt to obtain at least 5 years history)

Primary physician: _*Jill Hill, MD*_ of _*Candon*_ since _*Birth*_ frequency _*as needed*_

Dates	Purpose	In/Out pt.	Response to Tx	Professional
_____	*No significant Hx*	__ I __ O	_____	_____
_____	*"good health"*	__ I __ O	_____	_____
_____		__ I __ O	_____	_____

___ Check if continued on back

Current special services (___ social, ___ educational, ___ legal, ___ physical): _*None, school is*_
   _*considering EBD classes.*_____

Note and resolve any discrepancies between stated information and records: ___*None*_____

_____

Current Level of Daily Functioning

1. **Current Hobbies, Interests and Activities**

Hobby/interest (How persistently is it followed?)	Frequency	Duration
Coloring	_daily_	_5–10 min intervals_
TV/video games	_daily_	_1–2 hours_
Play outdoors	_daily_	_1–2 hours_
	weekends	_varies_

Realistic, appropriate, compare to previous functioning: _Normal range of behaviors._

2. **Activities**

_X_ Rent ___ Own: _X_ house ___ apartment ___ townhouse ___ duplex
___ condo ___ mobile home ___ other: _____

Who else lives there? (relationships, ages): _Both biological parents; 1 sister (10);_
1 brother (4)

What kind of things do you usually eat for:	Frequency	Problems
Breakfast: _Cereal_	_daily_	_no_
Lunch: _Soup-sandwiches_	_daily_	_sometimes_
Dinner: _Meat-potatoes-veg_	_daily_	_picky eater_

Physical challenges in bathing/grooming? _No_   Need reminders? _Age appropriate_

Daily Schedule Include chores, shopping, meals, meds, yard work, repairs, hobbies, employment, school. In time order, in and out of the house. What the client can do independently? Note persistence, pace, problems.

Time	Activity
	Typical school day as follows
_6:30_	_Get up, dress independently (with several prompts-prefers to play) Mother prompts her to get ready for school. Hygiene independently._
_7:45_	_Catch school bus–walk 1 block with sister to bus stop_
_8:15_	_School, 1st grade. Mainstream classes. Breakfast and lunch at school. Increasing disruptive behaviors in school (see attached school incident reports)_
_3:30_	_Home change clothes independently. Usually no homework given. Plays outside if weather is good, otherwise TV or video games. Usually with "best friend." Usually get along. Supposed to clean room before dinner. (Several prompts given) Often forgets to clean parts of room._
_5:30_	_Dinner with family. Eats very quickly. Can't sit still._
_6:00_	_Play outside. Sometimes goes to park with friend._
_7:30_	_Home. TV. Mother says she's always "on the go" in the house. Hard to settle her down._
_9:00_	_Gets ready for bed, may take 1–2 hours to fall asleep "playing with sister" in game room. Wakes up 1–2x/night. Toilet trained. No nightmares._

5 MINUTE MEMORY CHECK   _"House–Cat"_   = _2_ / _3_

Activities performed in the home (write letters, crafts, physical exercise, gardening, house repairs, cooking, drawing, painting, take care of pets, lifting, sewing, auto repairs, reading)

Activity	Frequency	Duration	Effects	Independent
Coloring	_daily_	_varies_		_yes_
TV/videos	_daily_	_1–2 hrs_	_attends if enjoyable_	_yes_

Activities outside the home (e.g., movies, eat out, meetings, dancing, go for walks, shopping, hunting, fishing, sports, bars, biking, bowling, volunteering, religious services, AA, classes, babysitting, travel)

Activity	Frequency	Duration	Effects	Independent
Play in park	_3–4x/wk_	_1 hr_	_calming_	_no_
Sunday School	_2–3x/m_	_1 hr_	_disruptive_	_N/A_

Ability to focus/concentrate on these activities (in and out of house): _If she is interested in something or receives 1–1 attention she concentrates better._

When Sx's increase how are these followed? _Tunes out everything and "climbs the walls"_

_N_ Drive   ___ Run errands   _N_ Use public transportation (___ bus,   ___ taxi)

_N_ Go shopping? How often? _____   Problems? _____   Independently? ___ N ___ Y

_N_ Walk places? How far? _____   How often? _____   Other: _____

How do you financially care for basic needs? _N/A_____

Who pays the bills? _____ _N/A_ _____   Who handles the finances? _____

___ Savings account   ___ Checking account   ___ Money orders

___ Others pay/write checks   ___ Figure change

3. Living Situation

Living conditions: (_X_ family, ___ alone, ___ group home; ___ crowded, ___ dysfunctional; ability to follow rules/procedures)

   Functional home environment—Eventually does most chores.

4. Ability to Relate to Others (e.g., ___ aggressive, ___ dependent, ___ defiant, ___ avoidant, ___ oppositional, ___ normal)

_____

Adults: _____ _Ignores_ _____   Authority figures: _____ _varies_ _____

Peers: _____ _Teased often in school_ _____   Police: _____

Family: _____ _Normal range of rivalry_ _____   Children: _____ _varies_ _____

Neighbors: _____ _Neutral_ _____   Other: _____

Have best friend? _____ _Yes_ _____   Group of friends? _____ _No_ _____

Activities with friends (include frequency, duration, and problems): _Play in park—video games._

How well did client relate (examiner, office personnel) during office visit? _Cooperated, but hyperactive._

5. **Substance Abuse** (if applicable)

Detailed history and current information regarding substance abuse patterns.

Age of onset: _____   Substances used historically: _____

History of usage: _____ *N/A* _____

_____

_____

6. **Self-help Skills** (Describe child's ability and assistance needed in the following)

Dressing: _____*OK, but needs prompts to begin task*_____

Grooming: _____*OK, but need prompts to begin task*_____

Feeding self: _____*OK, picky eater*_____

Avoiding dangers: _____*Often runs into street w/o looking. Often gets hurt "playing too hard"*_____

Independent activities outside the home: _____*Plays in park only (next to house)*_____

Making change($): _____*N/A*_____

Taking the bus: _____*School bus only*_____

7. **Concentration, Persistence and Pace** (age 3–18)

(Describe ability to concentrate, attend, persist and complete tasks in a timely manner.)

_____*Home: mother describes problems at home staying on task due to hyperactivity. Seems to*_____

_____*pay attention but has difficulty sitting still. Maintained conversation, but hurried through*_____

_____*tasks impulsively.*_____

Development

Pregnancy: _____*Normal*_____   Adverse factors? _____*None known*_____

Delivery: _____*Caesarian*_____   On time? _____*1 week late*_____

Early development: _____*Normal milestones*_____

Walked: _____*13m*_____   Talked: _____*20m*_____   Toilet trained: _____*3 1/2 yr*_____

(Provide specific information on how the child's symptoms impact performance of age appropriate developmental tasks and functional capacity.)

Age Group of Child (fill in appropriate age group)

A. Birth to 3 Years

Locomotion (e.g., crawling, walking, sitting up, pulling oneself into an upright position, etc.):

_____ *N/A* _____

_____

Language (e.g., vocalization, imitative sounds, talking, receptive skills, ability to follow commands, etc.): _____

_____

_____

Gross motor competence (e.g., reaching, throwing, jumping, grasping, pedaling a tricycle, etc.):

_____

_____

Fine motor competence (pincer grip, grasp, colors, uses pencils, reaches for objects, etc.):

_____

_____

Behavioral/social (e.g., excessive crying, hyperactivity, fear response to separation, aggressiveness, temper outbursts, lethargic, inability to bond, autistic features, efforts at toilet training, ability to relate to peers, siblings, parents, etc.): _____

_____

_____

B. 3 to 6 Years

Locomotion (describe any abnormalities as listed above, describe development of competency):

_____ *N/A* _____

_____

Communications (speech development, ability to form sentences, clarity of speech, expressive skills, receptive skills, ability to communicate needs, ability to respond to commands, ability to follow simple directions): _____

_____

_____

Motor (describe any abnormalities in fine or gross motor activity, can child use scissors, color within lines, copy simple designs [circle, square] Include observations of any impairments in coordination and/or balance): _____

_____

_____

Social/emotional (toilet training, aggressiveness, hyperactivity, ability to play with others, to share with others, to separate from caregivers, competency in feeding, dressing and grooming skills, temper outbursts, night terrors, manifestations of anxiety, phobias, fear response to separation, observations of bizarre or aberrant behavior): _____

_____

_____

Ability to concentrate, attend, persist, and complete tasks in a timely manner: _____

_____

_____

C. 6 to 16 Years

Locomotion (describe any abnormalities in walking, running, mobility): ___ *Normal range* ___

_____

Communication (reading, writing receptive and expressive language skills, speech): _____

Normal range _____

Motor skills (coordination, balance, perceptual motor skills, complex-integrated motor responses):

Normal range _____

_____

Ability to concentrate, attend, persist, and complete tasks in a timely manner: _____*OK when*_____

_____*interested or with 1–1 adult interaction. Concentration seems to be within normal limits.*_____

_____*Any concentration issues seem to be secondary to hyperactivity.*_____

D. 16 to 18 Years

Locomotion (describe any abnormalities in mobility): _____

_____

_____

Communications (any abnormalities noted): _____

_____

_____

Social/emotional (relationships to peer group, to school authority figures). Any evidence of oppositional, rebellious, antisocial, aggressive behavior, withdrawal. Assess stress tolerance, potential employment, potential for substance abuse, impairment in reality testing. Comment on identity issues and developing of body awareness: _____

_____

_____

Ability to concentrate, attend, persist, and complete tasks in a timely manner: _____

_____

_____

Other (Comment on any volunteer of after school work, vocational training, jobs associated with the school program in terms of work, ability to persist, complete tasks, and respond appropriately to supervision.): _____

_____

_____

Parents or Caregivers Leave Interview Room at This Time

Mental Status Exam

1. **Clinical Observations** (Entire page: Leave blank if normal. Check and comment if remarkable.)

   Appearance

   ___ Appears age, +/- ___ Grooming ___ Hair ___ Odor

   ___ Posture ___ Health _X_ Nails _X_ Demeanor

   Nails bitten very short. Very active.

   _____

   Activity Level

   ___ Mannerisms ___ Gestures ___ Alert ___ Lethargic ___ Limp

   ___ Rigid ___ Relaxed ___ Combative _X_ Hyperactive ___ Bored

   ___ Gait ___ Eye contact ___ Distracted ___ Preoccupied ___ Vigilance

   Rarely sat still. One time hid under desk. Ran out of room 3x. Agitated when didn't get

   her own way.

Speech

___ Vocabulary	___ Details	___ Volume	_X_ Pace
___ Reaction time	___ Pitch	___ Pressured	___ Hesitant
___ Monotonous	___ Slurred	___ Stuttering	___ Mumbled
___ Echolalia	___ Neologisms	_X_ Repetitions	___ Pronunciation

___ % Understood: ___95–98___

Rapid speech. Often repeated the questions asked. _____

_____

Attitude Toward Examiner

_X_ Attentive	___ Distracted	___ Cooperative	___ Friendly	___ Interested
___ Frank	___ Hostile	___ Defiant	___ Guarded	___ Defensive
___ Evasive	___ Hesitant	___ Manipulative	___ Humorous	___ Historian +/-

Held attention when interested, otherwise fidgety. _____

_____

2. Stream of Consciousness

Re: Speech:

___ Spontaneous	___ Inhibited	___ Blocked	___ Illogical
___ Vague	___ Pressured	___ Slowed	___ Disorganized
___ Rambling	___ Derailment	___ Coherent	___ Cause/effect
___ Neologisms			

Re: Thinking:

___ Relevant	___ Coherent	___ Goal directed	___ Loose & rambling

Re: Thought processes:

___ Number of ideas	___ Flight of ideas	___ Hesitance

No issues _____

_____

3. Thought Content

Preoccupations:

___ Obsessions	___ Compulsions	___ Phobias	___ Homicide	___ Antisocial

Suicidal:

Current:	___ Threats	___ Ideas	___ Plan
History:	___ Attempts	___ Threats	___ Ideas

Hallucinations:

___ Voices	___ Visions	___ Content	___ Setting	___ Sensory system

Illusions: _____

Delusions:

___ Persecutory	___ Somatic	___ Grandeur

Ideas of reference:

___ Controlled	___ Broadcasting	___ Antisocial	___ Validity
___ Content	___ Mood	___ Bizarre	

No issues _____

_____

4. Affect/Mood

Affective Observations

Range	_X_ Normal	___ Expansive	___ Restricted	___ Blunted	___ Flat
Appropriateness	_X_ Concordant		___ Discordant (with speech/ideas)		
Mobility	_X_ Normal	___ Decreased (constricted, fixed)	___ Increased (labile)		
Intensity	_X_ Normal	___ Mild	___ Strong		
Psychomotor	_X_ Normal	___ Retardation	___ Agitation		
Predominant mood	___ Neutral	_X_ Euthymic	___ Dysphoric	___ Euphoric	___ Manic
Level of anxiety	_X_ Normal	___ High (describe): _body/facial expression_			
Irritability	_X_ Normal	___ High (describe): _____			
Anger expression	_X_ Normal	___ High (describe): _____			

Mood (Rule in and rule out signs and symptoms)

Frequency/Intensity in Daily Life (give specific examples of impairments/strengths, frequency, duration.)

Clearly Validate with *DSM-IV* Criteria

Affection toward others: ___*Normal range*_____

Anger: ___ anger mng't issues _____ _X_ property destruction

___ explosive behaviors _____ ___ assaultive behaviors

How does the client act on anger?

Onset: _____*1st grade*_____ Frequency: _____*1x/wk*_____

Duration: ____*Brief*_____ Severity: _____*Mild*_____

Examples: ___*Growing concerns with temper tantrums since 1st grade*_____

_____

Panic Attacks: 4+, Abrupt development of:

___ palpitations	___ sweating	___ trembling
___ shortness of breath	___ feeling of choking	___ chest pain
___ nausea	___ dizziness	___ light-headed
___ derealization	___ fear of losing control	___ fear of dying
___ numbness	___ chills	___ hot flashes

___ Other: _None_____

_____

Onset: _____ Frequency: _____

Duration: _____ Severity: _____

Anxiety: GAD: 3+, most of time, 6 months:

___ restlessness	___ easily fatigued	___ concentration
___ irritability	___ muscle tension	___ sleep disturbance

___ Other: _Normal range_____

_____

Onset: _____ Frequency: _____

Duration: _____ Severity: _____

3.51

Depression: MDE: 2+ wks, 5+:

___ usually depressed   ___ anhedonia

___ wght +/- 5%/month   ___ appetite +/-

___ sleep +/-   ___ fatigue

___ psychomotor +/-   ___ worthlessness/guilt

___ concentration   ___ other: ___ crying spells   ___ withdrawal

___ death/suicidal ideation

___ Other: *Normal range* _____

_____

Onset: _____   Frequency: _____

Duration: _____   Severity: _____

Dysthymia: ___ depressed most of time   ___ onset; adult 2+ child/adolescent 1+ yrs, 2+ of:

___ +/- appetite or eating   ___ in/hypersomnia   ___ low energy/fatigue

___ low self-esteem   ___ low concentration/decisions   ___ hopelessness

___ Other: *No* _____

_____

Onset: _____   Frequency: _____

Duration: _____   Severity: _____

Mania: 3+:

___ grandiosity   ___ low sleep   ___ talkative   ___ flight of ideas

___ distractibility   ___ goals/agitation   ___ excessive pleasure

___ Other: *No* _____

_____

Onset: _____   Frequency: _____

Duration: _____   Severity: _____

PTSD: Traumatic event with intense response: 1+:

Distressing:

___ recollections   ___ dreams   ___ reliving

___ cues   ___ physiological reactivity with cues

3+:

___ avoid thoughts   ___ avoid environmental   ___ poor recall of events

___ low interest   ___ detachment   ___ restricted range of affect

___ foreshortened future

2+:

___ sleep   ___ anger   ___ concentration

___ hypervigilance   ___ startle response

___ Other: *No* _____

_____

Onset: _____   Frequency: _____

Duration: _____   Severity: _____

ODD: Pattern of negativistic, hostile and defiant behaviors > 6 months: 4+ of the following:

_X_ loses temper   ___ argues with adults

___ actively defies adults' requests   ___ deliberately annoys people

___ blames others for own mistakes or misbehavior   _X_ touchy/easily annoyed

___ angry/resentful   ___ spiteful/vindictive

1+ impairment:

___ social   ___ academic   ___ occupational

Increasing symptoms but not sufficient for diagnosis.

_____

Conduct: Repetitive/persistent behaviors violating rights of others. 3+ (past 12 month, 1 in past 6 months)

___ Aggression to people/animals:

___ bullies, threatens, intimidates   ___ initiates physical fights

___ has used harmful weapon   ___ physically cruel to: ___ people   ___ animals

___ stolen while confronting victim   ___ forces sexual activity

Destruction of property:

___ deliberate fire setting (intended damage)   ___ deliberate property destruction

Deceitfulness or theft:

___ broken into someone's property   ___ often lies/cons   ___ has stolen without confrontation

Serious violation of rules:

___ stays out at night against parents' rules before age 13

___ has run away 2+ or one extended   ___ often truant before age 13

1+ impairment:

___ social   ___ academic   ___ occupational

_No_

_____

ADHD: Inattention; 6+ Sx, 6+ months:

___ poor attn/careless mistakes   ___ difficult sustaining attn.   ___ forgetful

___ not listen when spoken to   _X_ not follow through

___ loses thing   _X_ easily distracted

___ difficult organizing, avoids tasks requiring sustained mental effort

AND/OR Hyperactivity/impulsivity, 6+, Hyperactivity:

_X_ fidgety   _X_ leaves seat often   _X_ runs/climbs

_X_ difficult being quiet   _X_ "on the go"   _X_ talks excessively

Impulsivity:

_X_ blurts out answers   _X_ difficulty awaiting turn   _X_ interrupts

_X_ Some Sx < age 7. 1+ impairment:

_X_ social   _X_ academic   ___ occupational

_____

Attention Span During Interview

_X_ Fidgety	_N_ Remained seated	_X_ Distracted
_X_ Blurted answers	___ Followed directions	___ Shifted focus
_X_ Talked excessively	_X_ Interrupted	___ Listened
_X_ Impulsivity	_X_ Understood questions	___ Attended to questions

___ Other: _____

Rule Out Clinical Syndromes

Pervasive developmental disorders, autistic disorders, specific developmental disabilities, learning disorders, incipient psychotic process, etc.:

_____ *Other disorders ruled out* _____

_____

_____

5. **Sensorium/Cognition**

Younger Children: Provide a basic assessment of the following:

A) **Consciousness** (ability to concentrate, confusion, attending): __ *N/A* _____

_____

B) **Orientation:** ___ Time ___ Place ___ Person   Notes: _____

_____

C) **Memory:** (recent, long-term, simple facts): _____

_____

D) **Estimated Intellectual Functioning:** _____

_____

Older Children:

A) **Reality Contact** (How in touch with reality is client?): _____ *Age-appropriate* _____

Able to hold normal conversation? _X_ Yes ___ No   Notes: _____

B) **Orientation X3:** _X_ Time _X_ Place _X_ Person   Notes: __ *Age-appropriate* ___

C) **Concentration** (age-appropriate measures):

Count by 1s: _____ *1–20* _____   Count by 2s: _____ *2–10* _____   Count by 3s: _____ *No* _____

Errors: _0_ Time: *Rapid*   Errors: _0_ Time: *Rapid*   Errors: ___ Time: _____

Count to 40 by 3s beginning at 1.

(__ 1, __ 4, __ 7, ___, 10, ___, 13, ___, 16, ___, 19, ___, 22, ___, 25, ___, 28, ___, 31, ___, 34, ___, 37, ___, 40)

Number of errors: _____   Time between digits: _____   Other: _____

Count backward by 7s from 100.

(100, 93, 86, 79, 72, 65, 58, 51, 44, 37, 30, 23, 16, 9, 2.) Errors: ___ Time: _____

$1 + 2 =$ _3_	$2 + 3 =$ _5_	$3 - 2 =$ _1_	$4 + 8 =$ _12_ *(fingers)*
$9 + 12 =$ _No_	$2 \times 3 =$ _No_	$4 \times 4 =$ ___	$7 \times 4 =$ ___
$12 \times 6 =$ ___	$65/5 =$ ___		

Digits forward and backward (for ages 6+)

FWD: _X_ 42 _X_ 394 _X_ 6385 ___ 96725 ___ 864972 ___ 5739481 ___ 31749852

BWD: ___ 73 ___ 582 ___ 9147 ___ 74812 ___ 839427 ___ 7392641 ___ 49521863

FWD = _4_ BWD = _0_ Evaluation: ___ Below average _X_ Average ___ Above average

Spell words: WORLD   _N_ FWD   _N_ BWD

                 STOP   _X_ FWD   _N_ BWD

                 CAT   _X_ FWD   _X_ BWD

D) Memory:

Remote Memory

Childhood data: _X_ Schools attended   _X_ Teacher's names/faces   _X_ Events of past holiday

              _X_ Street grew up on   _N_ Mother's maiden name

Recent Memory

___ Activities past few months   ___ Past few days   ___ Activities past weekend

___ Yesterday (events, meals, etc.)   ___ Today (events, meals, etc.)

___ Phone number   ___ Address

30 MINUTE MEMORY CHECK (5 = _2_ / 3) 30 = _"House–Cat"_ = _2_ / 3

Client's statements re: memory functioning: _____

Long-term: ___ L _X_ M ___ H   Short-term: ___ L _X_ M ___ H

Immediate: ___ L _X_ M ___ H

E) Information: (knowledge of current events)

Does the client: _N_ read newspaper?   How often? _____

             _N_ TV/radio news?   How often? _____

Name current local/national news: _No_   President's name: _No_   3 large cities: _No_

F) Judgment

"Find someone's purse in store": _Give to mother_ _____

"First one in theatre to see smoke and fire": _____

G) Abstractive Capacity

Interpretation of various proverbs   Interpretation Given

"Early bird catches the worm": _____ _N/A_ _____

"Strike while the iron is hot": _____

"Don't cry over spilled milk": _____

Interpretations: ___ "DK"   ___ Would not try   ___ Abstract

               ___ Concrete   ___ Age-appropriate   ___ Unusual: _____

H) Insight (awareness of issues: what level?)

___ Complete denial   _X_ Slight awareness

___ Awareness, but blames others   ___ Intellectual insight, but few changes likely

___ Emotional insight, understanding, changes can occur

Client's statement regarding actions needed to get better: _Listen to the teacher more_

_____

Comment on client's level of insight to problems: _Age-appropriate_ _____

I) Intellectual Level/Education/IQ Estimate

Grade in school: _1_   Ever repeat a grade? _No_   Grades/Progress: _S's and I's_

Special education classes: _No_   Estimated IQ: _Avg_

General knowledge: _Avg_   Selective nature of Sx: _____

J) Adverse Factors Affecting the Child's Ability to Function

(e.g., pain, side effects of meds, dysfunctional family, abuse, physical impairments, teasing, etc.)

None known

_____

_____

_____

Additional comments by caregiver of child: _None—Testing WISC-III-Low normal-see profile_

_____

_____

_____

_____

6. **Assessment**

Summary and Diagnostic Findings (Tie together history and mental status findings and relate to diagnosis. Include onset of current Sx of the condition and how far back it goes. Include evaluation of presenting problem vs. stated limitations vs. signs and symptoms. Include prognosis. Integrate collateral information.

This psychologist's confidence in the exam findings is ___ Poor _X_ Average ___ High

. . . test findings is ___ Poor _X_ Average ___ High

The claimant's ability to understand, retain, and follow instructions is:

___ Poor _X_ Average ___ High

Axis I   1: _314.01 ADHD, primarily hyperactive/impulsive type_

   2: _____

   3: _____

Axis II   1: _799.9 Deferred_

   2: _____

Axis III Defer to physician

Axis IV Current Stressors: _Social & academic problems_

Axis V Current GAF = _70_   Highest past year GAF = _70_

Prognosis: ___ Poor ___ Marginal ___ Guarded _X_ Moderate ___ Good ___ Excellent

Qualifiers to prognosis:

_X_ Med compliance   ___ Tx compliance   ___ Home environment

___ Activity changes   _X_ Behavioral changes   ___ Attitudinal changes

_X_ Education/training   ___ Other: _Need med eval_

Chapter 4

Treatment Plan
Forms and Procedures

Individual Treatment Plans

Effective treatment plans are designed to provide a clear picture of the client's specific treatment needs. Vague intake information leads to vague treatment plans, which leads to vague treatment, which leads to vague outcomes. No one would sign a contract to have a house built which simply stated, "Build house." The blueprints and contract provide specifications regarding time frame, cost, and outcome. The treatment plan is the blueprint for therapy.

Typical problems in writing treatment plans include making statements that are too vague or generic, not indicative of the assessment, unrealistic, or not assessable, measurable, or observable. Treatment plans must directly correspond to the assessment material (e.g., purpose, impairments, diagnosis, goals). The treatment plan is driven or documented by the assessment. It must clearly reflect a plan to alleviate impairments resulting from the mental disorder. Regulating sources (such as Medicare and the Joint Commission on Accreditation of Healthcare Organizations and most third-party payers) require that treatment plans provide measurable outcomes written in behavioral, objective, or measurable terms.

The process of writing a treatment plan begins with an accurate and specific assessment of the client's concerns. Assessment sources include the clinical interview, testing, observations, historical documents, and collateral information.

The plan should reflect both the client's presenting problem and the client's stated needs and goals, and it should also reflect the clinical judgment of the therapist. Both Medicare and Joint Commission guidelines call for specific measurable treatment outcomes to be attained by the client, not the therapist.

Treatment Plan Formats

Treatment plan formats vary, but the required information is fairly consistent. A three-column format (Problems/Symptoms, Goals/Objectives, and Treatment Strategies) will be used for examples in this book.

Column One, "Problems/Symptoms."   The first column identifies specific problem areas to be addressed in treatment. The stated symptoms must correspond to, and therefore validate, the client's diagnosis and impairments. Symptoms are not vague terms or constructs such as "depression," but rather symptoms of depression that are causing functional impairment. The symptoms listed must validate and be indicative of the Axis I diagnosis.

The listed symptoms, in themselves, should clearly define the diagnosis. If not, then the diagnosis is not clearly being treated. Some mental health professionals update treatment plans regularly (e.g., every 60 days); in such cases it is obviously not possible to address every symptom of a diagnosis. But nevertheless the symptoms addressed should be indicative of the diagnosis. Prolonged treatment of other diagnoses is not justified unless other diagnoses have been given.

Ethical concerns are noted when practitioners bill insurance companies under one diagnosis but treat a different diagnosis. Potential consequences could range from services not being covered to ethical charges.

Column Two, "Goals/Objectives."   The second column lists the client's intended outcomes of treatment, written in measurable, observable, and documentable terms in which the effectiveness of the treatment can be evaluated.

Both goals and objectives are to be listed for each symptom. Goals are defined as overall, global, long-term outcomes. Goals are often the opposite of the symptoms. For example, the goal for a depressed person might be to alleviate depression. It is difficult to measure goals, but they can be broken down into objectives which are observable. Objectives are defined as incremental steps by which goals are attained. They reflect specific improvements in adaptive behaviors resulting in reduction of symptoms. Objectives are revised throughout the course of therapy depending on progress and/or setbacks.

Objectives may be measured in a variety of ways, including successive testing, charting, subjective ratings by the client and/or others, and clinical observations. It is often difficult to write all objectives in measurable, observable, or quantifiable terms, but efforts should be taken to establish a baseline and objective points of comparison. Terms such as "increase" or "decrease" should be clarified with specific quantifiers and qualifiers. For example, an objective of "increase pleasurable social activities to four per week by October 13th" is much more specific and measurable than "increase pleasurable social activities." In the latter example, *any* increase (e.g., .0001 percent) would appear as progress. Specific treatment planning keeps therapy on course. Goals and objectives must be clear in order to be followed.

Column Three, "Strategies."   The third column describes treatment interventions in and out of the sessions by which the treatment goals and objectives will be addressed. Treatment strategies may include the type of therapy (e.g., group, family, individual), school of thought (e.g., cognitive, behavioral, psychoanalytic, Rational Emotive Therapy [RET]), therapeutic techniques (e.g., dream analysis, confrontation, systematic desensitization, role playing), and homework assignments.

Each aspect of the treatment plan requires client collaboration. The client must not only agree on the symptoms, goals and treatment strategies, he or she must also be willing to submit to their integrative process in therapy. The question, "What does the client want to get out of therapy?" is too often ignored. Client/therapist cooperation and collaboration go hand in hand.

Objectives should be written in small, attainable steps. For example, if a socially withdrawn person has a treatment plan objective of initiating five social interactions per week, the likelihood of success may be quite small. But since incremental increases in objective criteria are viewed as more attainable by the client, an initial objective in this case might be to initiate one social interaction per week. The high likelihood of success is in itself rewarding. As an objective is met, new objective criteria are set, up to the point at which impairment is alleviated. Treatment plans are meant to be revised as progress and/or setbacks take place.

Success of a treatment plan also depends on how realistic and achievable the goals are. For example, a treatment plan goal to "eliminate depression" can never be reached since depression is a normal and adaptive human emotion.

Client effort and motivation to fulfill treatment plan objectives merit close attention. The relationship between performance and motivation is curvilinear. That is, low levels or drive lead to low performance because little effort and low reinforcement are perceived. Likewise, high levels of drive generally lead to high levels of anxiety about performance, and thus performance is also low. For example, if a client is suffering from agoraphobia, an objective of going to a shopping mall during the week before Christmas would probably be too anxiety-provoking for any positive performance results. But if the objective is set too low, there might be little or no motivation to change behavior. A moderate amount of drive leads to optimal performance. Discussing specific goals and objectives with the client can certainly help determine the success of a treatment plan and subsequent treatment.

FORM 23
Individual Treatment Plan

FORM 23—Example of a Poor Treatment Plan

In the example of vague treatment plan statements on page 4.7, entries are neither descriptive, observable, measurable, nor client-specific with respect to functional impairments. No target dates are set. Goals are not broken down into objectives. It is not signed by the client or therapist.

Adult

Judy Doe's treatment plan (Form 23B) is the culmination of the presenting problem, testing, intake questions, clinical observations, and biographical information. During the second session, she and the therapist collaboratively set a course of treatment that met both the professional abilities of the therapist and the therapeutic wants and needs of the client.

The concerns noted in column 1 of the treatment plan serve a variety of functions. First, they validate the diagnosis. Her diagnosis of major depression is validated in her treatment plan for each of the following concerns:

1. Decreased energy level.

2. Low ego strength.

3. Difficulty concentrating.

4. Hopelessness feelings.

5. Diminished pleasure.

6. Social withdrawal.

The goals and objectives are based on, first, alleviation of the symptoms noted in Column 1, and second, on agreed-upon outcomes for Judy Doe to work on in a given time frame. Since not all mental health professionals are competent to treat all clients' concerns, the treatment strategies include referrals to other professionals when necessary. Judy Doe is to receive talk therapy from the psychologist but is referred to her physician for medication and to monitor a physical exercise program.

In this case, the psychologist's training does not permit her to prescribe medications or monitor physical procedures; therefore, a referral is given in these areas. Serious ethical violations may occur when mental health professionals practice outside of their competencies. For example, if a mental health professional were to suggest, or even monitor, a diet or exercise program and the client developed physical problems related to the program, the practitioner could be subject to litigation and possible license revocation.

Child

A treatment plan for children (Form 23C) differs from an adult treatment plan in that the initial sessions are not direct therapy; rather, the initial objectives are to establish a therapeutic relationship, acclimate the child to therapy, and establish rapport and trust. Without these initial sessions the prognosis would be poor.

FORM 24
Short-Term Therapy Treatment Plan

Form 24 depicts a sample treatment plan for short-term therapy in which session content is preplanned according to treatment goals and objectives. It differs from the traditional treatment plans in this book in that it outlines in advance the objectives for each session. Therapy is defined by a set number of sessions in which the focus of each is planned in the initial sessions.

FORM 25
Treatment Review

A Treatment Review (Form 25) is generally used in settings in which care is monitored by a supervisor or review committee. Organizations such as JCAHO require case reviews periodically or when changes are made in areas such as diagnosis, treatment plan, therapist, or an additional evaluation is requested. This document is designed for quality control within the clinic.

As treatment plan goals are met, they should be documented. New goals should be added as needed to best suit the client's needs. Clearly describe the purpose for any changes in treatment, rather than only listing changes. Changes such as progress and setbacks are documented to help assess the effectiveness of treatment.

When the estimated number of sessions to completion of treatment has been reached, but more sessions are needed, it should be clearly documented why more sessions are necessary. In such cases, the treatment plan is being changed. Any information that affects the course of treatment, such as additional life stressors, is documented to justify the changes. Diagnosis changes must be clearly validated according to the *DSM-IV.*

FORM 26
Treatment Update

The Treatment Update (Form 26) does not provide clinical details as in the Treatment Review. Rather, it summarizes the client's current standing in treatment and allows for a response from its recipient. It is communication between the therapist and a third-party. The form is usually used in cases such as when a third party (county social worker, guardian, parent, court, attorney, physician, etc.) has requested periodic summaries of the client's progress, or by others involved as collaterals or supports in therapy. Some clients may benefit from receiving this brief report of progress. A legal release of information is required to share this material in most cases.

Form 23   Individual Treatment Plan

Client's name: _____ DOB: _____ Date _____

Presenting problem: _____ Therapist: _____

Axis I: _____ Axis II: _____

Services Needed   **Anticipated Number of Sessions**

Treatment	0	1	2	3–5	6–10	11–20	21–40	40+
___ Assessment	___	___	___	___	___	___	___	___
___ Individual	___	___	___	___	___	___	___	___
___ Group	___	___	___	___	___	___	___	___
___ Family	___	___	___	___	___	___	___	___
___ Other	___	___	___	___	___	___	___	___

Problems/Symptoms	**GOALS/Objectives**	**Treatment Strategies**

I have discussed the information listed above, various treatment strategies, and their possible outcomes. I have received and/or read my copy of my rights as a client and procedures for reporting grievances. I concur with the above diagnosis and treatment plan.

Client's signature: _____ Date: ____/____/_____

Guardian's signature: _____ Date: ____/____/_____

Therapist's signature: _____ Date: ____/____/____

Clinical supervisor: _____ Date: ____/____/_____

Form 23A   Individual Treatment Plan

(Poor Example)

Client's name: _____JD_____   Date: _____

Problems/Symptoms	GOALS/Objectives	Treatment Strategies
Depression	Eliminate depression	Individual therapy and Prozac
Irritability	Stop mood swings	Therapy
Sadness	Increase outlook	Counseling
Conduct	Stop negative behaviors	Discuss feelings
Anger	Anger management	Listen to tapes
Budgeting	Balance budget	Marriage counseling
Marital discord	Communication skills	Talk therapy

Therapist's signature: _____

Form 23B Individual Treatment Plan—Adult

(Completed)

Client's name: _Doe, Judy_ DOB: _7/6/1948_ Date _3/15/1999_
Presenting problem: _Depressed mood, irritability_ Therapist: _DLB_
Axis I: _296.32 Major depression, recurrent, moderate_ Axis II: _Deferred_

Services Needed

Anticipated Number of Sessions

Treatment	0	1	2	3–5	6–10	11–20	21–40	40+
_X_ Assessment	—	—	X	—	—	—	—	—
_X_ Individual	—	—	—	—	—	X	—	—
___ Group	—	—	—	—	—	—	—	—
___ Family	—	—	—	—	—	—	—	—
___ Other	—	—	—	—	—	—	—	—

Problems/Symptoms	GOALS/Objectives	Treatment Strategies
DEPRESSED MOOD Address following symptoms:	Develop plan to alleviate emotional, occupational, and social impairment due to depressed mood. Return to previous functioning levels.	Individual therapy (cognitive behavioral). Med referral. Possible marital therapy. Successive BDI's. Charting.
1) Decreased energy level	INCREASE ENERGY LEVEL Participate in appropriate physical exercise daily	Medical evaluation referral. Physical program approved by physician.
2) Low ego strength	INCREASE EGO STRENGTH Accomplish at least one weekly homework assignment which leads to positive outcomes. Log at least one positive self-statement daily. Verbalize awareness of negative self-beliefs.	Focus on positive qualities. Chart and reinforce progress. Role playing. Logging. Experiencing and sharing feelings in session.
3) Difficulty concentrating	IMPROVE ABILITY TO FOCUS ON THOUGHTS/ACTIVITIES Complete an appropriate lesson plan in 45–60 minutes (as per previous functioning).	Learn strategies to break problems down into components.
4) Hopelessness feelings	RESTRUCTURE DYSFUNCTIONAL THOUGHTS/PROCESSES Chart one future plan daily. Develop insight as to relationship between stressors, anger, and depression.	Analyze dysfunctional thoughts. Keep dysfunctional thought record. Positive outcomes homework.
5) Diminished pleasure	INCREASE PLEASURE IN DAILY ACITIVITIES Increase/maintain selected pleasurable activities to 3x/week.	Incorporate effective time management of pleasurable vs. nonpleasurable activities. Chart and reinforce progress.
6) Social withdrawal	INCREASE SOCIAL INTERACTIONS Increase and maintain at least 2 new social interactions/week.	Role playing. Psychoeducational training. Chart and reinforce progress.

I have discussed the information listed above, various treatment strategies, and their possible outcomes. I have received and/or read my copy of my rights as a client and procedures for reporting grievances. I concur with the above diagnosis and treatment plan.

Client's signature: _Judy Doe_ Date: _3_ / _15_ / _1999_
Guardian's signature: _____ Date: ___/___/___
Therapist's signature: _Darlene L. Benton, PhD_ Date: _3_ / _15_ / _1999_
Clinical supervisor: _Sharon Bell, PhD_ Date: _3_ / _16_ / _1999_

Form 23C   Individual Treatment Plan—Child

(Completed)

Client's name: _Rentschler, Johnny_   DOB: _3/6/1993_   Date _1/29/1999_
Presenting problem: _Anger management, coping, withdrawal_   Therapist: _DLB_
Axis I: _Adjustment reaction/depressed mood and conduct_   Axis II: _None_

Services Needed   **Anticipated Number of Sessions**

Treatment	0	1	2	3–5	6–10	11–20	21–40	40+
_X_ Assessment	—	—	X	—	—	—	—	—
_X_ Individual	—	—	—	—	—	X	—	—
___ Group	—	—	—	—	—	—	—	—
_X_ Family	—	—	—	—	X	—	—	—
___ Other	—	—	—	—	—	—	—	—

Problems/Symptoms	GOALS/Objectives	Treatment Strategies
Behavioral and affective dysfunctioning since recent divorce of parents.	*Develop plan to alleviate emotional, behavioral, and social impairment, and increase coping skills.*	*Individual play therapy. Collateral sessions with mother. Charting.*
INITIAL CONCERNS *1) Lack of trust*	*INCREASE LEVEL OF TRUST* *Develop nonthreatening therapeutic relationship.* *ENGAGE IN PLAY THERAPY* *Enactment of psychological conflicts in therapy session.*	*Initial sessions incorporating drawings (e.g., draw pictures of family as an expression of affect and to help become comfortable in therapeutic setting). Increasing use of play therapy and rapport- and trust-building strategies.*
SYMPTOMS *2) Anger/behavioral management* • *Recurrent outbursts toward mother* • *Property damage in the home* • *Bullying/hitting younger sister*	*INCREASE ABILITY TO EXPRESS, CLARIFY, AND LABEL ANGER FEELINGS POSITIVELY* *Current: 4–5 daily outbursts toward family.* *3-month objective: 0–2 daily outbursts.* *Current: 0 interactions discussing feelings.* *3-month objective: discuss, label feelings 1/day*	*Play therapy utilizing safe expression of hostility. Role playing means of appropriately verbalizing related feelings. Charting at home with selective reinforcers such as verbal praise.*
3) Difficulties coping with changes in environment resulting in increased stress levels	*Learn socially acceptable means of coping with loss and resultant anger management issues.*	*Play therapy. Psychoeducation. Role playing.*
4) Social withdrawal	*INCREASE TIME SPENT WITH SIGNIGICANT OTHERS, ACTIVITIES, AND RECREATION* *Current hours in above activities:4/week.* *3-month objective: 20/week.*	*Family assignments encouraging positive social activities. Charting.*

I have discussed the information listed above, various treatment strategies, and their possible outcomes. I have received and/or read my copy of my rights as a client and procedures for reporting grievances. I concur with the above diagnosis and treatment plan.

Client's signature: _____   Date: ___/___/_____
Guardian's signature: _Linda Rentschler_   Date: _1_/_29_/_1999_
Therapist's signature: _Darlene L. Benton, PhD_   Date: _1_/_29_/_1999_
Clinical supervisor: _Sharon Bell, PhD_   Date: _2_/_3_/_1999_

Form 24   Individual Treatment Plan—Short-Term Therapy

Client's name: _____   DOB: _____   Date _____

Presenting problem: _____   Therapist: _____

Axis I: _____   Axis II: _____

Services Needed   **Anticipated Number of Sessions**

Treatment	0	1	2	3–5	6–10	11–20	21–40	40+
___ Assessment	___	___	___	___	___	___	___	___
___ Individual	___	___	___	___	___	___	___	___
___ Group	___	___	___	___	___	___	___	___
___ Family	___	___	___	___	___	___	___	___
___ Other	___	___	___	___	___	___	___	___

Problems/Symptoms	**GOALS/Objectives**	**Treatment Strategies**

Schedule of Topics

Session(s)	Topic(s)	Session(s)	Topic(s)

I have discussed the information listed above, various treatment strategies, and their possible outcomes. I have received and/or read my copy of my rights as a client and procedures for reporting grievances. I concur with the above diagnosis and treatment plan.

Client's signature: _____   Date: ____/____/_____

Guardian's signature: _____   Date: ____/____/_____

Therapist's signature: _____   Date: ____/____/_____

Clinical supervisor: _____   Date: ____/____/_____

Form 24A   Individual Treatment Plan—Short-Term Therapy
(Completed)

Client's name: _Roe, Sheila_   DOB: _6/4/1958_   Date _5/7/1999_
Presenting problem: _Depressed mood, irritability_   Therapist: _PS_
Axis I: _300.4 Dysthymic Disorder_   Axis II: _Deferred_

Services Needed

Anticipated Number of Sessions

Treatment	0	1	2	3–5	6–10	11–20	21–40	40+
_X_ Assessment	___	X	___	___	___	___	___	___
_X_ Individual	___	___	___	___	X	___	___	___
___ Group	___	___	___	___	___	___	___	___
___ Family	___	___	___	___	___	___	___	___
___ Other	___	___	___	___	___	___	___	___

Problems/Symptoms	GOALS/Objectives	Treatment Strategies
DEPRESSED MOOD Address following symptoms:	Develop plan to alleviate emotional, occupational, and social impairment due to depressed mood.	Individual therapy (cognitive behavioral). Possible marital therapy. Successive BDIs.
1) Decreased energy level	INCREASE ENERGY LEVEL Participate in increased physical activities.	Medical evaluation referral. Discuss exercise program (M.D. approval).
2) Hopelessness feelings	RESTRUCTURE THOUGHTS TO VIEW FUTURE MORE POSITIVELY Chart one future plan daily.	Analyze dysfunctional thoughts. Keep dysfunctional thought record. Positive outcomes homework.
3) Diminished pleasure	INCREASE PLEASURE IN DAILY ACITIVITIES Increase/maintain selected pleasurable activities to 3x/week.	Incorporate effective time management of pleasurable vs. nonpleasurable activities. Chart progress.
4) Social withdrawal	INCREASE SOCIAL INTERACTIONS Increase/maintain at least 2 new social interactions per week.	Role playing. Psychoeducational training. Chart progress.

Schedule of Topics

Session(s)	Topic(s)	Session(s)	Topic(s)
1	Assessment	5–6	Social withdrawal
2	Treatment planning		Diminished pleasure
3	Diminished pleasure	7	Review progress
4	Hopelessness feelings	8–9	Hopelessness feelings
	Diminished pleasure		Social withdrawal
		10	Closure

I have discussed the information listed above, various treatment strategies, and their possible outcomes. I have received and/or read my copy of my rights as a client and procedures for reporting grievances. I concur with the above diagnosis and treatment plan.

Client's signature: _Sheila Roe_   Date: _5_ / _7_ / _1999_
Guardian's signature: _____   Date: ___ / ___ / ___
Therapist's signature: _Phillip Schultz, MSW_   Date: _5_ / _7_ / _1999_
Clinical supervisor: _Sharon Bell, PhD_   Date: _5_ / _7_ / _1999_

Form 25   Treatment Review

Client's name: _____ DOB: _____ Date _____

ID no: _____ No. of session since last review: _____ Intake date: _____

Initial Diagnosis   **Current Diagnosis**

Axis I   _____   Axis I   _____

_____   _____

Axis II   _____   Axis II   _____

Axis III   _____   Axis III   _____

Axis IV   _____   Axis IV   _____

Axis V   _____   Axis V   _____

Purpose of Treatment Review

____ Change in diagnosis   ____ Significant change in treatment plan

____ Estimated length of treatment reached   ____ Change in treatment or therapist

____ Required periodic review   ____ Significant change in functioning level

____ Increased or attempted suicidal concerns ____ Other: _____

Describe any changes in the client's condition noted above: _____

_____

_____

_____

_____

Progresses: _____

_____

_____

_____

_____

Setbacks/impairments: _____

_____

_____

_____

What actions are needed at this time?   Describe needed services:

____ Referral   _____

____ Transfer   _____

____ Psychiatric eval   _____

____ Psychological eval   _____

____ Physical eval   _____

____ Other   _____

4.13

Treatment Plan Review Refer to previous Treatment Plan or Treatment Review

Current Goal 1   Met yet?   Target date if not met yet
_____   ___ Y ___ N   _____
Describe current progress toward objectives: _____
_____
_____

Current Goal 2   Met yet?   Target date if not met yet
_____   ___ Y ___ N   _____
Describe current progress toward objectives: _____
_____
_____

Current Goal 3   Met yet?   Target date if not met yet
_____   ___ Y ___ N   _____
Describe current progress toward objectives: _____
_____
_____

Current Goal 4   Met yet?   Target date if not met yet
_____   ___ Y ___ N   _____
Describe current progress toward objectives: _____
_____
_____

New Goal 1
_____   Target date: _____
Problem area: _____
Objectives: _____
                    _____
Treatment: _____
Services (and frequency) needed: _____
_____

New Goal 2
_____   Target date: _____
Problem area: _____
Objectives: _____
                    _____
Treatment: _____
Services (and frequency) needed: _____
_____

Therapist: _____   Date: ____/____/_____
Reviewed by: _____   Date: ____/____/_____

Form 25A   Treatment Review

(Completed)

Client's name: _William Olden_   DOB: _3/7/1973_   Date _7/9/1998_

ID no: _OW040498_   No. of session since last review: _12_   Intake date: _4/4/1998_

Initial Diagnosis	**Current Diagnosis**
Axis I _Oppositional Defiant Disorder_ _Adj Disorder, conduct, Chronic_	Axis I _Oppositional Defiant Disorder_
Axis II _No diagnosis_	Axis II _No diagnosis_
Axis III _Defer to physician_	Axis III _Defer to physician_
Axis IV _Social, family, academic problems_	Axis IV
Axis V _58_	Axis V

Purpose of Treatment Review

___ Change in diagnosis   ___ Significant change in treatment plan

___ Estimated length of treatment reached   ___ Change in treatment or therapist

_X_ Required periodic review   ___ Significant change in functioning level

___ Increased or attempted suicidal concerns   ___ Other: _____

Describe any changes in the client's condition noted above: _School year ended, is in required_ _summer school. Decreased conduct and defiance._

Progresses: _Catching up in school in summer program. Seldom over 1 or 2 disruptive behaviors_ _in school weekly for past month. Is initiating cooperative behaviors to family and peers._

Setbacks/impairments: _Continued blaming mother for "ruining my family." Was found sneaking_ _alcohol one time at home. Continued foul language._

What actions are needed at this time?   Describe needed services:

   _X_ Referral   _Join summer anger management_

   ___ Transfer   _group for adolescents_

   ___ Psychiatric eval

   ___ Psychological eval

   ___ Physical eval

   ___ Other

4.15

Treatment Plan Review Refer to previous Treatment Plan or Treatment Review

Current Goal 1   Met yet?   Target date if not met yet
___*Decrease oppositional behaviors*___   __ Y _X_ N   ___*9/30/1998*___

Describe current progress toward objectives: ___*Has decreased oppositional behaviors at home*___
___*and school by 50%.*___

Current Goal 2   Met yet?   Target date if not met yet
___*Initiate and maintain one peer friendship*___   _X_ Y __ N   _____

Describe current progress toward objectives: ___*Has maintained positive and cooperative friendship*___
___*with neighbor (same age).*___

Current Goal 3   Met yet?   Target date if not met yet
___*Decrease temper tantrums*___   __ Y _X_ N   ___*6/20/1998*___

Describe current progress toward objectives: ___*Mother reports that temper tantrums have decreased*___
___*from 6/week to 2/week.*___

Current Goal 4   Met yet?   Target date if not met yet
___*Cease initiating fights with peers*___   _X_ Y __ N   _____

Describe current progress toward objectives: ___*Has not initiated a fight with peers for three weeks.*___

New Goal 1

___*Develop positive relationship with step-father*___   Target date: ___*10/5/1998*___

Problem area: ___*Ignores step-father 80% of time, often sarcastic*___

Objectives: ___*—Initiate at least one conversation with step-father daily*___
___*—Attend one outing 2x/month with step-father*___

Treatment: ___*Incorporate into individual and family counseling*___

Services (and frequency) needed: ___*Behavioral assignments, cognitive therapy*___

New Goal 2

_____   Target date: _____

Problem area: _____

Objectives: _____

_____

Treatment: _____

Services (and frequency) needed: _____

Therapist: ___*Samuel Jones, MSW*___   Date: _7_ / _9_ / _1998_

Reviewed by: ___*Charles Wollat, LICSW*___   Date: _7_ / _14_ / _1998_

Form 26   Treatment Update

Client's name: _____   Report prepared for: _____

Therapist: _____   No. of sessions since last update: _____

Current treatment Plan Goals Being Addressed in Therapy

_____

_____

_____

_____

Recent Progresses

_____

_____

_____

_____

Recent Setbacks or Lack of Progress

_____

_____

_____

_____

Suggestions for Improved Progress

_____

_____

_____

_____

Summary Checklist of Therapeutic Progress

Topic	Low		Progress Moderate		High
Attendance	(__)	(__)	(__)	(__)	(__)
Discusses ongoing issues	(__)	(__)	(__)	(__)	(__)
Acknowledges problem areas	(__)	(__)	(__)	(__)	(__)
Developing insight into behaviors/emotions	(__)	(__)	(__)	(__)	(__)
Motivation to change	(__)	(__)	(__)	(__)	(__)
Objectives being met in timely manner	(__)	(__)	(__)	(__)	(__)
Therapy seems beneficial	(__)	(__)	(__)	(__)	(__)

Therapist: _____   Date: _____/_____/_____

Form 26A   Treatment Update

(Completed)

Client's name: _William Olden_   Report prepared for: _Lanna Olden, mother_

Therapist: _Samuel Jones, MSW_   No. of sessions since last update: _4_

Current treatment Plan Goals Being Addressed in Therapy

(1) Decreased temper tantrums

(2) Develop positive relationship with step-father

Recent Progresses

(1) Role played and discussed four alternative behaviors which have better consequences

(2) Revised roles in an attempt to empathize with step-father

Recent Setbacks or Lack of Progress

States that he still has little desire to get close to step-father. Seems to believe that he will betray

biological father.

Suggestions for Improved Progress

Do not allow his behavior to visibly affect marriage and family relationships. Reinforce his

efforts to control temper tantrums.

Summary Checklist of Therapeutic Progress

Topic	Low		Moderate		High
Attendance	(__)	(__)	(__)	(_X_)	(__)
Discusses ongoing issues	(__)	(__)	(_X_)	(__)	(__)
Acknowledges problem areas	(__)	(_X_)	(__)	(__)	(__)
Developing insight into behaviors/emotions	(__)	(__)	(_X_)	(__)	(__)
Motivation to change	(__)	(_X_)	(__)	(__)	(__)
Objectives being met in timely manner	(__)	(__)	(__)	(_X_)	(__)
Therapy seems beneficial	(__)	(__)	(_X_)	(__)	(__)

Therapist: _Samuel Jones, MSW_   Date: _8_ / _1_ / _1998_

4.18

Chapter 5

Progress Notes and Prior Authorization Request Forms and Procedures

In-Session Progress Notes

Progress notes are designed to document the course of therapy. They should clearly reflect the implementation of the treatment plan and assessment. The treatment plan symptoms, objectives, and treatment strategies must be documented regularly in the progress notes.

Various formats for writing progress notes such as DAP and SOAP are commonly used. Organized progress notes provide structure to progress note writing, rather than simply summarizing a session. The acronym DAP stands for data, assessment, and plan. SOAP stands for subjective, objective, assessment, and plan. The DAP format will be used for examples in this book.

Data

The Data section of the progress notes is oriented to address a number of clinical concerns or questions. Although the progress notes may not specifically cover each of the following areas of documentation, overall they should reflect:

What specifically took place in the session.

Therapeutic interventions.

Clinical observations.

Test results.

Homework assignments.

Current documentation of the diagnosis.

Current stressors, impairments, and affective and cognitive concerns.

Current behavioral concerns.

As in the scientific method, data provides information by which to assess a client's current condition, assess the progress of therapy, and plan upcoming interventions based on current data and assessment. Specifically, documentation in the Data section includes the following.

Clinical Diagnosis. An outside reader should be able to determine the diagnosis, current issues, treatment, and interventions by the content of the progress notes. For example, if the diagnosis is an adjustment disorder, the progress notes should document an adjustment disorder by addressing the current stressor(s) and the resulting affective/behavioral issues noted in the diagnosis. Likewise, if the diagnosis is a conduct disorder, progress notes should clearly address treatment of conduct, not depression, unless there is a secondary diagnosis of depression. Of course, secondary issues may be documented and noted, but progress notes must be consistent with the primary diagnosis and treatment objectives of the session.

Functional Impairments. Medical necessity of treatment is defined as "significant impairment or dysfunction as a result of a mental disorder." Symptoms and impairments differ in that symptoms help define the DSM-IV diagnosis, but do not adequately specify which areas of the client's life are adversely affected. The specific ways in which symptoms adversely affect the client's life are referred to as impairments. The course of treatment is aimed at alleviating the functional impairments resulting from the DSM symptoms of the diagnosis. As treatment progresses, functional impairments decrease. Regular charting of ongoing functional impairments is crucial to documentation of the course of treatment. When functional impairments no longer validate or justify a diagnosis, most third-party payers no longer cover services. But if progress notes do not validate functional impairments, there is no "documented behavioral evidence"; thus an audit or case review could result in funds paid for services being returned. As the treatment is revised, it addresses current functional impairments.

Types of functional impairments include social, family, occupational, affective, physical, cognitive, sexual, educational, biopsychological, and other areas in life that could lead to dysfunction. Documentation of functional impairments includes providing specific examples that are measurable. For example, a client with major depression might be impaired occupationally by significant decreases in work production; thus his or her job future might be in jeopardy. Documentation could include comparisons of previous functioning (e.g., producing 10 widgets per week) to current functioning (e.g., producing 3 widgets per week due to fatigue, low motivation, missing work, etc.). Progress notes could document specific interventions to alleviate fatigue, low motivation, and missing work, and subsequently document the resulting production at work. Charting such as Figure 5.1 could aid the documentation. The goal of such documentation is not to produce a graph, but rather to provide evidence of progress or setbacks in order to monitor and document therapeutic effectiveness of therapy and client participation.

Treatment Plan Symptoms, Goals, and Objectives. The documentation of clinical symptoms is similar to that of functional impairments. In the previous example, a functional impairment was less production at work, while symptoms include fatigue, low motivation, and missing work. Documentation of symptoms includes noting ongoing frequency, duration, and intensity of symptoms. Charting techniques may be employed, and may include simple notation in the chart for later comparisons. Each therapeutic session has specific objectives taken directly from the treatment plan.

Therapeutic Interventions. Documentation of clinical interventions is required in progress notes. Charting statements both reflect and document accepted therapeutic interventions. Most third-party payers require that the techniques employed in therapy are not experimental in nature. Notes should reflect specific techniques, interventions, and their outcomes. Such information will provide an empirical rationale

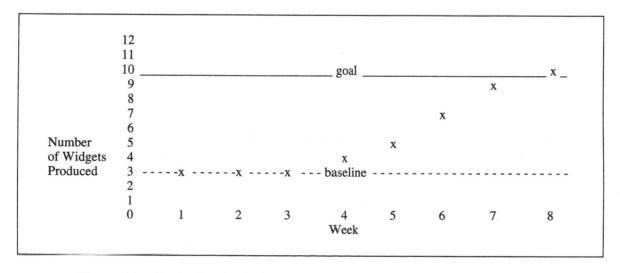

Figure 5.1 Graph Charting Patient Progress Based on Effectiveness of Therapy.

to continue, discontinue, or modify the specific course of therapy. Intervention statements also include evaluation of client homework assignments prescribed in therapy.

Current Issues/Stressors.   Progress notes should provide ongoing evidence of current stressors and problems, as well as positive aspects in the client's life. Documented therapeutic interventions are directed at alleviating impairments resulting from these stressors. Therapeutic techniques are noted that document interventions designed to cope with current issues and stressors. Ongoing documentation assesses therapeutic results.

Observations.   Clinical observations written in the progress notes provide ongoing statements in areas such as affect, mental status, contact with reality, nonverbal behaviors, unusual behaviors or statements, contradictory statements, and so forth that provide additional documentation of the need for services. Examples of affective observations include psychomotor retardation/agitation and level of affect (e.g., normal, restricted, blunted, or flat). Other examples may be found on pages 2.122–2.125 in the Mental Status Exam section of the Diagnostic Assessment Report and in the Diagnostic Interview Form. Several publications are available describing such terminology (see Bibliography).

Assessment

The Assessment section of the progress notes is used for evaluation of the course of therapy based on the most recent data (results of the current session). Assessment may include the current session and a cumulative assessment of the therapy in general. The following areas may be evaluated:

The session.

The course of therapy.

Client cooperation/insight/motivation.

Client progress/setbacks.

Areas needing more work.

Impairments.

Treatment strategies.

How treatment plan objectives are being met.

Changes needed to say on target.

Plan

The Plan section of the progress notes is based on the Assessment. The question asked is, "Based on the current assessment, what will be done to most effectively meet the treatment plan objectives?" A confirmation and/or revision of the treatment plan, this section may include plans for:

Homework assignments.

Upcoming interventions.

The next session or series of sessions.

Treatment plan revisions in objectives or strategies.

Common Errors in Progress Notes

Form 27A illustrates several common errors.

Errors of Omission

1. No date (M/D/Y)

2. No stated objectives for the session. The content of the session should follow specific treatment plan objectives and be documented in the progress notes.

3. No signature of therapist. Initials are not sufficient.

4. No start and ending time. Notations such as "1 hr" are often not sufficient for documentation unless exact times are documented in a ledger or date book.

Errors of Commission. Each progress note statement is quite vague and does not validate any diagnosis or impairments.

5. "Did his homework."

   Although this statement may suggest client compliance, it does not provide information on the therapeutic effectiveness of the activity or suggest how it meets treatment plan objectives. Homework assignments should be documented concerning their therapeutic effectiveness and should be consistent with accepted procedures in the mental health field.

6. "Took test."

   Ongoing testing is certainly an effective means of documentation, but the specific test given and the results are needed to provide data for reference. It is possible to chart results of ongoing testing. A brief interpretation is also suggested.

7. "Talked about. . . . Went over. . . . Discussed. . . ."

   Statements such as these indicate to some degree the content of the session, but provide no indication of how the treatment plan is being followed or documented.

8. There should be no open spaces left where additional information could later be added to the progress notes. Lines should fill up this space to prevent fabricating information after the fact. When a therapist recalls information at a later date, it should be written as an addendum, rather than simply penciled in.

9. "Waive co-payment. . . ."

   Such procedures are illegal and constitute insurance fraud.

Saving Time in Progress Note Writing

Approximately 75 percent of the therapists surveyed by this author have indicated that they write progress notes after the session (see pages 5.11 and 5.12). They believe that if they took progress notes during the session they would not be able to attend to the client as well and that writing progress notes after the session helps to provide an overall picture of the session.

However, other therapists have stated that their progress note details and accuracy have increased when they started writing the notes during the session. They add that the transition often takes a few months. The form on page 5.13 entitled Progress Notes—Outline can be used during the transition from taking progress notes after the session to taking them during the session.

In some cases, writing progress notes during the session can increase rapport and empathy. When the therapist nonverbally portrays the message, "What you say is important, so I must write it down," progress note writing during the session can be both time-saving and therapeutic.

FORM 27
Sample Progress Notes

Two sample progress notes are included. The first, on page 5.11 is for an adult client named John Doe and is designed to document evidence of the course of therapy and follow the DAP guidelines discussed previously. The second, on page 5.12, is for a child. It follows the treatment plan from page 4.10.

FORM 28
Progress Notes—Outline

Form 28 provides structure and reminders to the therapist as to what areas of documentation are helpful in progress notes. Although the information contained in the progress notes is the same as previous examples, this form breaks down the DAP format into specific content areas. The form is not designed to model a particular type of treatment, but rather to provide evidence of on-target treatment for any therapeutic stance.

Some therapists using this form prefer to jot brief notes during the session to be used as reminders when they write the final copy of their progress notes. Others use this form as a final product. This form can also serve as a transition for therapists in the process of changing their procedure from writing progress notes after the session to writing them during the session.

A Progress Note—Outline form for Judy Doe's third session in therapy is provided as Form 28A. The DAP format is used, but the specific documentation needed for each section is addressed.

FORM 29
Group Therapy Progress Notes

Few group therapists have time to write separate and concise progress notes for an entire group. Some therapists have reported that they spend more time after the session writing progress notes than the time spent in the session. Others report that they use the same progress note for the entire session, noting contributions for each client. The latter practice poses ethics problems due to confidentiality being broken if any of the group members' files are released to an outside source.

The Group Therapy Progress Notes form on page 5.15 is designed to enable the therapist to take separate notes on each group member during the session. Information that is common to all group members (treatment plan objectives for the session) is listed under Group Topics Discussed. Twelve group behaviors are rated in the Group Behavior Ratings section. Over the course of group therapy these ratings can be assessed for various areas of progress. The remaining space on the form allows for Individual Contributions, which may be documented as the client speaks.

The group progress note form also includes a periodic summary that is helpful when progress notes are regularly forwarded to others such as parents, guardians, social workers, or group homes.

FORMS 30 and 30A
Third-Party Prior Authorization
Request for Continued Services

Many third-party payers initially approve fewer than three initial sessions for assessment and then request a prior authorization (PA) for continued services at regular intervals. Every third-party payer has its own form for requesting continued services. Therapists often complain of their requests usually being turned down, causing services to be quickly terminated due to lack of insurance coverage. As a result, cognitive dissonance persists. Often, the true issue is the therapist's lack of training in writing the PA request, rather than the third-party payer's refusal to continue services. Requesting a PA for services requires concise writing skills in which documenting medical necessity is essential.

The forms on pages 5.17 and 5.18 represent PAs from the file of Judy Doe. These samples represent a typical PA format. The first is completed vaguely and does not provide sufficient documentation of diagnosis, symptoms, impairments, therapeutic progress/setbacks, and so on. It is written in a manner suggesting that the client has improved significantly and does not need further services. If this were the case, further services should not be requested. But, if additional mental health services are medically necessary, the documentation provided in this form would be a disservice to the client.

Some therapists have noted that writing a PA request is a "Catch-22" situation. That is, if significant improvements are noted as in this form, the PA will be denied because goals apparently have been met sufficiently. On the other hand, if continued severe impairments are noted, it may appear that treatment is ineffective, so the PA will likewise be denied.

The form on page 5.18 provides specific examples of Judy Doe's progress in therapy and documents a continued need to work on other treatment plan goals. This one-page document attempts to summarize the entire course of treatment. The quantified examples are taken directly from the well-documented progress notes, rather than offering a nondocumented opinion at the time of writing the PA request.

FORM 31
Clinical Outcomes Questionnaire

The Clinical Outcomes Questionnaire (Form 31) provides a brief checklist for the client to fill out after treatment has been terminated. Some clinics mail it to the client with a self-addressed, stamped envelope at the time the termination letter is sent. It is designed to measure consumer satisfaction within a number of realms of services provided. It provides feedback to both the clinician and the therapist as to areas of strengths and weakness in a quantified manner. Agencies such as JCAHO may request that evidence is shown how the clinic attains and responds to the client feedback.

FORM 32
Chart Review

A Chart Review (Form 32) may take place any time during the course of therapy. The specific timing is a clinical policy. While some clinics randomly review a set number of charts after termination, others review every chart. Reviewing charts is a very time consuming and expensive process, but it is designed to increase the quality of care.

The Chart Review Form lists the most important aspects of the various areas of documentation including:

Background Information.

Diagnostic Information.

Treatment Plan.

Progress Notes.

Termination Procedures.

For comparative reasons there is a quantified score by which the reviewer can provide feedback to the therapist. The therapist's progress in documentation may then be monitored over time.

Form 27　Progress Notes

Client's name: _____　Session: _____　Date _____

Diagnosis: _____

Tx goals: _____　Therapist: _____

Time started: _____　Time finished: _____　Duration: _____

Next appointment:　Date: _____　Time: _____

Therapist's signature: _____

Form 27A   Progress Notes

Client's name: _____John_____   Date _____Monday_____

John was on time for his appointment. Did his homework. Took test. Talked about his homework. Went over marital relationship. Discussed events of week and how they relate to counseling. Was happy about talking to his uncle on the phone.

Went over homework and made plans. Worked on communication skills. Positive communication is important. Will come again.

(Note: waive co-payment if insurance pays their portion)

Therapist's signature: _____   Date: _____/_____/_____

Form 27B   Progress Notes—Adult

(Completed)

Client's name: _John Doe_   Session: _5_   Date _2/13/1999_

Diagnosis: _300.4 Dysthymia_

Tx goals: _Ego strength/Positive thoughts_   Therapist: _PS_

(D) *Completed homework assignment of identifying dysfunctional thoughts. Reviewed five positive qualities and five perceived negative characteristics from previous session. Several self-deprecating statements. Current BDI score = 29 (previous week = 32). Difficulties believing that he is capable of being happy. Describes self as being easily irritated and less capable than most other people. Fairly upset about continued spousal discord. Two divorce threats this week. Now sleeping in guest room; angry, frustrated, sad. States much guilt and remorse over his irritability, which he believes courses others to reject him. Charted progress of social contacts. Continues to meet current homework goals of one new social interaction per week. Describes affective level past week as sad about 50% of the time. (Charting indicates previous four weeks = 60–75% of time feeling sad.) Missed one day at work this week due to feelings of boredom/fatigue. **Sessions Topics: Ego strength.** Role-played speaking with assertiveness to spouse, employer, and in job interview. **Positive thoughts.** States no positive plan or goals for future. History of others making his decisions (parents, relatives, spouse). Identified three attainable short-term goals that he is interested in pursuing: 1) enrolling in community education course or seminar, 2) weekend trip, 3) volunteering at nursing home once per week.*

(A) *Increased focus on personal responsibility for behavioral/affective change and in self-direction. Viewing self more positively in past few weeks. Continued concerns with level of irritability and spousal discord. Progress in individual concerns, but low motivation in spousal issues and missing work. Compliant in homework assignments, but level of insight moderately low. Behavioral techniques seem most helpful.*

(P) *Homework: Implement one of three above listed short-term goals. Continue dysfunctional thought record. Client is considering spousal involvement in therapy in 3–4 weeks.*

Time started: _4:00 p.m._   Time finished: _4:51 p.m._   Duration: _51 minutes_

Next appointment: Date: _2/20/1999_   Time: _2:00 p.m._

Therapist's signature: _Phillip Schultz, MSW_

Form 27C   Progress Notes—Child

Client's name: _Johnny Rentschler_   Session: _3_   Date   _2/12/1999_

Diagnosis: _Adjustment reaction with depressed mood/conduct_

Tx goals: _Establish trust/Engage in play therapy_   Therapist: _SB_

(D) *1st session since assessment.* **Mother present.** *Began session with mother bringing in chart of 38 physical aggressions in past week directed toward people, and 12 incidents of property damage in the home. Major aggression toward sister after two attempts by Johnny to phone father who did not return phone calls. Mother further noted receiving two notes from teacher describing initiating fights in school. Possible suspension impending. Mother further notes that Johnny refused to go on family outing to visit friends in old neighborhood. Spent most of weekend in his room watching TV and playing video games. Refused to play with same-aged cousin, whom mother invited to home. Loaned mother copy of "Parental Consistency Manuel."* **Mother not present.** *Asked Johnny to draw portrait of his family. Quickly drew colorful picture with all family members in a boxing ring. Everyone in the family except Johnny had hands tied. Mother was kicking at him. He was the only one able to fight with his hands. (See drawing dated 2/12/1995.) Note father's placement on other side of ropes in opposite corner. When invited to discuss the drawing, Johnny stated that dad is far away and can't be reached because his mother is in the way and his sister is on his mother's side. He further noted that his mother and sister can not hurt him, like his father did before, or they will also get in trouble.*

(A) *Much blaming of mother for father's absence. Resentment and anger toward family, whom he views as responsible for father now being unapproachable. Deep sense of loss. Seems to view family as choosing sides against him, but they are unable to control his behaviors without getting into legal trouble. Views situation as having few available options to cope with perceived rejection. Insight into source of anger slowly developing. Views control as rewarding.*

(P) *"Functional Analysis of Behavior" form to be completed by mother. Continue with drawings in which he draws/discusses changes he desires and related affect. Continue nonthreatening enactments of family dynamics. Continue rapport/trust building.*

Time started: _2:00 p.m._   Time finished: _2:49 p.m._   Duration: _49 minutes_

Next appointment: Date: _2/19/1999_   Time: _2:00 p.m._

Therapist's signature: _Sharon Bell, PhD_

Form 28   Progress Notes—Outline

Name: _____   Therapist: _____   Date: _____

Axis I: _____   Axis II: _____

Session goals/objectives: _____

Data

Homework from past session(s): _____
_____
_____
_____

Functional impairment (e.g., emotional, social, occupational, legal, behavioral; include degree, frequency, duration): _____
_____
_____
_____

Current issues/topics/stressors: _____
_____
_____
_____

Interventions: _____
_____
_____
_____

Observations: _____
_____
_____
_____

Other: _____
_____

Assessment (Progress/Impairment/Effectiveness of interventions): _____
_____
_____
_____

Plan (Homework, objectives next session, changes, testing): _____
_____
_____
_____

Time started: _____   Time finished: _____   Duration: _____

Next appointment: Date: _____   Time: _____

Therapist's signature: _____

5.13

Form 28A Progress Notes—Outline

(Completed)

Name: _Judy Doe_   Therapist: _DLB_   Date: _3/22/1999_

Axis I: _296.32 Major depression, recurrent, moderate_   Axis II: _Deferred_

Session goals/objectives: _Hopelessness: Restructure dysfuntional thoughts_

Data

Homework from past session(s): _Completed homework assigned; identified uncomfortable situations leading to depression and hopelessness._

Functional impairment (e.g., emotional, social, occupational, legal, behavioral; include degree, frequency, duration): _Poor appetite. One meal/day, increasing fatigue. Little social support at home. Very little time spent with spouse or children this week, no sexual desire in 2–3 months. Continues usually feeling depressed, guilty, and angry. Low motivation to teach students. Missed one day of work: no energy, motivation._

Current issues/topics/stressors: _Angry because both students and her family will not become motivated to her expectations. States it is her fault. Increasing anger toward spouse due to not supporting her parenting decisions. Much self-blame for others not performing. Notes guilt feelings if she does not chauffeur her children like "other parents."_

Interventions: _Discussed and identified 3 dysfunctional thoughts and their respective situations and associated feelings. Vented feelings of anger toward her family and students via empty chair. Confronted defensiveness about accepting others' negative treatment toward her as acceptable._

Observations: _Poor eye contact, slumped posture, closed body position, monotonous speech, restricted affect. less psychomotor agitation during periods of insight._

Other: _SUDs level of depression = 88. Baseline = 95. See Subjective Units of Distress (SUDs) charts._

Assessment (Progress/Impairment/Effectiveness of interventions): _Increased insight into relationship between "shoulds" from parents and current affective/behavioral concerns. Differentiating thoughts and feelings is quite helpful. Difficulties accepting that she is angry at others._

Plan (Homework, objectives next session, changes, testing): _Dysfunctional thought record as homework. Read "Escape form Co-dependency." Next session: Pleasurable activities._

Time started: _1:00 p.m._   Time finished: _1:52 p.m._   Duration: _52 minutes_

Next appointment: Date: _3/29/1999_   Time: _1:00 p.m._

Therapist's signature: _Darlene L. Benton, PhD_

5.14

Form 29   Group Therapy Progress Notes

Client: _____   Group: _____   Date: _____

Agenda: Group Topics Discussed

_____

_____

Group Behavior Ratings

	Low		Medium		High
Seemed interested in the group	(__)	(__)	(__)	(__)	(__)
Initiated positive interactions	(__)	(__)	(__)	(__)	(__)
Shared emotions	(__)	(__)	(__)	(__)	(__)
Helpful to others	(__)	(__)	(__)	(__)	(__)
Focused on group tasks	(__)	(__)	(__)	(__)	(__)
Disclosed information about self	(__)	(__)	(__)	(__)	(__)
Understood group topics	(__)	(__)	(__)	(__)	(__)
Participated in group exercises	(__)	(__)	(__)	(__)	(__)
Showed listening skills/empathy	(__)	(__)	(__)	(__)	(__)
Offered opinions/suggestions/feedback	(__)	(__)	(__)	(__)	(__)
Seemed to benefit from the session	(__)	(__)	(__)	(__)	(__)
Treatment considerations addressed	(__)	(__)	(__)	(__)	(__)

Monthly Evaluation (fill out last group of each month)

Topic	Progress		
	Low	Medium	High
Participation	(__)	(__)	(__)
Discusses issues	(__)	(__)	(__)
Insight	(__)	(__)	(__)
Motivation	(__)	(__)	(__)
Emotional expression	(__)	(__)	(__)
Stays on task	(__)	(__)	(__)
Objectives being met	(__)	(__)	(__)

Suggestions

___ Individual counseling   ___ Evaluation for meds   ___Other: _____

Individual Contributions This Session

_____

_____

_____

_____

_____

_____

_____

Time started: _____   Time finished: _____   Duration: _____

Therapist: _____

Cotherapist: _____

Client: __Pat Anderson_____   Group: __Grief___   Date: __3/10/1999__

Agenda: Group Topics Discussed

__Session 6 Agenda: 1) Expressing grief; 2) Coping with changes_____

__Next week: 1) Saying "good-bye"; 2) Future plans_____

Group Behavior Ratings

	Low		Medium		High
Seemed interested in the group	( )	( )	(X)	( )	( )
Initiated positive interactions	( )	(X)	( )	( )	( )
Shared emotions	( )	( )	(X)	( )	( )
Helpful to others	( )	(X)	( )	( )	( )
Focused on group tasks	( )	( )	(X)	( )	( )
Disclosed information about self	( )	( )	(X)	( )	( )
Understood group topics	( )	( )	(X)	( )	( )
Participated in group exercises	( )	( )	(X)	( )	( )
Showed listening skills/empathy	( )	( )	( )	(X)	( )
Offered opinions/suggestions/feedback	( )	( )	(X)	( )	( )
Seemed to benefit from the session	( )	( )	(X)	( )	( )
Treatment considerations addressed	( )	( )	( )	(X)	( )

Monthly Evaluation (fill out last group of each month)

Topic	Progress		
	Low	Medium	High
Participation	( )	( )	( )
Discusses issues	( )	( )	( )
Insight	( )	( )	( )
Motivation	( )	( )	( )
Emotional expression	( )	( )	( )
Stays on task	( )	( )	( )
Objectives being met	( )	( )	( )

Suggestions

___ Individual counseling   ___ Evaluation for meds   ___Other: _____

Individual Contributions This Session

__Pat was 10 minutes late for the session. Did not seem interested in discussing how he is currently__

__handling death of his parents in auto accident. During a group exercise he disclosed that he cries__

__every night before going to sleep and wakes up 3–4 times per night thinking that his parents are__

__in the room. Has not been doing most of his homework in college, but reports slight increases in__

__homework compliance in past 2 weeks. Generally quiet (but seemed to listen/empathize) when__

__other people discussed their coping strategies dealing with loss of loved ones.__

Time started: __7:00 p.m.__   Time finished: __8:30 p.m.__   Duration: __90 minutes__

Therapist: ____Clara Nielson, LCSW_____

Cotherapist: ____Fred Jorbell, MA_____

Form 30   Third-Party Prior Authorization Request

(Poor Example)

(Provider information)   _____Judy Doe_____   (Patient information)

ICD   or   DSM

Primary diagnosis: ___Depression_____   _____   _____

Secondary diagnosis: _____   _____   _____

Initial service date: _____   Dates requested: From: ___9/7/1999___ through ___9/7/2000___

Hours used: ___10___   Type(s) of service(s) and hours requested: ___Counseling_____

Describe mental health history and current mental status with documentation of diagnosis.

Has been in counseling several times in life. History of marital issues. Mental status indicates
need for counseling. Continues to meet diagnostic criteria for depression.

Current stressors and functional impairment. Include psychological impairment as a result of this disorder.

Marital conflict. Does not like her job. Psychological impairment due to issues relating to people
who upset her.

Rating of patient's progress in therapy.   Poor   1   2   3   4   5   (6)   High

Documentation of progress.

Client is doing very well in therapy. Able to discuss issues which are difficult to discuss with
spouse.

Rating of patient's cooperation.   Poor   1   2   3   4   5   (6)   High

Describe willingness to follow treatment plan.

Always willing to participate in discussions in treatment sessions.

Current medications. Therapist's contact with primary care physician.

None needed. No referrals necessary.

Discharge plans. Include objective criteria.

Client agrees to remain in treatment until marriage issues are resolved.

Signature: _____   Date: ____/____/_____

Form 30A   Third-Party Prior Authorization Request

(Provider information)   _Judy Doe_   (Patient information)

		ICD	or	DSM

Primary diagnosis: _Major depression, moderate, recurrent_ _____ _296.32_

Secondary diagnosis: _____ _____ _____

Initial service date: _1/27/1999_   Dates requested: From: _3/29/1999_ through _12/7/1999_

Hours used: _6_   Type(s) of service(s) and hours requested: _Individual psychotherapy—15 hrs_

Describe mental health history and current mental status with documentation of diagnosis. *Hx of mental health; Dx of Major depression since 1976. Three in-patient hospitalizations due to suicidal threats/attempts. Other Tx since 1976 includes 6 months of group therapy. 3 attempts of individual therapy (each <10 sessions), and ongoing med management. Appears depressed/psychomotor retardation/fatigued/low motivation/weight loss of 20# in past 3 months/sleeping 12 hrs/day. Oriented x3. No evidence of thought disorder. Family Hx of depression (Dx, Tx, hospital).*

Current stressors and functional impairment. Include psychological impairment as a result of this disorder. *Unemployment due to being fired from job (excessive absences). Few/no friends. Divorced six weeks ago. No immediate family in geographic area. Excessive social withdrawal (spends most of day in home, has refused invitations of former friends to attend social functions). Sad most of time, low motivation. Notes difficulty concentrating when filling out job applications.*

Rating of patient's progress in therapy.   Poor   1   2   3   (4)   5   6   High

Documentation of progress. *Documentation of Progress. Client notes that she wants to change her outlook on life. Has successfully accomplished two of four homework assignments involving initiating social interactions, time management, and involving herself in pleasurable activities. Increase insight regarding dysfunctional thought processes. Gains in ability to make positive self-statements. Continued concerns in social withdrawal and low motivation. Presently focusing on assertiveness skills.*

Rating of patient's cooperation.   Poor   1   2   3   4   5   (6)   High

Describe willingness to follow treatment plan. *High degree of cooperation, but perhaps due to overdependence. Generally agrees with interpretative statements, but in a seemingly dependent manner. Recent attempts at role playing assertiveness have been facilitative.*

Current medications. Therapist's contact with primary care physician. *Current meds include Prozac from MD. Noted compliance. Collaborative treatment with MD. Shared Tx plans. Summary of sessions exchanged monthly.*

Discharge plans. Include objective criteria. *See attached Tx plan for specific goals to be accomplished during course of therapy including: Consistent BDI score of < 15. 8 hrs of sleep per night/5 job applications per week until job is acquired/acceptable subjective rating of level of impairment due to depression. Tapering off of sessions. Current weekly visits will become every other week as of session 10.*

Signature/Professional title: _Darlene L. Benton, PhD, Clinical Psychologist_ Date: _3_ / _15_ / _1999_

Form 31   Clinical Outcomes Questionnaire

Name (optional): _____   Therapist: _____   Date: _____

No. of sessions attended: _____   Purpose of counseling (e.g., depression, anxiety): _____

Type(s) of counseling: ___ Individual ___ Group ___ Family ___ Marriage ___ Other: _____

Please circle the response under each statement which most closely indicates your level of agreement or disagreement.

Highly Disagree 1	Moderately Disagree 2	Slightly Disagree 3	Neutral 4	Slightly Agree 5	Moderately Agree 6	Highly Agree 7

"I was given choices about my treatment."

| 1 | 2 | 3 | 4 | 5 | 6 | 7 |

"The therapist explained the benefits and risks of therapy to me."

| 1 | 2 | 3 | 4 | 5 | 6 | 7 |

"I was treated with respect and dignity by the therapist."

| 1 | 2 | 3 | 4 | 5 | 6 | 7 |

"The therapist listened to my concerns."

| 1 | 2 | 3 | 4 | 5 | 6 | 7 |

"The treatment plan was clearly explained to me."

| 1 | 2 | 3 | 4 | 5 | 6 | 7 |

"Services were performed in a time-efficient manner."

| 1 | 2 | 3 | 4 | 5 | 6 | 7 |

"The clinic's policies were clearly explained to me."

| 1 | 2 | 3 | 4 | 5 | 6 | 7 |

"The counseling was directed toward helping my problem areas."

| 1 | 2 | 3 | 4 | 5 | 6 | 7 |

"I was satisfied with the counseling I received."

| 1 | 2 | 3 | 4 | 5 | 6 | 7 |

"The services I received were helpful."

| 1 | 2 | 3 | 4 | 5 | 6 | 7 |

"I would return to the therapist for services in the future if needed."

| 1 | 2 | 3 | 4 | 5 | 6 | 7 |

Comments: _____

_____

_____

_____

Form 32   Chart Review

Client's name: _____   ID#: _____   Date of review: _____

Therapist: _____   Reviewed by: _____

Check the appropriate column.   Key :   0 = No   1 = Somewhat   2 = Yes

Background Information

0   1   2

___ ___ ___   Do the signs and symptoms coincide with and clarify the presenting problem?

___ ___ ___   Are the signs and symptoms clearly documented?

___ ___ ___   Does the history indicate stressors and/or circumstances demonstrating a need for services?

___ ___ ___   Is a relevant medical history included?

___ ___ ___   Does the biopsychosocial information include relevant areas of strength/weakness?

___ ___ ___   Does the biopsychosocial information depict cultural/spiritual concerns?

_____/12 total

Remarks: _____

_____

Diagnostic Information

0   1   2

___ ___ ___   Is the diagnosis concordant with observations?

___ ___ ___   Is the diagnosis clearly validated by DSM symptoms criteria?

___ ___ ___   Are specific impairments due to the diagnosis listed?

_____/6 total

Remarks: _____

_____

Treatment Plan

0   1   2

___ ___ ___   Are the treatment plan problem areas concordant with the diagnosis?

___ ___ ___   Does the treatment plan outline the type and number of sessions needed?

___ ___ ___   Are the goals and objectives realistic or attainable within the estimated time frames?

___ ___ ___   Are the specific objectives measurable or observable?

___ ___ ___   Are the treatment strategies appropriate?

_____/10 total

Remarks: _____

_____

Progress Notes

   0   1   2

___ ___ ___   Do the progress notes reflect the diagnosis and treatment plan?

___ ___ ___   Do the progress notes include specific data supporting continued need for services?

___ ___ ___   Are treatment strategies (including meds) clearly identified and assessed?

___ ___ ___   Are progress and setbacks of each session assessed?

___ ___ ___   Is a specific plan for each subsequent session noted?

___ ___ ___   If there are health/safety issues, are they addressed?

_____/12 total

Remarks: _____

_____

Termination Procedures

   0   1   2

___ ___ ___   Is the reason for termination noted?

___ ___ ___   Is the progress toward each goal documented?

___ ___ ___   Is the timing of termination appropriate?

___ ___ ___   Was a termination letter sent?

___ ___ ___   Is a 5 Axis discharge diagnosis included?

_____/10 total

Remarks: _____

_____

Total score: _____ 50

Areas of concern: _____

Areas of strength: _____

Reviewers Comments/Suggestions: _____

_____

_____

_____

_____

_____

_____

_____

_____

_____

Reviewer's signature: _____   Date: ____/____/_____

Therapist's signature: _____   Date: ____/____/_____

Chapter 6

Relationship Counseling
Forms and Procedures

FORMS 33 and 34
Marital and Couple's
Information Forms

Although similar in format, the Marital Information Form (Form 33) and the Couple's Information Form (Form 34) differ in the choice of wording in the questions. The marital form refers to the "spouse" and to concerns in the "marriage," while the couple's form addresses the "relationship." Experience has taught that using the same form for married and nonmarried clients may cause complaints.

Each form provides valuable information regarding strengths and weaknesses in the relationship. Each partner's point of view and perspective on their partner's point of view are assessed to help increase clients' understanding of each other. The forms end with a written consent for the therapist to discuss each other's responses.

FORM 35
Analysis of Target Behaviors

The Analysis of Target Behaviors Form (Form 35) is designed to increase communication by breaking down negative behaviors in the relationship into causal and affective components. In this homework assignment, clients are asked to indicate how they believe their partner felt after each disagreement and also to list positive alternative actions that could have been taken in place of the negative behavior.

FORM 36
Cooperating in Child Rearing

Form 36 begins on page 6.18 with a narrative regarding various reasons why parents' diverse backgrounds and personalities may make it difficult for them to agree on child-rearing practices, followed by a discussion regarding various ways in which the parents may have been raised and how the disparity could cause conflict with the partner's view of parenting. In a homework assignment, each partner is asked to provide information regarding his or her upbringing compared to the partner's. Understanding and compromises are subsequently suggested.

FORM 37
Sharing Your Feelings

In Form 37, couples are asked to complete sentences in the presence of their partner in which opportunities are given to discuss their commitment to the relationship. This exercise has been helpful for individuals who have difficulties expressing their feelings.

Form 33   Marital Information Form

1) Name: _____ 2) Age: _____ 3) Date: _____

4) Address: _____ City: _____ State: _____ Zip: _____

5) Briefly, what is your main purpose in coming to marital therapy? _____

_____

Instructions: To assist us in helping you, please fill out this form as fully and openly as possible. Your answers will help plan a course of marital therapy that is most suitable for you and your spouse. Do not exchange this information with your spouse.

Several of your answers on this form may be shared later with your spouse during joint therapy sessions if you give us permission to share this information. For this reason you are advised to respond honestly and carefully to each item. If certain questions do not apply to you or you do not want to share this information, please leave them blank.

6) Is this your first marriage? ___ Yes   ___ No
   If No, which marriage is it for you?   2   3   4   5+

7) How long have you and your present spouse been married? _____

8) Are you and your spouse presently living together? ___ Yes   ___ No
   If No, why not? _____

9) How many times have you and your spouse separated? _____

10) Fill out the following information for each child of whom the natural parent is both you and your partner, children from previous relationships, and adopted children.

   *"Whose child?" answering options: B = Both of ours, natural child

   BA = Both of ours, adopted (or taken on)

   M = My natural child

   MA = My child, adopted (or taken on)

   S = Spouse's natural child

   SA = Spouse's child, adopted (or taken on)

	Child's name	Age	Sex	*Whose child?	Lives with you and spouse?
1)	_____	_____	F M	_____	___ Yes ___ No
2)	_____	_____	F M	_____	___ Yes ___ No
3)	_____	_____	F M	_____	___ Yes ___ No
4)	_____	_____	F M	_____	___ Yes ___ No
5)	_____	_____	F M	_____	___ Yes ___ No
6)	_____	_____	F M	_____	___ Yes ___ No
7)	_____	_____	F M	_____	___ Yes ___ No
8)	_____	_____	F M	_____	___ Yes ___ No

11) List five qualities that initially attracted you to
    your spouse:

Does your spouse still possess this trait?

1) _____ ___ Yes ___ No
2) _____ ___ Yes ___ No
3) _____ ___ Yes ___ No
4) _____ ___ Yes ___ No
5) _____ ___ Yes ___ No

12) List four negative concerns that you initially
    had in the relationship:

Does your spouse still possess this trait?

1) _____ ___ Yes ___ No
2) _____ ___ Yes ___ No
3) _____ ___ Yes ___ No
4) _____ ___ Yes ___ No

13) List five present positive attributes of
    your spouse:

Do you often praise your spouse for this trait?

1) _____ ___ Yes ___ No
2) _____ ___ Yes ___ No
3) _____ ___ Yes ___ No
4) _____ ___ Yes ___ No
5) _____ ___ Yes ___ No

14) List five present negative attributes of
    your spouse:

Do you nag your spouse about this trait?

1) _____ ___ Yes ___ No
2) _____ ___ Yes ___ No
3) _____ ___ Yes ___ No
4) _____ ___ Yes ___ No
5) _____ ___ Yes ___ No

15) List five things you do (or could do) to make
    the marriage more fulfilling for your spouse:

Do you often implement this behavior?

1) _____ ___ Yes ___ No
2) _____ ___ Yes ___ No
3) _____ ___ Yes ___ No
4) _____ ___ Yes ___ No
5) _____ ___ Yes ___ No

16) List five things that your spouse does (or could do)
    to make the marriage more fulfilling for you:

Does your spouse often implement this behavior?

1) _____ ___ Yes ___ No
2) _____ ___ Yes ___ No
3) _____ ___ Yes ___ No
4) _____ ___ Yes ___ No
5) _____ ___ Yes ___ No

17) List five expectations or dreams you had about marriage before you married your spouse:

Has this been fulfilled?

1) _____ ___ Yes ___ No
2) _____ ___ Yes ___ No
3) _____ ___ Yes ___ No
4) _____ ___ Yes ___ No
5) _____ ___ Yes ___ No

18) On a scale of 1 to 5 rate the following items as they pertain to:

1) The present state of the marriage
2) Your need or desire for it
3) Your spouse's need or desire for it

Circle the Appropriate Response for Each

	Present state of the marriage	Your need or desire	Spouse's need or desire
	Poor Great	Low High	Low High
1) Affection	1 2 3 4 5	1 2 3 4 5	1 2 3 4 5
2) Childrearing rules	1 2 3 4 5	1 2 3 4 5	1 2 3 4 5
3) Commitment together	1 2 3 4 5	1 2 3 4 5	1 2 3 4 5
4) Communication	1 2 3 4 5	1 2 3 4 5	1 2 3 4 5
5) Emotional closeness	1 2 3 4 5	1 2 3 4 5	1 2 3 4 5
6) Financial security	1 2 3 4 5	1 2 3 4 5	1 2 3 4 5
7) Honesty	1 2 3 4 5	1 2 3 4 5	1 2 3 4 5
8) Housework sharing	1 2 3 4 5	1 2 3 4 5	1 2 3 4 5
9) Love	1 2 3 4 5	1 2 3 4 5	1 2 3 4 5
10) Physical attraction	1 2 3 4 5	1 2 3 4 5	1 2 3 4 5
11) Religious commitment	1 2 3 4 5	1 2 3 4 5	1 2 3 4 5
12) Respect	1 2 3 4 5	1 2 3 4 5	1 2 3 4 5
13) Sexual fulfillment	1 2 3 4 5	1 2 3 4 5	1 2 3 4 5
14) Social life together	1 2 3 4 5	1 2 3 4 5	1 2 3 4 5
15) Time together	1 2 3 4 5	1 2 3 4 5	1 2 3 4 5
16) Trust	1 2 3 4 5	1 2 3 4 5	1 2 3 4 5
Other (specify)			
17) _____	1 2 3 4 5	1 2 3 4 5	1 2 3 4 5
18) _____	1 2 3 4 5	1 2 3 4 5	1 2 3 4 5
19) _____	1 2 3 4 5	1 2 3 4 5	1 2 3 4 5
20) _____	1 2 3 4 5	1 2 3 4 5	1 2 3 4 5

19) Which partner spends more time conducting the following activities?

Circle the Appropriate Response for Each

(M = Me   S = Spouse   E = Equal time)

		Is this equitable (fair)?	Comments
1) Auto repairs	M S E	___ Yes ___ No	_____
2) Child care	M S E	___ Yes ___ No	_____
3) Child discipline	M S E	___ Yes ___ No	_____
4) Cleaning bathrooms	M S E	___ Yes ___ No	_____
5) Cooking	M S E	___ Yes ___ No	_____
6) Employment	M S E	___ Yes ___ No	_____
7) Grocery shopping	M S E	___ Yes ___ No	_____

8) House cleaning	M	S	E	___ Yes	___ No	_____
9) Inside repairs	M	S	E	___ Yes	___ No	_____
10) Laundry	M	S	E	___ Yes	___ No	_____
11) Making bed	M	S	E	___ Yes	___ No	_____
12) Outside repairs	M	S	E	___ Yes	___ No	_____
13) Recreational events	M	S	E	___ Yes	___ No	_____
14) Social activities	M	S	E	___ Yes	___ No	_____
15) Sweeping kitchen	M	S	E	___ Yes	___ No	_____
16) Taking out garbage	M	S	E	___ Yes	___ No	_____
17) Washing dishes	M	S	E	___ Yes	___ No	_____
18) Yard work	M	S	E	___ Yes	___ No	_____
19) Other: _____	M	S	E	___ Yes	___ No	_____
20) Other: _____	M	S	E	___ Yes	___ No	_____

20) If some of the following behaviors take place only during MILD arguments circle an "M" in the appropriate blanks. If they take place only during SEVERE arguments, circle an "S." If they take place during ALL arguments circle an "A." Fill this out for you and you impression of your spouse. If certain behaviors do not take place, leave them blank.

Circle the Appropriate Response for Each

(M = Mild arguments only   S = Severe arguments only   A = All arguments)

Behavior	By me			By spouse			Should this change?	
1) Apologize	M	S	A	M	S	A	___ Yes	___ No
2) Become silent	M	S	A	M	S	A	___ Yes	___ No
3) Bring up the past	M	S	A	M	S	A	___ Yes	___ No
4) Criticize	M	S	A	M	S	A	___ Yes	___ No
5) Cruel accusations	M	S	A	M	S	A	___ Yes	___ No
6) Cry	M	S	A	M	S	A	___ Yes	___ No
7) Destroy property	M	S	A	M	S	A	___ Yes	___ No
8) Leave the house	M	S	A	M	S	A	___ Yes	___ No
9) Make peace	M	S	A	M	S	A	___ Yes	___ No
10) Moodiness	M	S	A	M	S	A	___ Yes	___ No
11) Not listen	M	S	A	M	S	A	___ Yes	___ No
12) Physical abuse	M	S	A	M	S	A	___ Yes	___ No
13) Physical threats	M	S	A	M	S	A	___ Yes	___ No
14) Sarcasm	M	S	A	M	S	A	___ Yes	___ No
15) Scream	M	S	A	M	S	A	___ Yes	___ No
16) Slam doors	M	S	A	M	S	A	___ Yes	___ No
17) Speak irrationally	M	S	A	M	S	A	___ Yes	___ No
18) Speak rationally	M	S	A	M	S	A	___ Yes	___ No
19) Sulk	M	S	A	M	S	A	___ Yes	___ No
20) Swear	M	S	A	M	S	A	___ Yes	___ No
21) Threaten divorce	M	S	A	M	S	A	___ Yes	___ No
22) Threaten to take kids	M	S	A	M	S	A	___ Yes	___ No
23) Throw things	M	S	A	M	S	A	___ Yes	___ No
24) Verbal abuse	M	S	A	M	S	A	___ Yes	___ No
25) Yell	M	S	A	M	S	A	___ Yes	___ No
26) _____	M	S	A	M	S	A	___ Yes	___ No
27) _____	M	S	A	M	S	A	___ Yes	___ No
28) _____	M	S	A	M	S	A	___ Yes	___ No

21) How often do you have: Mild arguments? _____

                                                 Severe arguments? _____

22) When a MILD argument is over how do you usually feel?

Check Appropriate Responses

___ Angry   ___ Lonely
___ Anxious   ___ Nauseous
___ Childish   ___ Numb
___ Defeated   ___ Regretful
___ Depressed   ___ Relieved
___ Guilty   ___ Stupid
___ Happy   ___ Victimized
___ Hopeless   ___ Worthless
___ Irritable

23) When a SEVERE argument is over how do you usually feel?

Check Appropriate Responses

___ Angry   ___ Lonely
___ Anxious   ___ Nauseous
___ Childish   ___ Numb
___ Defeated   ___ Regretful
___ Depressed   ___ Relieved
___ Guilty   ___ Stupid
___ Happy   ___ Victimized
___ Hopeless   ___ Worthless
___ Irritable

24) Which of the following issues or behaviors of you and/or your spouse may be attributable to your marital or personal conflicts? If an item does not apply, leave it blank.

Circle the Appropriate Responses

(M = My behavior   S = Spouse's behavior   B = Both)

Alcohol consumption	M	S	B	Perfectionist	M	S	B
Childishness	M	S	B	Possessive	M	S	B
Controlling	M	S	B	Spends too much	M	S	B
Defensiveness	M	S	B	Steals	M	S	B
Degrading	M	S	B	Stubbornness	M	S	B
Demanding	M	S	B	Uncaring	M	S	B
Drugs	M	S	B	Unstable	M	S	B
Flirts with others	M	S	B	Violent	M	S	B
Gambling	M	S	B	Withdrawn	M	S	B
Irresponsibility	M	S	B	Works too much	M	S	B
Lies	M	S	B	Other (specify)			
Past marriage(s)	M	S	B	_____	M	S	B
Other's advice	M	S	B	_____	M	S	B
Outside interests	M	S	B	_____	M	S	B
Past failures	M	S	B	_____	M	S	B

25) In the remaining space please provide additional information that would be helpful:

_____

_____

_____

I, _____ , hereby give my permission for this clinic to share the information that I provide on this form to _____ (spouse) when it is deemed appropriate by an agreement between me, my spouse, and out therapist. This sharing of information may take place only during a joint counseling session (both spouses present).

Client's signature: _____   Date: ____/____/_____

PLEASE RETURN THIS AND OTHER ASSESSMENT MATERIALS TO THIS OFFICE AT LEAST TWO DAYS BEFORE YOUR NEXT APPOINTMENT.

1) Name: _____   2) Age: _____   3) Date: _____

4) Address: _____   City: _____   State: _____   Zip: _____

5) Briefly, what is your main purpose in coming to couple's counseling? _____

_____

Instructions: To assist us in helping you, please fill out this form as fully and openly as possible. Your answers will help plan a course of couple's therapy that is most suitable for you and your partner. Do not exchange this information with your partner at this time.

Several of your answers on this form may be shared later with your partner during joint therapy sessions if you give us permission to share this information. For this reason you are advised to respond honestly and carefully to each item. If certain questions do not apply to you or you do not want to share this information, please leave them blank.

6) Have you been married before? ___ Yes   ___ No

   If Yes, how many previous marriages have you had?   1   2   3   4   5+

7) How long have you and your partner been in this relationship? _____

8) Are you and your partner presently living together? ___ Yes   ___ No

9) Are you and your partner engaged to be married? ___ Yes When? _____   ___ No

10) Fill out the following information for each child of whom the natural parent is both you and your partner, children from previous relationships, and adopted children.

   ___ Neither of us has children (go to next page)   ___ One or each of us has children (continue)

   *"Whose child?" answering options: B = Both of ours, natural child

   BA = Both of ours, adopted (or taken on)

   M = My natural child

   MA = My child, adopted (or taken on)

   P = Partner's natural child

   PA = Partner's child, adopted (or taken on)

	Child's name	Age	Sex	*Whose child?	Lives with whom?
1)	_____	_____	F M	_____	___ Yes ___ No
2)	_____	_____	F M	_____	___ Yes ___ No
3)	_____	_____	F M	_____	___ Yes ___ No
4)	_____	_____	F M	_____	___ Yes ___ No
5)	_____	_____	F M	_____	___ Yes ___ No
6)	_____	_____	F M	_____	___ Yes ___ No
7)	_____	_____	F M	_____	___ Yes ___ No
8)	_____	_____	F M	_____	___ Yes ___ No

11) List five qualities that initially attracted you to
    your partner:

    1) _____

    2) _____

    3) _____

    4) _____

    5) _____

Does your partner still
possess this trait?

___ Yes   ___ No

___ Yes   ___ No

___ Yes   ___ No

___ Yes   ___ No

___ Yes   ___ No

12) List four negative concerns that you initially
    had in the relationship:

    1) _____

    2) _____

    3) _____

    4) _____

Does your partner still
possess this trait?

___ Yes   ___ No

___ Yes   ___ No

___ Yes   ___ No

___ Yes   ___ No

13) List five present positive attributes of
    your partner:

    1) _____

    2) _____

    3) _____

    4) _____

    5) _____

Do you often praise your
partner for this trait?

___ Yes   ___ No

___ Yes   ___ No

___ Yes   ___ No

___ Yes   ___ No

___ Yes   ___ No

14) List five present negative attributes of
    your partner:

    1) _____

    2) _____

    3) _____

    4) _____

    5) _____

Do you nag your partner
about this trait?

___ Yes   ___ No

___ Yes   ___ No

___ Yes   ___ No

___ Yes   ___ No

___ Yes   ___ No

15) List five things you do (or could do) to make
    the marriage more fulfilling for your partner:

    1) _____

    2) _____

    3) _____

    4) _____

    5) _____

Do you often implement
this behavior?

___ Yes   ___ No

___ Yes   ___ No

___ Yes   ___ No

___ Yes   ___ No

___ Yes   ___ No

16) List five things that your partner does (or could do)
    to make the marriage more fulfilling for you:

    1) _____

    2) _____

    3) _____

    4) _____

    5) _____

Does your partner often
implement this behavior?

___ Yes   ___ No

___ Yes   ___ No

___ Yes   ___ No

___ Yes   ___ No

___ Yes   ___ No

17) List five expectations or dreams you had about relationships before you met your partner:

                                                     Has this been fulfilled?

1) _____ ___ Yes ___ No

2) _____ ___ Yes ___ No

3) _____ ___ Yes ___ No

4) _____ ___ Yes ___ No

5) _____ ___ Yes ___ No

18) On a scale of 1 to 5 rate the following items as they pertain to:

1) The present state of the relationship

2) Your need or desire for it

3) Your partner's need or desire for it

Circle the Appropriate Response for Each (If not applicable, leave blank.)

	Present state of the relationship	Your need or desire	Partner's need or desire
	Poor — Great	Low — High	Low — High
1) Affection	1 2 3 4 5	1 2 3 4 5	1 2 3 4 5
2) Childrearing rules	1 2 3 4 5	1 2 3 4 5	1 2 3 4 5
3) Commitment together	1 2 3 4 5	1 2 3 4 5	1 2 3 4 5
4) Communication	1 2 3 4 5	1 2 3 4 5	1 2 3 4 5
5) Emotional closeness	1 2 3 4 5	1 2 3 4 5	1 2 3 4 5
6) Financial security	1 2 3 4 5	1 2 3 4 5	1 2 3 4 5
7) Honesty	1 2 3 4 5	1 2 3 4 5	1 2 3 4 5
8) Housework sharing	1 2 3 4 5	1 2 3 4 5	1 2 3 4 5
9) Love	1 2 3 4 5	1 2 3 4 5	1 2 3 4 5
10) Physical attraction	1 2 3 4 5	1 2 3 4 5	1 2 3 4 5
11) Religious commitment	1 2 3 4 5	1 2 3 4 5	1 2 3 4 5
12) Respect	1 2 3 4 5	1 2 3 4 5	1 2 3 4 5
13) Sexual fulfillment	1 2 3 4 5	1 2 3 4 5	1 2 3 4 5
14) Social life together	1 2 3 4 5	1 2 3 4 5	1 2 3 4 5
15) Time together	1 2 3 4 5	1 2 3 4 5	1 2 3 4 5
16) Trust	1 2 3 4 5	1 2 3 4 5	1 2 3 4 5
Other (specify)			
17) _____	1 2 3 4 5	1 2 3 4 5	1 2 3 4 5
18) _____	1 2 3 4 5	1 2 3 4 5	1 2 3 4 5
19) _____	1 2 3 4 5	1 2 3 4 5	1 2 3 4 5
20) _____	1 2 3 4 5	1 2 3 4 5	1 2 3 4 5

19) For couples living together. Which partner spends more time conducting the following activities?

Circle the Appropriate Response for Each (If not applicable, leave blank.)

(M = Me   P = Partner   E = Equal time)

		Is this equitable (fair)?	Comments
1) Auto repairs	M P E	___ Yes ___ No	_____
2) Child care	M P E	___ Yes ___ No	_____
3) Child discipline	M P E	___ Yes ___ No	_____
4) Cleaning bathrooms	M P E	___ Yes ___ No	_____
5) Cooking	M P E	___ Yes ___ No	_____
6) Employment	M P E	___ Yes ___ No	_____
7) Grocery shopping	M P E	___ Yes ___ No	_____

8) House cleaning	M P E	___ Yes ___ No	_____
9) Inside repairs	M P E	___ Yes ___ No	_____
10) Laundry	M P E	___ Yes ___ No	_____
11) Making bed	M P E	___ Yes ___ No	_____
12) Outside repairs	M P E	___ Yes ___ No	_____
13) Recreational events	M P E	___ Yes ___ No	_____
14) Social activities	M P E	___ Yes ___ No	_____
15) Sweeping kitchen	M P E	___ Yes ___ No	_____
16) Taking out garbage	M P E	___ Yes ___ No	_____
17) Washing dishes	M P E	___ Yes ___ No	_____
18) Yard work	M P E	___ Yes ___ No	_____
19) Other: _____	M P E	___ Yes ___ No	_____
20) Other: _____	M S E	___ Yes ___ No	_____

20) If some of the following behaviors take place only during MILD arguments circle an "M" in the appropriate blanks. If they take place only during SEVERE arguments, circle an "S." If they take place during ALL arguments circle an "A." Fill this out for you and you impression of your partner. If certain behaviors do not take place, leave them blank.

Circle the Appropriate Response for Each

(M = Mild arguments only   S = Severe arguments only   A = All arguments)

Behavior	By me	By partner	Should this change?
1) Apologize	M S A	M S A	___ Yes ___ No
2) Become silent	M S A	M S A	___ Yes ___ No
3) Bring up the past	M S A	M S A	___ Yes ___ No
4) Criticize	M S A	M S A	___ Yes ___ No
5) Cruel accusations	M S A	M S A	___ Yes ___ No
6) Cry	M S A	M S A	___ Yes ___ No
7) Destroy property	M S A	M S A	___ Yes ___ No
8) Leave the house	M S A	M S A	___ Yes ___ No
9) Make peace	M S A	M S A	___ Yes ___ No
10) Moodiness	M S A	M S A	___ Yes ___ No
11) Not listen	M S A	M S A	___ Yes ___ No
12) Physical abuse	M S A	M S A	___ Yes ___ No
13) Physical threats	M S A	M S A	___ Yes ___ No
14) Sarcasm	M S A	M S A	___ Yes ___ No
15) Scream	M S A	M S A	___ Yes ___ No
16) Slam doors	M S A	M S A	___ Yes ___ No
17) Speak irrationally	M S A	M S A	___ Yes ___ No
18) Speak rationally	M S A	M S A	___ Yes ___ No
19) Sulk	M S A	M S A	___ Yes ___ No
20) Swear	M S A	M S A	___ Yes ___ No
21) Threaten breaking up	M S A	M S A	___ Yes ___ No
22) Threaten to take kids	M S A	M S A	___ Yes ___ No
23) Throw things	M S A	M S A	___ Yes ___ No
24) Verbal abuse	M S A	M S A	___ Yes ___ No
25) Yell	M S A	M S A	___ Yes ___ No
26) _____	M S A	M S A	___ Yes ___ No
27) _____	M S A	M S A	___ Yes ___ No
28) _____	M S A	M S A	___ Yes ___ No

21) How often do you have: Mild arguments? _____
                            Severe arguments? _____

22) When a MILD argument is over how do you usually feel?

Check Appropriate Responses

___ Angry	___ Lonely
___ Anxious	___ Nauseous
___ Childish	___ Numb
___ Defeated	___ Regretful
___ Depressed	___ Relieved
___ Guilty	___ Stupid
___ Happy	___ Victimized
___ Hopeless	___ Worthless
___ Irritable	

23) When a SEVERE argument is over how do you usually feel?

Check Appropriate Responses

___ Angry	___ Lonely
___ Anxious	___ Nauseous
___ Childish	___ Numb
___ Defeated	___ Regretful
___ Depressed	___ Relieved
___ Guilty	___ Stupid
___ Happy	___ Victimized
___ Hopeless	___ Worthless
___ Irritable	

24) Which of the following issues or behaviors of you and/or your partner may be attributable to your relationship or personal conflicts? If an item does not apply, leave it blank.

Circle the Appropriate Responses

(M = My behavior   P = Partner's behavior   B = Both)

Alcohol consumption	M	P	B	Perfectionist	M	P	B
Childishness	M	P	B	Possessive	M	P	B
Controlling	M	P	B	Spends too much	M	P	B
Defensiveness	M	P	B	Steals	M	P	B
Degrading	M	P	B	Stubbornness	M	P	B
Demanding	M	P	B	Uncaring	M	P	B
Drugs	M	P	B	Unstable	M	P	B
Flirts with others	M	P	B	Violent	M	P	B
Gambling	M	P	B	Withdrawn	M	P	B
Irresponsibility	M	P	B	Works too much	M	P	B
Lies	M	P	B	Other (specify)			
Past marriage(s)/relationship(s)	M	P	B	_____	M	P	B
Other's advice	M	P	B	_____	M	P	B
Outside interests	M	P	B	_____	M	P	B
Past failures	M	P	B	_____	M	P	B

25) In the remaining space please provide additional information that would be helpful:

_____

_____

_____

I, _____ , hereby give my permission for this clinic to share the information that I provide on this form to _____ (partner) when it is deemed appropriate by an agreement between me, my partner, and out therapist. This sharing of information may take place only during a joint counseling session (both partners present).

Client's signature: _____   Date: _____/_____/_____

PLEASE RETURN THIS AND OTHER ASSESSMENT MATERIALS TO THIS
OFFICE AT LEAST TWO DAYS BEFORE YOUR NEXT APPOINTMENT.

Form 35   Analysis of Target Behaviors

Your name: _____   Date: _____

Spouse's name: _____

Every couple encounters misunderstandings, disagreements, hurt, and anger, as well as happy times, fulfillment, encouragement, and cooperation. Unfortunately, when relationships are on the down side, too many people dwell on the negatives. Not all people intentionally try to hurt their partners, but, when arguments heat up, they often fall back into selfish attitudes and behaviors that only serve as ammunition for their own cause. Such defenses never facilitate a happy relationship.

A few examples of detrimental behaviors include the following:

- Belittling/putting down
- Blaming or accusing
- Bringing up the past
- Constantly refusing sex
- Controlling
- Dwelling on negatives
- Flirting with others
- Guilt trips
- Lack of affection
- Lying
- Not sharing responsibilities

- Physical abuse
- Pouting
- Refusing to talk/shunning
- Sarcasm
- Shifting attention to family/friends
- Spending or hoarding money
- Substance abuse
- Threatening suicide
- Threatening to leave
- Verbal abuse
- Yelling

Enjoying a successful relationship involves much more than simply eliminating negative behaviors. Some couples would leave therapy with little to talk about if the counseling only involved discarding the negative. Mutually rewarding, positive actions must replace the negative.

Directions: During the next week list all interactions between you and your partner in which negative interactions (such as those above) take place. Mark down the day and approximate time when each take place. Do not share this list with your partner or compare notes. We will go over the lists in the next counseling session. Use as many of the attached sheets as necessary.

This list must contain behaviors acted out by you, your partner, and both. The purpose of this exercise is to learn about and enrich your relationship, not to blame or find fault. We are not interested in determining "who is right," but rather "what is right" for your relationship.

Also include alternative positive actions that could have been taken instead of the negative behavior, and what seemed to cause the behavior (if you know).

Date: _____ Time: _____

Negative behavior(s): _____

_____

_____

_____

Acted out by whom: _____ ___ Both

What caused it to happen? _____

_____

_____

_____

How did you feel afterward? _____

_____

How do you think your partner felt afterward? _____

_____

What positive actions could have been taken instead of the negative: _____

_____

_____

_____

_____

Date: _____ Time: _____

Negative behavior(s): _____

_____

_____

_____

Acted out by whom: _____ ___ Both

What caused it to happen? _____

_____

_____

_____

How did you feel afterward? _____

_____

How do you think your partner felt afterward? _____

_____

What positive actions could have been taken instead of the negative? _____

_____

_____

_____

_____

Your name: _____Linda Schommer_____   Date: ___3/9/1999___

Spouse's name: ___Paul Schommer_____

Every couple encounters misunderstandings, disagreements, hurt, and anger, as well as happy times, fulfillment, encouragement, and cooperation. Unfortunately, when relationships are on the down side, too many people dwell on the negatives. Not all people intentionally try to hurt their partners, but, when arguments heat up, they often fall back into selfish attitudes and behaviors that only serve as ammunition for their own cause. Such defenses never facilitate a happy relationship.

A few examples of detrimental behaviors include the following:

- Belittling/putting down
- Blaming or accusing
- Bringing up the past
- Constantly refusing sex
- Controlling
- Dwelling on negatives
- Flirting with others
- Guilt trips
- Lack of affection
- Lying
- Not sharing responsibilities

- Physical abuse
- Pouting
- Refusing to talk/shunning
- Sarcasm
- Shifting attention to family/friends
- Spending or hoarding money
- Substance abuse
- Threatening suicide
- Threatening to leave
- Verbal abuse
- Yelling

Enjoying a successful relationship involves much more than simply eliminating negative behaviors. Some couples would leave therapy with little to talk about if the counseling only involved discarding the negative. Mutually rewarding, positive actions must replace the negative.

Directions: During the next week list all interactions between you and your partner in which negative interactions (such as those above) take place. Mark down the day and approximate time when each take place. Do not share this list with your partner or compare notes. We will go over the lists in the next counseling session. Use as many of the attached sheets as necessary.

This list must contain behaviors acted out by you, your partner, and both. The purpose of this exercise is to learn about and enrich your relationship, not to blame or find fault. We are not interested in determining "who is right," but rather "what is right" for your relationship.

Also include alternative positive actions that could have been taken instead of the negative behavior, and what seemed to cause the behavior (if you know).

Date: _3/12/1999_   **Time:** _6:45 a.m._

Negative behavior(s): _Paul kept telling me that the only reason I spend so much time getting_ _ready in the morning is to impress the men at work. Even though there are no other men, I told_ _him, "At least some people care about me."_

Acted out by whom: _____   _X_ Both

What caused it to happen? _When pressures between us build up we become quite sarcastic and_ _belittling of each other. When he accuses me I don't try to reason, but rather I try to hurt his_ _feelings and make him feel inadequate._

How did you feel afterward? _Guilty for implying I might have admirers and good because I was_ _one up on him._

How do you think your partner felt afterward? _Angry and put down._

What positive actions could have been taken instead of the negative: _We could let the other_ _know on a regular basis how important we are to each other. When I feel like I'm being put down,_ _I could discuss my feelings with him rather than spout off. He could avoid making judgmental_ _statements about me by telling me when he is down._

Date: _31/5/1999_   **Time:** _8:30 p.m._

Negative behavior(s): _He yelled at me for spending $200 on a new outfit. I shouted back that he_ _is not my father and I can spend what I want. Then I drove off and did not come back until_ _3:00 a.m. and said, "I went where people appreciate me."_

Acted out by whom: _____   _X_ Both

What caused it to happen? _We have several unpaid bills, but I spent $200 on a whim. He was_ _very upset and I reacted._

How did you feel afterward? _Angry because he has no right to tell me how much I can spend._ _Guilty, because we are in debt. Childish, because he lectured me._

How do you think your partner felt afterward? _Frustrated, because I often overspend when we_ _have other bills to pay._

What positive actions could have been taken instead of the negative? _This could have been_ _prevented if we had an agreed-on budget. He didn't have to yell at me. I didn't have to drive off_ _for several hours. We should agree on expenditures over a certain amount._

6.17

Form 36   Cooperating in Child Rearing

No two people totally agree on all child-rearing principles. The same individual will often seem strict in some matters but quite lax in others. What you view as strict may be thought of as lenient by your partner. What you consider to be fun might be seen as dangerous by your partner.

Most parents tend to raise their children in a similar manner to how they grew up. Of course there are exceptions, but many of the child-rearing techniques we use were learned because our parents (by their example) taught them to us. Unless your parents were just like your partner's parents, your schooling was identical to your partner's schooling, your ideas are the same as your partner's ideas, and so forth, it is inevitable that some of your child-rearing techniques will conflict with those of your partner.

Two important issues involved in child-rearing practices include:
1) the degree of **warmth vs. hostility** in the household, and
2) the degree of **independence vs. control** rendered to the child.

1) WARMTH VS. HOSTILITY. The amount of warmth shown in a family can range from extremely warm (too much smothering and affection) to extremely hostile (little or no love shown).

Extremely warm families often smother their children with so much affection that the children may grow up demanding that others take care of their needs. If you were raised in an extremely warm family it is possible that you might have some difficulties separating your identity from that of your children and family.

Being raised in a warm, loving family can be quite rewarding provided that it doesn't lead to constant smothering. Warm families tend to be affectionate, accepting, and low in physical punishment; parents don't openly criticize one another and are family-centered, rather than self-centered.

Extremely hostile families are often prone to extreme disciplinary measures toward their children. The words "I love you" are rarely spoken. Parents are often rejecting, cold, disapproving, and quite critical of family members. If you were raised in a hostile family it is possible that you might have some difficulties listening to your children's points of view, showing affection, and controlling your temper.

Some families seem to go back and forth between warmth and hostility. When things are going quite well (e.g., children are obeying, finances are in order, parents are getting along, etc.) these families tend to be warm. But when pressures confront the family, there may be times when the parents vent their hostilities on each other and/or the children. This type of situation becomes confusing to the children because of the mixed messages they are receiving. These parents must learn how to be consistent.

2) INDEPENDENCE VS. CONTROL. The amount of independence granted to children can range from extreme independence (children having few or no rules) to extreme control (children allowed to make few or no decisions).

Extreme independence in a family allows the children to do almost whatever they want to do. Parents reason that the children will learn from their mistakes and grow from the experiences. Few restrictions are imposed, and little enforcement is provided for these restriction. If you were raised in an extremely independent child-rearing family, it is quite possible that you are somewhat uncomfortable when it comes to setting limits or enforcing family rules.

Extreme control in a family allows few decisions to be made without the approval of the "head of the house." Children are expected to do exactly what they are told, even when no logical reason is given. There are many restrictions and high enforcement of the rules. If you were raised in an extremely controlling family, perhaps you experience great discomfort or anger whenever someone doesn't agree with you or behaves contrary to your ideas, advice, or rules.

Most people were raised in families in which the family atmosphere is somewhere between extremely warm and extremely hostile. Perhaps there was some hostility, but most of the time warmth was shown. Likewise, few people were raised on either extreme of independence or control. Most children are gradually granted more independence as they get older.

CONSIDERATIONS: You and your partner might find it difficult agreeing or cooperating on how to raise you children. You learned from different teachers! Now is the time for both of you to objectively appraise the benefits and drawbacks of your own upbringing, and purposely create the type of family atmosphere that is best for your family.

Your children need stability and consistency in their family life. When they are presented with dissimilar messages from you and your partner it may be quite difficult for them to develop a consistent value system. Although you both may not at present agree on certain techniques of child rearing, you must come to some agreement for the children's sake. Although compromise and cooperation may be difficult at first, you will find that the harmony they eventually produce will enhance your relationship and your family stability.

First, make compromises. Families function more smoothly when each partner practices the give-and-take process of cooperation. The will of one spouse should not impose on the rights of the other partner. Selfish desires of one partner may often lead to long-lasting hurts and resentments on the part of the other. Many compromises may not immediately feel good to the individual, but the cooperation and agreement lead to a more stable relationship.

Second, be consistent. When you agree upon how you will handle certain issues, tell the children about the process you went through to come to your decisions. That is, let them know that the rules of the house have been formulated by both you and your partner. When issues come up you may be tempted to go back to your old ways of dealing with them, but stay consistent for the family's sake. In the long run your children will respect the newfound strength of family unity.

Third, be patient. Change takes time. Your children will do their best to test the parent they see as the more lenient. At first expect a certain amount of protest when family rules are changed or added. But over time the children will realize that you and your spouse are together when it comes to discipline. Remember, a parent is a child's most influential teacher.

Your name: _____ Date _____

Partner's name: _____

Please respond to the following items. Do not share this information with your partner until the next counseling session.

1) Which of the following best describes the family in which you grew up?

WARM AND ACCEPTING				AVERAGE			HOSTILE AND FIGHTING	
1	2	3	4	5	6	7	8	9

Comments: _____
_____
_____

2) Which of these describes the way in which your parents raised you?

ALLOWED ME TO BE VERY INDEPENDENT				AVERAGE			ATTEMPTED TO CONTOL ME	
1	2	3	4	5	6	7	8	9

Comments: _____
_____
_____

3) Which of the following best describes the family in which your partner grew up?

WARM AND ACCEPTING				AVERAGE			HOSTILE AND FIGHTING	
1	2	3	4	5	6	7	8	9

Comments: _____
_____
_____

4) Which of these best describes the way in which your partner's parents raised your partner?

ALLOWED MY PARTNER TO BE VERY INDEPENDENT				AVERAGE			ATTEMPTED TO CONTROL MY PARTNER	
1	2	3	4	5	6	7	8	9

Comments: _____
_____
_____

5) Which of the following best describes your family style?

I AM WARM AND ACCEPTING				AVERAGE			I AM HOSTILE AND FIGHTING	
1	2	3	4	5	6	7	8	9

Comments: _____
_____
_____

6.20

6) Which of these describes the way in which you are raising your children?

I ALLOW THEM TO BE VERY INDEPENDENT				AVERAGE			I ATTEMPT TO CONTROL THEM	
1	2	3	4	5	6	7	8	9

Comments: _____

_____

_____

7) Which of the following best describes your partner's family style?

PARTNER IS WARM AND ACCEPTING				AVERAGE			PARTNER IS HOSTILE AND FIGHTING	
1	2	3	4	5	6	7	8	9

Comments: _____

_____

_____

8) Which of these describes the way in which your partner is raising your children?

PARTNER ALLOWS THEM TO BE VERY INDEPENDENT				AVERAGE			PARTNER ATTEMPTS TO CONTROL THEM	
1	2	3	4	5	6	7	8	9

Comments: _____

_____

_____

9) Which of the following best describes the family style you would like you and your partner to have?

WARM AND ACCEPTING				AVERAGE			HOSTILE AND FIGHTING	
1	2	3	4	5	6	7	8	9

Comments: _____

_____

_____

10) Which of these describes the way in which you would like you and your partner to raise you children?

BOTH ALLOW TO BE VERY INDEPENDENT				AVERAGE			BOTH ATTEMPT TO CONTROL THEM	
1	2	3	4	5	6	7	8	9

Comments: _____

_____

_____

11) List the child-rearing issues about which you and your partner have very different opinions or practices:

    A) **Issue:** _____

        How do you differ? _____

        _____

        Problems arising: _____

        _____

        Your willingness to compromise: _____

        _____

        Comments: _____

        _____

    B) **Issue:** _____

        How do you differ? _____

        _____

        Problems arising: _____

        _____

        Your willingness to compromise: _____

        _____

        Comments: _____

        _____

    C) **Issue:** _____

        How do you differ? _____

        _____

        Problems arising: _____

        _____

        Your willingness to compromise: _____

        _____

        Comments: _____

        _____

    D) **Issue:** _____

        How do you differ? _____

        _____

        Problems arising: _____

        _____

        Your willingness to compromise: _____

        _____

        Comments: _____

        _____

Form 37   Sharing Your Feelings

Your name: _____   Date: _____

Spouse's name: _____

Directions: Both partners are to face each other, hold hands, and look into one another's eyes during the following communication assignment.

Both partners take turns reading and elaborating on each of the following statements. One partner is first to share feelings on the odd-numbered items, while the other partner is first on the even-numbered items. Both partners respond to all items.

Do not make any remarks regarding your partner's statements. Just listen attentively.

Do not write down your spouse's responses during the exercise. When you have completed all the items write down what you remember from your partner's responses.

1) I fell in love with you because: _____
   _____

2) You make me so happy when you: _____
   _____

3) I'm sorry about: _____
   _____

4) I wish we could: _____
   _____

5) To help you be more happy I should probably: _____
   _____

6) We need to spend more time: _____
   _____

7) I am lonely when: _____
   _____

8) I am proud of you when: _____
   _____

9) You seem to get angry when I: _____
   _____

10) Try to understand that I: _____
    _____

11) I'll try to stop: _____
    _____

12) One thing I need more of from you is: _____

_____

13) It is hard for me to express my feelings about: _____

_____

14) To make our relationship better I will: _____

_____

15) We need to stop: _____

_____

16) We need to start: _____

_____

17) If we try, I believe we can: _____

_____

18) We seem to stop communicating whenever: _____

_____

19) We need better planning when it comes to: _____

_____

20) The one thing that has changed the most in our relationship is: _____

_____

21) It is getting harder for me to: _____

_____

22) A happy marriage (or relationship) means that: _____

_____

23) Whatever it takes, I will: _____

_____

24) I wish we could somehow go back to the time when: _____

_____

25) We don't understand each other when it comes to: _____

_____

26) I don't understand how to please you when: _____

_____

27) I feel guilty after: _____

_____

28) I get scared whenever: _____

_____

29) Please help me to: _____

_____

Form 37A   Sharing Your Feelings

(Completed)

Your name: _____Sergio Allecio_____   Date: ___4/2/1999____

Spouse's name: __Monica Allecio_____

Directions: Both partners are to face each other, hold hands, and look into one another's eyes during the following communication assignment.

Both partners take turns reading and elaborating on each of the following statements. One partner is first to share feelings on the odd-numbered items, while the other partner is first on the even-numbered items. Both partners respond to all items.

Do not make any remarks regarding your partner's statements. Just listen attentively.

Do not write down your spouse's responses during the exercise. When you have completed all the items write down what you remember from your partner's responses.

1) I fell in love with you because: _you treated me better than anyone else had ever treated me. You were special to me._

2) You make me so happy when you: _tell me that you love me._

3) I'm sorry about: _blaming you every time we have money problems._

4) I wish we could: _talk about things before we blow up at each other._

5) To help you be more happy I should probably: _let you know that I believe in you._

6) We need to spend more time: _making future plans and sticking to them._

7) I am lonely when: _we argue and don't talk for a while._

8) I am proud of you when: _you play so well with the children even though I know you are very busy._

9) You seem to get angry when I: _act as if your opinion is not important to me._

10) Try to understand that I: _think the world of you._

11) I'll try to stop: _acting like only my opinion counts._

12) One thing I need more of from you is: _thanks for all I do around the house that rarely is appreciated._

13) It is hard for me to express my feelings about: _how upset I get when you seem to be flirting with other women._

14) To make our relationship better I will: _look at marriage as a partnership and treat you the way I want to be treated._

15) We need to stop: _competing and beating up on the other._

16) We need to start: _acting like we are married and love each other._

17) If we try, I believe we can: _renew our commitment—this time for good._

18) We seem to stop communicating whenever: _it seems like one of us if right and the other is not._

19) We need better planning when it comes to: _finances and spending._

20) The one thing that has changed the most in our relationship is: _how we treat each other. The level of respect has really gotten poor._

21) It is getting harder for me to: _confide in you, because when we argue you use it against me._

22) A happy marriage (or relationship) means that: _each person puts the relationship first, but is allowed to be an individual._

23) Whatever it takes, I will: _make compromises to make this marriage grow._

24) I wish we could somehow go back to the time when: _we wouldn't even think of cutting down the other person._

25) We don't understand each other when it comes to: _the give-and-take process in a happy marriage._

26) I don't understand how to please you when: _you ask my opinion about something, but almost never follow my advice. It's like you want to do the opposite._

27) I feel guilty after: _I throw mistakes in your face._

28) I get scared whenever: _you seem to care more about the women at work than me._

29) Please help me to: _be myself._

Bibliography and Suggested Readings

American Psychiatric Association. (1994). *Diagnostic and Statistic Manual of Mental Disorders* (4th ed.). Washington, DC: American Psychiatric Association.

American Psychological Association. (1992). *Ethical Principles for Psychologists and Code of Conduct.* Washington, DC: American Psychological Association.

_____. (1987). General Guidelines for Providers of Psychological Services. *American Psychologist, 42,* 7.

Barlow, D. H. (1993). *Clinical Handbook of Psychological Disorders: A Step-by-Step Treatment Manual* (2d ed.). New York, NY: Guilford Press.

Brown, S. L. (1991). *The Quality Management Professional's Study Guide.* Pasadena, CA: Managed Care Consultants.

Browning, C. H. (1996). "Practice Survival Strategies: Business Basics for Effective Marketing to Managed Care." In N. A. Commings, et al. (Eds.), *Surviving the Demise of Solo Practice: Mental Health Practitioners Prospering in the Era of Managed Care.* New York, NY: Psychosocial Press.

Browning, C. H., & Browning, B. J. (1996). *How to Partner with Managed Care.* New York, NY: John Wiley & Sons, Inc.

Galasso, D. (1987). "Guidelines for Developing Multi-Disciplinary Treatment Plans." *Hospital and Community Psychiatry, 38,* 394–397.

Goldstein, G., & Hersen, M. (1990). *Handbook of Psychological Assessment* (2d ed.). New York, NY: Pergamon Press.

Goodman, M., Brown, J., & Deitz, P. (1992). *Managing Managed Care: A Mental Health Practitioner's Guide.* Washington, DC: American Psychiatric Press.

Grant, R. L. (1981). "The Capacity of the Psychiatric Record to Meet Changing Needs." In C. Siegel & S. K. Fischer (Eds.), *Psychiatric Records in Mental Health Care.* New York, NY: Brunner/Mazel.

Groth-Marnat, G. (1990). *Handbook of Psychological Assessment* (2d ed.). New York, NY: John Wiley & Sons, Inc.

Joint Commission on Accreditation of Healthcare Organizations. (1994). *Accreditation Manual for Mental Health, Chemical Dependency, and Mental Retardation Developmental Disabilities Services.* OakBrook Terrace, IL: Joint Commission on Accreditation of Healthcare Organizations.

Jongsma, A. E., & Peterson, L. M. (1995). *The Complete Psychotherapy Treatment Planner.* New York, NY: John Wiley & Sons, Inc.

Jongsma, A. E., Peterson, L. M., & McInnis, W. P. (1996). *The Child and Adolescent Psychotherapy Treatment Planner.* New York, NY: John Wiley & Sons, Inc.

Kennedy, J. A. (1992). *Fundamentals of Psychiatric Treatment Planning.* Washington, DC: American Psychiatric Press.

Maxmen, J. S., & Ward, N. G. (1995). *Essential Psychopathology and Its Treatment.* New York, NY: W. W. Norton, Inc.

*Medicare Program: Prospective Payment for Medicare Final Rule: Federal Register 49 (January 3):*234–240. (1984).

Morrison, J. R. (1993). *The First Interview.* New York, NY: Guilford Press.

Bibliography

Othmer, E., & Othmer, S. C. (1994). *The Clinical Interview Using DSM IV,* Vol. 1: *Fundamentals;* Vol. 2: *The Difficult Patient.* Washington, DC: American Psychiatric Press.

Phares, E. J. (1988). *Clinical Psychology: Concepts, Methods, and Profession* (3d ed.). Pacific Grove, CA: Brooks/Cole Publishing Co.

Social Security Regulations. (1981). *Rules for Determining Disability and Blindness.* Washington, DC: U.S. Department of Health and Human Services, Social Security Administration, Office of Operational Policy and Procedures, SSA No. 64-014, ICN 436850.

Soreff, S. M., & McDuffee, M. A. (1993). *Documentation Survival Handbook: A Clinician's Guide to Charting for Better Care, Certification, Reimbursement, and Risk Management.* Seattle, WA: Hogrefe & Huber.

Trzepacz, P. T., & Baker, R. W. (1993). *The Psychiatric Mental Status Examination.* New York, NY: Oxford University Press.

U.S. Department of Health and Human Services. (1983). Medicare Program: Prospective Payments for Medicare Inpatient Hospital Services. *Federal Register 48(171):*39752-890.

Wiger, D. E. (1997). *The Clinical Documentation Sourcebook: A Comprehensive Collection of Mental Health Practice Forms, Handouts, and Records.* New York, NY: Wiley.

Wiger, D. E. (1999). *The Clinical Documentation Primer.* New York, NY: Wiley.

Zuckerman, E. L. (1995). *Clinician's Thesaurus: A Guidebook for Writing Psychological Reports.* New York, NY: Guilford Press.

Zuckerman, E. L. (1997). *The Paper Office: Forms, Guidelines, and Resources* (2d ed.). New York, NY: Guilford Press.

Practice Planners™ offer mental health professionals a full array of practice management tools. These easy-to-use resources include *Treatment Planners*, which cover all the necessary elements for developing formal treatment plans, including detailed problem definitions, long-term goals, short-term objectives, therapeutic interventions, and DSM-IV diagnoses; *Homework Planners* featuring behaviorally-based, ready-to-use assignments which are designed for use between sessions; and *Documentation Sourcebooks* that provide all the forms and records that therapists need to run their practice.

Practice *Planners* ™

For more information on the titles listed below, fill out and return this form to: John Wiley & Sons, Attn: M.Fellin, 605 Third Avenue, New York, NY 10158.

Name _____

Address _____

Address _____

City/State/Zip _____

Telephone _____ Email _____

Please send me more information on:

- ❑ The Child and Adolescent Psychotherapy Treatment Planner / 240pp / 0-471-15647-7 / $39.95
- ❑ The Chemical Dependence Treatment Planner / 208pp / 0-471-23795-7 / $39.95
- ❑ The Continuum of Care Treatment Planner / 208pp / 0-471-19568-5 / $39.95
- ❑ The Couples Therapy Treatment Planner / 208pp / 0-471-24711-1 / $39.95
- ❑ The Employee Assistance (EAP) Treatment Planner / 176pp / 0-471-24709-X / $39.95
- ❑ The Pastoral Counseling Treatment Planner / 208pp / 0-471-25416-9 / $39.95
- ❑ The Older Adult Psychotherapy Treatment Planner / 176pp / 0-471-29574-4 / $39.95
- ❑ The Behavioral Medicine Treatment Planner / 176pp / 0-471-31923-6 / $39.95
- ❑ The Complete Adult Psychotherapy Treatment Planner, Second Edition / 224pp / 0-471-31922-4 / $39.95
- ❑ TheraScribe® 3.0 for Windows®: The Computerized Assistant to Psychotherapy Treatment Planning Software / 0-471-18415-2 / $450.00 (For network pricing, call 1-800-0655x4708)
- ❑ TheraBiller™ w/TheraScheduler: The Computerized Mental Health Office Manager Software / 0-471-17102-2 / $599.00 (For network pricing, call 1-800-0655x4708)
- ❑ Brief Therapy Homework Planner / 256pp / 0-471-24611-5 / $49.95
- ❑ Brief Couples Therapy Homework Planner / 256pp / 0-471-29511-6 / $49.95
- ❑ The Child & Adolescent Homework Planner / 256pp / 0-471-32366-7 / $49.95
- ❑ The Psychotherapy Documentation Primer / 224pp / 0-471-28990-6 / $39.95
- ❑ The Forensic Documentation Sourcebook / 0-471-25459-2 / 224pp / $75.00
- ❑ The Couples & Family Clinical Documentation Sourcebook / 240pp / 0-471-25234-4 / $49.95
- ❑ The Chemical Dependence Treatment Documentation Sourcebook / 0-471-31285-1 / 304pp / $49.95
- ❑ The Child Clinical Documentation Sourcebook / 256pp / 0-471-29111-0 / $49.95

Order the above products through your local bookseller, or by calling 1-800-225-5945, from 8:30 a.m. to 5:30 p.m., est. You can also order via our web site: www.wiley.com/practiceplanners

WILEY
Publishers Since 1807

About the Disk

Disk Contents

Introduction

The forms on the enclosed disk are saved in Microsoft Word for Windows version 7.0. In order to use the forms, you will need to have word processing software capable of reading Microsoft Word for Windows version 7.0 files.

System Requirements

- IBM PC or compatible computer.

- 3.5|inch| floppy disk drive.

- Windows 95 or later.

- Microsoft Word for Windows version 7.0 or later or other word processing software capable of reading Microsoft Word for Windows 7.0 files.

  NOTE: Many popular word processing programs are capable of reading Microsoft Word for Windows 7.0 files. However, users should be aware that a slight amount of formatting might be lost when using a program other than Microsoft Word. If your word processor cannot read Microsoft Word for Windows 7.0 files, unformatted text files have been provided in the TXT directory on the floppy disk.

How to Install the Files onto Your Computer

To install the files follow the instructions below.

1. Insert the enclosed disk into the floppy disk drive of your computer.

2. From the Start Menu, choose **Run.**

3. Type **A:\SETUP** and press **OK.**

4. The opening screen of the installation program will appear. Press **OK** to continue.

5. The default destination directory is C:\WIGER. If you wish to change the default destination, you may do so now.

6. Press **OK** to continue. The installation program will copy all files to your hard drive in the C:\WIGER or user-designated directory.

Using the Files

LOADING FILES

To use the word processing files, launch your word processing program. Select **File, Open** from the pull-down menu. Select the appropriate drive and directory. If you installed the files to the default directory, the files will be located in the C:\WIGER directory. A list of files should appear. If you do not see a list of files in the directory, you need to select **WORD DOCUMENT (*.DOC)** under **Files of Type.** Double click on the file you want to open. Edit the file according to your needs.

PRINTING FILES

If you want to print the files, select **File, Print** from the pull-down menu.

SAVING FILES

When you have finished editing a file, you should save it under a new file name by selecting **File, Save As** from the pull-down menu.

User Assistance

If you need assistance with installation or if you have a damaged disk, please contact Wiley Technical Support at:

Phone: (212) 850-6753
Fax: (212) 850-6800 (Attention: Wiley Technical Support)
Email: techhelp@wiley.com

To place additional orders or to request information about other Wiley products, please call (800) 225-5945.

For information about the disk see the **About the Disk** section on page D.1.

CUSTOMER NOTE: IF THIS BOOK IS ACCOMPANIED BY SOFTWARE, PLEASE READ THE FOLLOWING BEFORE OPENING THE PACKAGE.

This software contains files to help you utilize the models described in the accompanying book. By opening the package, you are agreeing to be bound by the following agreement:

This software product is protected by copyright and all rights are reserved by the author, John Wiley & Sons, Inc., or their licensors. You are licensed to use this software on a single computer. Copying the software to another medium or format for use on a single computer does not violate the U.S. Copyright Law. Copying the software for any other purpose is a violation of the U.S. Copyright Law.

This software product is sold as is without warranty of any kind, either express or implied, including but not limited to the implied warranty of merchantability and fitness for a particular purpose. Neither Wiley nor its dealers or distributors assumes any liability for any alleged or actual damages arising from the use of or the inability to use this software. (Some states do not allow the exclusion of implied warranties, so the exclusion may not apply to you.)